Environmental Citizenship

D0912177

Environmental Citizenship

edited by Andrew Dobson and Derek Bell

The MIT Press
Cambridge, Massachusetts
London, England

WITHDRAWN

NOV 1 1 2015

PROPERTY OF
SENECA COLLEGE
LIBRARIES
NEWNHAM CAMPUS

© 2006 Massachusetts Institute of Technology

All rights reserved. No part of this book may be reproduced in any form by any electronic or mechanical means (including photocopying, recording, or information storage and retrieval) without permission in writing from the publisher.

MIT Press books may be purchased at special quantity discounts for business or sales promotional use. For information, please e-mail <special_sales@mitpress.mit.edu> or write to Special Sales Department, The MIT Press, 55 Hayward Street, Cambridge, MA 02142.

This book was set in Sabon by SPI Publisher Services. Printed and bound in the United States of America.

Library of Congress Cataloging-in-Publication Data

Environmental citizenship / edited by Andrew Dobson and Derek Bell.
    p. cm.
Includes bibliographical references and index.
ISBN 0-262-02590-6—ISBN 0-262-52446-5 (pbk.)
1. Sustainable development. 2. Environmental policy. 3. Citizenship. 4. Political ecology.
I. Dobson, Andrew. II. Bell, Derek, 1968–

HC79.E5E5755 2005
338.9′27—dc22

2005050472

Printed on recycled paper.

10 9 8 7 6 5 4 3 2 1

Contents

Introduction

Andrew Dobson and Derek Bell

Most governments around the world have made a commitment to "sustainable development," and they are therefore confronted with a key question: how to achieve it. Overwhelming confidence has been placed in the efficacy of fiscal sticks and carrots in this connection. The idea is that financial rewards and penalties can be used to nudge individuals, as well as public and private corporations and institutions, toward environmentally responsible behavior. If the sticks and carrots are appropriately placed and priced, self-interested rational actors—so the theory goes—will be induced to push their own appropriate behavioral buttons without further government intervention. It is this last aspect of the scheme that makes it so enticing for liberal-capitalist governments. They—and their subject populations too—are supposedly averse to government intervention, so the idea that individuals might be encouraged to choose sustainable paths for themselves—albeit within a fiscal framework set by a government—is an attractive one.

There is no doubt that fiscal measures of this sort have a place in the environmental policy toolbox. Such evidence as there is suggests that behavior can indeed be tweaked by measures of this sort, and even a moment's self-examination will reveal how susceptible we are to inducements and punishments that focus on the money in our pockets. Governments would be foolish to eschew these sources of motivation and the political possibilities they produce.

But it would seem equally foolish to put all our environmental eggs in the fiscal basket. There are a number of reasons for thinking that other approaches to the business of getting people, corporations, and institutions to behave sustainably are worth exploring. First, the belief that all human beings at all times and in all places are irrevocably moved to act only according to monetary self-interest is probably wrong. "Self-interest" itself can take many forms, and need not always be interpreted in financial ways. Parents of young children, for example, may regard sustainable behavior as being grounded in a broader interpretation of self-interest, one that takes account of the futures of those people—their children—in whom they have an immediate interest.

Similarly, behaving sustainably, in some social circles, can be an increasingly important esteem factor. In such circles, individuals' stock rises and falls with the contribution they make to environmental and other forms of sustainability. This esteem contributes, in turn, to the individual's sense of well-being and self-worth, and so the sustainable behavior it generates can quite properly be regarded as prompted by self-interest.

So even if we believe self-interest to be the most fundamental well-spring of environmental behavior, we should not take this to be always and only a matter of fiscal stops and starts. But there is a more fundamental reason to be concerned at the almost exclusive focus on these types of sticks and carrots—a reason that gets us closer to the subject matter of this book than a reinterpretation of self-interest enables us to do. We can probably all think of some penalty- and/or reward-based scheme for encouraging environmentally sustainable behavior. One that comes to mind is the Plastic Bag Environmental Levy (PBEL) introduced as a charge on plastic shopping bags throughout Ireland on March 4, 2002. From that date on, nonexempt bags have cost shoppers fifteen cents each. The twin stated aims of the scheme were, and are, "to encourage the use of reusable bags and to change people's attitudes to litter and pollution in Ireland" (Department of the Environment and Local Government 2002). As far as the first aim is concerned, the evidence indicates that the PBEL has been a success. The use of plastic bags has been cut by more than 90 percent, removing over one billion plastic bags from circulation each year (BBC News 2002; Friends of the Irish Environment 2004).

Success in regard to the second aim—that of changing people's attitudes to litter and pollution—is much harder to assess, and to our knowledge no specific follow-up research on this issue has been done.[1]

One research difficulty would be that of correlating any observed change in attitudes to *this particular* policy, rather than to any other type of attitude-changing prompt. But the main point turns on the key distinction between changing *behavior* and changing *attitudes*. The PBEL is designed to do both, and the levy's aims are couched in such a way as to make us think that there is an uncomplicated reciprocal relationship between the two: changes in behavior will lead to changes in attitude, and vice versa. A moment's reflection might lead us to believe that the latter is more likely than the former. It makes sense that if our underlying attitudes to waste and pollution change, we could reach the conclusion that plastic bags are bad news, and consequently reduce our consumption of them.

The reverse effect—that a change in behavior will lead to a change in underlying attitudes—seems less likely. There would be nothing necessarily odd or inconsistent in changing our behavior in respect to the consumption of plastic bags without that change of behavior "overflowing" into a more general change of attitude as far as waste and pollution are concerned. So while the PBEL might prompt some individuals to reflect more broadly on their consumption habits, the chances are that they would already have had some predisposition to do so.[2]

A general worry with policy instruments like the PBEL is that people's behavior will be affected much more by the levy itself than by the reasons that lie behind it. Such instruments are much better, in other words, at getting at people's behavior in respect to the policy's specific problem than at the attitudes that underlie it. It is not impossible to imagine a future Irish government repealing the levy. What would happen then? Would people revert to using a new plastic bag for each couple of items of shopping, or would the levy have had the effect of changing people's attitudes to the point that more sustainable behavior was cemented in place? In truth, we don't know. (The Irish government could do the research community—if not the environment—a massive favor by repealing the levy for six months so we could see what would happen.)

It is at least plausible to suppose that different kinds of policy instruments are appropriate for different kinds of objectives. Market-based instruments, which are by far the most widely used in liberal-capitalist and social democratic societies, such as the PBEL are potentially good at changing behavior, but may be less good at getting at attitudes. Once again, this is not to say that market-based instruments don't have their place in the policy toolkit, yet it should equally be recognized by market-based enthusiasts that these particular tools probably won't achieve all their objectives. In the consultancy study paper on plastic bags that eventually led to the PBEL, the Irish government makes it clear that other policy instruments were considered (Minister for the Environment and Local Government 1999), but it is also clear that these instruments (such as "enhanced litter control measures by local authorities") were aimed at the "behavior-changing" rather than the "attitude-altering" end of things. It is our view that governments committed to sustainable development—that is, practically every government on the planet, at least formally—need to give some thought to changing attitudes as well as altering behavior, since both are key to achieving the objective of sustainability.

This is easier said than done. Just where do we start? It would certainly help to begin with a broader picture of human motivation. The policies we have talked about thus far are all grounded in theories that have individuals acting out of self-interest. But we all know that some of us, some of the time, do things because we think they are the right thing to do, even if they conflict with our perceived self-interest. This is the kind of behavioral structure that some aspects of sustainable development would seem to demand. It is surely a fantasy to think that sustainability can always be a win-win policy objective, in which each gain for the common good will also be a gain for each and every individual member of society. It is at this point that thoughts of environmental citizenship begin to emerge from the fog of policy options. There is no determinate thing called "environmental citizenship," as will become clear from the rest of this book, and one of us has even made a point of muddying the waters still further by distinguishing between environmental and ecological citizenship (Dobson 2003), but within the broadest possible compass, such citizenship will/ can/may surely have something to do with the relationship between individuals and the common good. (Whatever the common good, in the context of sustainability, might mean. And we take it that part of what being an environmental citizen might mean is to participate in the never-ending process of defining what sustainability does mean.) In the terms we introduced above, the environmental citizen's behavior will be influenced by an attitude that is—in part, at least—informed by the knowledge that what is good for me as an individual is not necessarily good for me as a member of a social collectivity. Market-based instruments do not raise this possibility in any systematic way, and so are incomplete as prompts for social learning.

Jean-Jacques Rousseau wrote that "every individual as a man may have a private will contrary to, or different from, the general will that he has as a citizen" (1762, 63). This observation led him to formulate the famous distinction between the will of all and the general will, according to which "the general will studies only the common interest while the will of all studies private interest" (72). One way of thinking about the contrast between market- and citizen-based routes to sustainability is in terms of Rousseau's distinction, with the latter focusing on individuals making decisions in virtue of what they perceive to be the common sustainability interest, rather than in terms of what they—as individuals—might or might not gain from pursuing particular courses of action. This distinction maps, roughly, onto that drawn above between behavior and attitudes. Market-based instruments allow individuals to keep behaving self-interestedly, while citizenship approaches acknowledge a potential gap between self-interest and environmentally responsible behavior—the closing of which may require attitude as well as (or leading to) behavior change.

This starting point prompts a host of questions. What do we mean by environmental or ecological citizenship? Might it mean different things in different places? What are the ethics and the values that might inform it? How should it be promoted? What are the obstacles to its promotion? How and where might it be "done"? What is the role of the state in all this? In this new field of inquiry, perhaps the central issue is the relationship between environmental or ecological citizenship and the (long) history of citizenship itself. Is environmental citizenship new, or is it an inflection of a citizenship of which we already have historical experience? In citizenship theory, a standard distinction is drawn between liberal and republican citizenship. Within a broad and bold compass, this distinction turns on two contrasts. The first is between citizen rights (liberal) and citizen responsibilities (republican)—a distinction that has a presence in environmental reflections on citizenship in the guise of citizens' environmental rights, on the one hand, and the responsibility to contribute to sustainability, on the other. The second distinction is drawn in terms of virtue. It is often said that liberal citizenship puts little stress on citizen virtue while its republican counterpart depends on it, in the form of a willingness to work for the common good, and the inculcation of the virtues of duty and sacrifice. In truth, liberal citizenship has its virtues too—tolerance, and openness to argument and information, for example. Environmentalists might argue that sustainability as process and social objective requires the exercise of virtues of all these types. And put like this, it might seem that environmental citizenship draws on both the liberal and republican traditions—a supposition that is fruitfully put to the test in several of the chapters that follow.

Another important issue for contemporary citizenship is the political space in which it operates. The history of citizenship suggests a number of possibilities: for example, the municipality, the city-state, and overwhelmingly nowadays, the state itself. In recent years, there has been something of a challenge to this almost exclusive focus on the state (or its homologues) as the "container" of citizenship, and this has come in the guise of cosmopolitanism. For cosmopolitans, the political-moral space within which citizenship operates is the whole of humanity. This trans- or international conception of citizenship is of interest to environmental citizenship for the rather obvious reason that many environmental problems are trans- or international in nature. There are those, though, who will argue that citizenship is by definition about the relationships between people, and between people and their governments, in particular states. If this is the case, then predicating "environmental" or "ecological" of "citizenship" might be a category mistake, at least in the trans- or international dimension on which environmentalists will probably insist. In any event, not all environmental problems are international anyway; many are local, regional, or national. Does this mean that environmental or ecological citizenship must be promiscuous as far as "political space" is concerned? And if it must, can citizenship stand the conceptual strain this brings with it? Once again, these key research questions are broached in the chapters that follow.

One final area of debate in the context of the relationship between environmental or ecological citizenship and the tradition of citizenship itself deserves mention: the so-called public-private divide. In the Aristotelian tradition, so influential in this regard, being a citizen involves political activity in the public realm. Indeed, in this tradition politics itself is definitionally associated with this realm, the realm of the πόλις, which is contrasted with the realm of οικος, the household. Both the liberal and republican traditions, so apparently different in a number of respects, have this in common: that citizenship is about political relationships and activity in the public arena. According to one way of thinking, environmental or ecological citizenship calls this into question. One key environmental point has always been that "private" actions can have important public consequences. Decisions, for example, as to how we heat or cool our homes, or how and what we choose to buy to consume in them, are decisions that have public consequences in terms of the environmental impact (which may be far afield indeed) they entail. In this regard, environmental citizenship invites us to take a fresh look at a crucial piece of the architecture of citizenship with a view, perhaps, toward recasting the mold in which it has traditionally been formed.

So the relationship between environmental or ecological citizenship and the 2,000-year-old tradition of citizenship itself is an interesting and developing one. Because it is developing, there is no definitive perspective on any of the issues raised above. This book is part of that development, and the contributors to it consider these issues as part of an inquiry into the nature, possibilities, and limits of citizenship as a way of promoting sustainability.

The chapters, outlined below, are ten carefully selected and thoroughly reworked papers from a conference on citizenship and the environment that took place at Newcastle University, UK, in September 2003. The conference was organized by this book's editors, Andrew Dobson (Open University, UK) and Derek Bell (Newcastle University, UK). The conference was, and therefore the book is, multidisciplinary. The book draws on expert work in the fields of sociology, political theory, philosophy, psychology, and educational studies, and it ranges from high theory to ethnography. This range of disciplines and methodologies converges on the relationship between citizenship and sustainability, and our work is badged under four themes, reflected in the two parts of the book: "Theory and Practice," and "Obstacles and Opportunities." The book is thus theoretically informed and policy relevant. Every chapter is original and previously unpublished.[3]

Key themes in John Barry's pathbreaking work in green social and political theory reappear here in the context of citizenship and the environment (chapter 1). He argues that the environmental citizen will be concerned not only about the environment but about the social and economic practices that are connected with and serve to sustain unsustainability. Environmental citizenship, for Barry, is a totalizing and holistic political condition, which demands consistency in individual and collective practice across a range of contexts. Can the environmental citizen recycle their domestic waste and work in the nuclear power industry?

Barry locates environmental citizenship in the civic republican tradition, and perhaps the most striking aspect of his intervention is to reclaim the notion of "service" that goes with that tradition. Pointing out that voluntary approaches to sustainability have had limited success, Barry suggests that the state should play a more forceful role. One aspect of this might be to ask citizens to carry out occasional sustainability-related activities, in the spirit and context of the civic republican demand that citizens contribute to the common good—in this case, a broad conception of sustainability. Barry knows that this will be an uncomfortable—even an illegitimate—message in "liberal" societies where compulsion of this sort is regarded as an inappropriate assault on individual liberties. In response, he holds out the possibility that such service might be rewarded in some way—through fiscal incentives, for example.

This "realism" takes another form, for Barry, in the context of the public-private distinction. On the face of it, citizenship—and particularly, perhaps the civic republican sort—demands the suppression of private interests in favor of public ones. Barry regards this as unrealistic or, better, as a misreading of the public-private relationship in late modern societies. The private realm, he says, is no longer a sphere of "privation," and we should not think of citizenship behavior as ineluctably connected only with the public realm. He thus rejects the commonly held distinction between the citizen and the consumer in favor of the view that citizenly behavior as a consumer is possible.

Barry's green civic republicanism also draws on the language of virtue available to that tradition, and James Connelly (chapter 2) coaxes the idea into the foreground of environmental citizenship theorising in his chapter. Virtues as well as fiscal incentives, he argues, will be essential to achieving sustainability. Connelly's virtues are not—or are not only—directed at achieving human flourishing but at achieving worthwhile environmental ends. They are social, aimed at the common good, and in this case they are deliberative, in the sense that environmental citizens will not take sustainability as an objective that is objectively given but as a moving target that is constructed through deliberation. Connelly is not at all committed to the view that environmental citizenship requires the establishing of new virtues of an explicitly ecological sort—deep ecological virtues, for example. He believes that the resources we already possess, provided by the long traditions of common good theorising, are up to the task of providing the basis for an account of environmental citizenship virtue.

Connelly deals with some big themes: whether an account of virtue requires a view of the good for humans, the duties that virtues entail, and to whom or to what those duties are owed. These questions are dealt with in a way that will surely make this chapter a fundamental reference point as debates on the nature of environmental citizenship unfold. At the end of the chapter, Connelly takes the plunge and tells us what he thinks the key environmental citizenship virtues actually are. He also grapples with a question familiar from Barry's chapter: How is virtue to be promoted? Connelly focuses less on service and more on the legislative framework within which virtues can be exercised: "to merely live by rule is no virtue; but without rules there can be no virtues." Virtue cannot be legislated, he says, but the state can encourage it indirectly through the appropriate use of sanctions and incentives. Both Connelly and Barry agree, then, that a "do-it-yourself" approach to environmental citizenship will only take us part of the way there; environmental citizenship also requires an active state.

In chapter 3, Bronislaw Szerszynski asks us to pause for thought. Is environmental citizenship about caring for particular places or for the earth "as a whole"? Or is it about both? But then *can* it be about both? Is not the universal normative injunction to care for the earth in tension—at least—with the apparent need to dwell "in place"? In common with much of the developing theory around environmental citizenship,

Szerszynski points out that citizenship has traditionally been taken to be an affair of public spaces, and that this has involved an absenting of the citizen from the quotidian business of the reproduction of daily life. He employs three metaphors to evoke this "self-absenting"—blindness, distance, and movement—and suggests that they are as present in theories of environmental citizenship as they are in more traditional conceptions. Universalizing conceptions of environmental citizenship seem to demand blindness of us as far as particular places are concerned, distance from those same places, and a movement that "can be both a source and expression of commitments that transcend the local and the particular"—a movement, in other words, toward the universal.

Szerszynski argues that it would be a mistake to see the universalisms present in environmental citizenship as the whole story. He agrees that an "enlarged citizenship" is required, but that this is achieved through a *dialectic* between blindness and vision, distance and proximity, mobility and staying still. Our view of the local needs to be transformed by considering it in connection with the wider global, but the transformation is incomplete without it coming to rest in particular places at particular times. These fascinating theoretical reflections are prompted and buttressed by two pieces of empirical research, relating to research on the production and reception of global images, on the one hand, and to perceptions of local landscape character in West Cumbria, England, on the other. According to Szerszynski, this latter research suggests that there may be limits to how far universalizing, disembodied, unlocated notions of environmental citizenship can take us. His respondents' experiences and vocabulary, located in and referring to known and local spaces, point to the need for a rooted "wayfinding," along with an abstract "cartographic," approach to environmental citizenship. In a word, this new citizenship needs to take account of our condition as *denizens* as well as citizens.

In chapter 4, Sherilyn MacGregor notes that feminists and environmentalists have both posted their challenges to citizenship theory and practice, but that reflections taking gender, the environment, and citizenship into account simultaneously are few and far between. Here, she offers a critique of emerging notions of environmental citizenship for their gender blindness. Chief among environmental citizenship's problems from this perspective are the tensions (to say the least) between its advo-cating for more labor- and time-intensive lifestyle changes at the same time as working for more political time spent in the public sphere; the way in which the intensification of green lifestyles may assist neoliberal efforts to download public services to the private sphere; and the lack of attention paid to the unjust ways in which responsibilities for the repro-duction of life are shared out. This last point undercuts environmental cit-izenship attempts to make societies sustainable in the broadest and most acceptable senses of the word.

MacGregor asks the critical question, What kind of subject would one have to be to fulfill the requirements of environmental citizenship as it is developing at present? Her answer effectively takes environmental citi-zenship theory—and most especially, us "white, male academics living in advanced capitalist societies" who are among its articulators—to task for paying too little attention to the organization of socially necessary work that will underpin the radical democratic injunctions and lifestyle changes present in most of this theory. Lifestyle changes—"more duty with less time," as MacGregor puts it—will merely make women work harder than they already are. MacGregor is wary of taking the well-worn environmental citizenship path that leads to the enlisting of care as a cit-izenship virtue due to its tactical and strategic naivety. This powerful cri-tique of environmental citizenship from the point of view of gender is essential reading for those of us in any danger of resting contentedly on our socially progressive laurels.

What kind of lives should environmental citizens lead? Dave Horton (chapter 5) answers this question through a fine-grained study of envi-ronmental activists in the town of Lancaster in northwestern England. This is an exploration of the quotidian, mundane aspects of the lives of people who demonstrate their environmental commitment not only through membership in environmental organizations but by living their lives in particular ways. It is an examination, then, of the everyday, rather than campaigns, protests, and participation in organizations. Horton brings a number of themes to our attention: how activists try to make their personal lives and their political commitments consistent with one another; how these lives are lived locally; and how these lives are demand-ing ones in the transformative contrast they draw with business as usual.

Is this a specific case—or set of cases—from which we can draw general lessons? Do we not count as environmental citizens unless we lead our lives along the lines of Horton's activists? Horton stops short of this conclusion, suggesting that these lives are at the same time "elite" and "exemplary" (the first word is Horton's, and the second is ours).

In common with other authors in this book (MacGregor, for instance, as well as Gough and Scott), and in line with a developing consensus in work on environmental citizenship, Horton contends that more education and better knowledge are not sufficient for the creation of such citizenship. His analysis indicates that green activists occupy a specific cultural world, inhabiting and creating green spaces, using green materialities (such as bicycles and organic food) and refusing brown ones (televisions and cars), and carving out green times. This, in turn, suggests that environmental citizenship requires the broadening of the cultural and material conditions within which it develops, and in which—a key point for Horton—it can be practiced. Horton refers to these conditions as an "architecture," understood in a broad sense, and he offers examples of actually existing green architecture that could be built on to produce the "trickle-out" effect he thinks is required. In sum, Horton offers us a rich panoply of detailed observation and thoroughly original general as well as inductive categories through which to examine environmental citizenship and—especially important—the ways in which it might be fomented.

Nicholas Nash and Alan Lewis (chapter 6) offer us a view from psychology. They grapple with the key question of the apparent dissonance between people's stated attitudes toward the environment (sustainability is crucial) and their everyday practices (often unsustainable). In common with other commentators, Nash and Lewis use the notion of a "Dominant Social Paradigm" (DSP) as their point of departure. Previous research has indicated an inverse relationship between cleaving to the DSP and environmental concern. Adherence to the DSP—a belief in technological solutions to environmental problems, for example—can actually lead to a *reduction* in environmental concern. Nash and Lewis's striking finding, arrived at through statistical analysis of responses to a greenfield development near Swindon, UK, is that while the DSP indeed exerts a powerful influence at the *general* level, its effects are less potent at the *local* level. This leads directly to the recommendation that attempts to encourage environmental citizenship should be focused at the local level where the grip of the DSP is less secure.

Nash and Lewis surmise that while concern for global environmental problems may be high, people generally feel unable to do anything about them, and are therefore more likely to defer to existing political, economic, and technological arrangements (the DSP, in other words) to deal with them. In contrast, local environmental problems seem more amenable to action, and this creates a "noise" that "drowns out" (in Nash and Lewis's words) the DSP signal. Nash and Lewis relate these findings to debates about the emerging notion of environmental citizenship, and conclude that traditional liberal and civic-republican conceptions are found wanting in their adherence to contractual notions of citizenship, and in their reluctance to think of the private sphere as a place where citizenship might be enacted. This key research reveals locally based commitments to the idea of responsibility that might be built on to encompass broader arenas of political, social, and economic life.

In chapter 7, Julian Agyeman and Bob Evans act as friendly critics of the notion of environmental citizenship. Their principal concern is that to the extent that it focuses too much on the issue of the environment, it pays too little attention to the broader social and economic aspects of sustainable development. In particular, they say, it has too little to say about social justice, and they conclude that environmental justice, rather than environmental citizenship, has a better chance of mobilizing people to achieve the kinds of change required for wide-ranging sustainability. Agyeman and Evans carry through their argument via an examination of the contemporary situation in the United States and Europe. They draw a distinction between broad and narrow focus civic environmentalism, in which the latter focuses on the environmental aspects of sustainability while the former takes wider social and economic issues into account. Agyeman and Evans believe that civic environmentalism in the United States is currently dominated by the narrow focus option, and that this hampers the coalition building between progressive groups that sustainable development requires.

They maintain that in Europe, by contrast, at the formal level of public plans and pronouncements at least, the commitment is to a broader, justice-based conception of sustainable development in which equity, justice, and democratic governance play key roles. While implementation of these principles and governments' engagement with sustainable development is patchy, the authors are guardedly optimistic that steps are being taken in the right direction. A principal problem with environmental citizenship, say Agyeman and Evans, is its reluctance to take into account the ways in which large numbers of people are excluded from citizenship of any sort. This leads them, once again and in conclusion, to wonder why we bother with environmental citizenship at all, given that the vocabulary and practices of environmental justice more appropriately reflect the causes of unsustainability, and are better able to mobilize people to do something about it.

What might mobilization in the context of environmental citizenship mean anyway? David Schlosberg, Stuart Shulman, and Stephen Zavestoski (chapter 8) take the unpromising-sounding U.S. Administrative Procedures Act (APA) of 1946 and show how the age of electronic communication is potentially opening up new avenues for citizen participation in rule making. The APA enjoins agencies to respond to public input regarding the development of rules, and so in principle the act has considerable democratic potential. Schlosberg and his colleagues pay special attention to the potential for the transformation, rather than the simple aggregation, of positions because of the discursive nature of virtual participation. Early empirical evidence suggests that citizens will take the opportunity to participate in the decision-making process electronically, rather than just use portals to download government information. The opportunities for environmental citizenship are especially interesting, say the authors, because of the high level of public interest and participation in environmental issues, because of the way in which such issues are already a part of Web-based comment, and because if the common good aspect of environmental citizenship is to be developed, then perhaps virtual discussion provides a route to doing so. The relationship between democracy and environmental issues has often been a tense one: What happens if democratic processes produce the "wrong" environmental outcomes? Even those who support deliberative democratic processes as a way of dealing with the politics of the environment are typically cautious as to whether such processes will come up with the environmental goods. In conclusion, and in contrast to the Jeremiahs, Schlosberg, Shulman, and Zavestoski offer us the striking thought that we've perhaps been looking at this the wrong way around: the already-existing citizen commitment to debating the environment could kick-start deliberative approaches to doing democracy. The environment as the mother of democratic invention? Now there's a thought.

In chapter 9, Monica Carlsson and Bjarne Bruun Jensen offer us the first of two concluding reflections on the role of education in promoting environmental citizenship, drawing on experiences in Denmark. A key issue in discussing this role is one that ghosts many of the contributions to this book: the extent to which the "mere" transfer of knowledge can lead to more environmentally responsible behavior. Carlsson and Jensen suggest that two elements can enhance the chances of successful environmental education (that is, education for the environment) in schools. The first is that students decide what to do for themselves, and the second is that activities focus on practical problem solving. These general observations are both derived from and explored through two case studies in Danish schools, demonstrating that student participation and problem solving are complex notions in themselves. Projects aimed at successful environmental education in schools need to pay careful attention to dialogic relations between pupils, teachers, parents, and other collaborators, and to interrogate these relations at every turn for any sign of the imposition of agendas on pupils. Projects must be internally defined, and pupil participation must be real rather than symbolic.

The likelihood that these prerequisites are in place seems to be enhanced by schools having a sense of their place and role in society as political agents for transformation, rather than as transmission belts for society's reproduction. All this is important, say Carlsson and Jensen, because the ability to "take action"—understood as an activity that has been consciously decided on rather than as an instinctive response—is a prerequisite for acts of environmental citizenship. Schools that do *not* follow the careful guidelines for environmental education set out by Carlsson and Jensen, in contrast, may actually inhibit the development of the habits required for environmental citizenship.

Stephen Gough and William Scott (chapter 10) also explore the relationship between learning and (environmental) citizenship. They make the important point that given that citizenship can't be made compulsory in liberal democratic states, the education system provides an arena within which it might be learned and encouraged. They offer a threefold typology of approaches to learning in connection with sustainable development: first, one in which environmental problems are deemed to have environmental causes, leading to an emphasis on natural scientific education; second, one in which the causes of environmental problems are reckoned to be social, leading to social-scientific forms of education; and third, one which analyzes environmental problems as an aspect of the coevolution of society and its environment, leading to education aimed at enabling us "to manage, individually and collectively, a nexus of environmental and citizen behavior in the context of problems that may have multiple, contested definitions and shifting, contingent solutions."

Each of these three types bears on the citizenship question in that they contain an account of the "skills" required for effective citizenship. The skills associated with the third type, suggest Gough and Scott, are the most appropriate for environmental citizenship in that they correspond to aspects of the "sustainability question" that the others ignore: the role of values in determining the meaning of sustainability, and the issues of risk, complexity, and indeterminacy that feature in many environmental problems. The three types of learning are given concrete manifestation in a fascinating case study on education and sustainable development in North Borneo. Elements of the three types are teased out of the students' experiences, and it becomes apparent that a curriculum organized solely around types 1 and 2 would have inhibited the exploration of many of the sustainability questions that turned out to be important to students. In conjunction, then, these final two chapters offer richly textured and empirically based accounts of the kinds of conditions required for deep and broad citizenship education for sustainable development.

From Lancaster to Borneo, from gender to class (and classrooms), from culture to nature, from liberalism to civic republicanism, from cybercafes to cyberspace itself, the authors in this book cover plenty of ground. Neither they nor we, though, claim to have done much more than scratch the surface of the practical inquiry that environmental citizenship deserves and requires. We are, all of us, in the early days of this enquiry, and our aim here has been a modest one: to lighten the gloom just enough to outline the contours that the inquiry might take.

Notes

1. Our attempts to get Ireland's Department of the Environment and Local Government to provide us with evidence one way or the other have proved fruitless.

2. Even this slightly more complex account is still probably too simplistic. See Kolmuss and Agyeman (2002), whose work is discussed in Stephen Gough and William Scott's chapter in this book.

3. Each of the chapters has gone through a rigorous redrafting process. After the first draft produced for the September 2003 conference, authors wrote a second draft, which was then commented on in detail by the book's editors. A third draft was produced, for comment on by expert reviewers with The MIT Press. Final revisions were then made in December 2004, prior to the publication of the book you now have in your hands. The work here was therefore scrupulously reworked and refereed.

References

BBC News, 2002. Irish Bag Tax Hailed Success. August 20. <http://news.bbc.co. uk/1/hi/ world/europe/2205419.stm>.

Department of the Environment and Local Government, Ireland. 2002. Plastic Bag Environmental Levy in Ireland. March 4. <http://www.mindfully.org/ Plastic/Laws/Plastic-Bag-Levy-Ireland4mar02.htm>.

Dobson, Andrew. 2003. *Citizenship and the Environment*, Oxford: Oxford University Press.

Friends of the Irish Environment. 2004. Plastic Bag Levy Continued Success. February 6. <http://www.friendsoftheirishenvironment. net/main/article.php?sid= 415>.

Kolmuss, A., and Agyeman, J. 2002. Mind the Gap: Why Do People Act Environmentally and What Are the Barriers to Pro-environmental Behaviour? *Environmental Education Research* 8, no. 3: 239–260.

Minister for the Environment and Local Government, Ireland. 1999. Consultancy Study on Plastic Bags Recommends Tax on Plastic Bags. August 19. <http://www .mindfully.org/Plastic/Laws/Plastic-Bag-Levy-Ireland4mar02.htm#2>.

Rousseau, J.-J. 1762. *The Social Contract*. Repr., Harmondsworth, UK: Penguin, 1968.

I
Theory and Practice

1

Resistance Is Fertile: From Environmental to Sustainability Citizenship

John Barry

Those who profess to favour freedom and yet depreciate agitation are men who want crops without plowing up the ground. They want rain without thunder and lightning. . . . Power concedes nothing without a demand. It never has and never will.
—Frederick Douglass, freed slave and antislavery campaigner *North Star,* August 4, 1857

Environmental citizenship is fast becoming a buzzword within green political theorizing, but more important, it is also gaining currency outside the academy in the decision- and policymaking discourses of state, corporate/business, and civil society/nongovernmental organizations.[1] Rather like sustainable development before it, this extension of environmental citizenship is evidence of it being open to a wide variety of interpretations, not all of which are reconcilable with one another.

The aim of this chapter is to highlight the normative and sociological/empirical dimensions of environmental citizenship with particular emphasis on some of the dangers of an overly narrow conception of environmental citizenship that limits it to state-based or state-backed practices encouraging individuals to do their bit for the environment. Taking a green political approach, there is a danger that the practices of environmental citizenship can be limited to environmental issues, potentially neglecting the economic, political, and cultural dimensions of sustainability and sustainable development. Thus, the chapter explores the centrality of conceptions and practices of resistance, or "critical citizenship," to the achievement of a less unsustainable society.

In explicating this notion of resistance, green citizenship, I use the republican tradition and conception of citizenship to explore the possible practices of green citizenship. The adoption of a green republican per-spective is undertaken not just because it represents one of the most robust and long-standing political traditions in which active citizenship is central but also because of its openness to virtue-based moral/political perspectives. Given the emphasis many have placed on notions of obli-gation and duty in connection with green citizenship (Dobson 2003; Mills 2001; Barry 1999), often expressed as standing in sharp opposition to liberal citizenship, an exploration of the republican political tradition seems a useful place to start thinking about green citizenship.

The Co-optation of Environmental Citizenship

It is clear that many firms and public bodies are adopting the language of environmental citizenship. Motivated either by compliance with corporate environmental reporting or to demonstrate evidence of good corporate environmental practice, or as evidence of a commitment to some version of corporate social responsibility, many large corporations and parts of the state system are increasingly making use of the language of "environment citizenship" to describe their employee environmental education programs and other environmental practices.

For many, encouraging their employees to be environmental citizens is simply an integral part of either internal environmental management systems or conformity with the International Standards Organization's Environmental Management System such as ISO 140001. While doubt-less raising awareness of environmental issues, it is also likely that such in-house environmental citizen programs will be largely focused on reduc-ing costs (especially energy and material) and ensuring that the company or public agency is compliant with environmental regulations and stan-dards. That is, environmental citizenship is rather narrowly circumscribed to actions and behavior that individuals have as employees, not some-thing that guides their action outside of work (although of course it may). Being an environmental citizen is therefore a part-time occupation, some-thing one engages in during working hours. It goes without saying that this understanding of the environmental citizen does not, for example, challenge the undemocratic manner in which work is organized, nor does it include a provision for addressing the ethical and wider socioeconomic or political aspects or impacts of work and production.

Given this view, one could be a good environmental citizen even while working for a nuclear power plant or a firm producing and exporting toxic wastes. This co-optation or interpretation (if one wishes to be more objective or neutral) of the concept and practice of environmental citizenship should not surprise us. Like sustainable development before it, environmental citizenship is yet another term or idea that can be defined in a number of ways, by different actors and for different purposes.

One of the dimensions missing from corporate/job-based notions of environmental citizenship is the wider context within which environmental questions and issues are placed. Such narrow environmental and work-based initiatives focus on dealing with the environmental, pollution, and resource effects, rather than on an exploration of the underlying structural (political, economic, and social) causes of environmental problems.[2] It is not the aim or intention of job-based environmental citizen programs to either foster a wider environmental awareness about the macrolevel political and economic dynamics of environmental problems and solutions, or to connect the environmental behavior of individuals at work with what they do outside it. Of course, this may happen; some individuals might make the connections and develop a more critical awareness of the political, economic, and cultural dimensions of environmental problems. It is highly unlikely, however, that any such employment-based conception of environmental citizenship will encourage individuals to reduce consumption or buy fair trade products, to promote active citizenship by joining environmental groups or parties, or to engage in nonviolent environmental protest aimed at altering the unequal structures of political and economic power. At most, such conceptions address the environmental effects rather than the underlying nonenvironmental effects—that is, the political, structural, and economic causes—of unsustainable development.

Toward Sustainability Citizenship

In terms of passive/active minimal/extensive notions of citizenship, one can view the greening of citizenship as stretching along a continuum from environmental to sustainability citizenship.[3] The latter conception signals a shift from environmental citizenship, which confines acts of citizenship to environmental actions or behavior that have beneficial environmental effects, toward sustainability citizenship, which I take to be a more ambitious, multifaceted, and challenging mode of green citizenship, which focuses on the underlying structural causes of environmental degradation and other infringements of sustainable development such as human rights abuses or social injustice.

Sustainability citizenship, while of course centered on environmental issues, is not only incompletely defined by environmental actions but indeed must go beyond such actions to encompass economic, social, political, and cultural spheres in its remit. For example, sustainable development includes not just the achievement of environmental protection, long-term development, and other aspects of ecological sustainability but in going beyond the purely environmental sphere, it includes human rights, democracy, equality, quality of life, participation, and good governance (Jacobs 1999, 26–27). That is, despite its various flaws, sustainable development does (at least rhetorically or discursively) commit those who agree with it, or sign treaties or policies based on it, to changes in economic and political structures and practices that go beyond a narrow concern with ensuring resource efficiency or environmental protection. Sustainable development can be interpreted as denoting a commitment to a different type of society, at the heart of which is a commitment to a new view of development that includes economic, environmental, and social bottom lines. In keeping with this wide view of sustainable development, sustainability citizenship is that form of citizen action that addresses and focuses on this broad and radical understanding of sustainable development, rather than narrowly focusing on its environmental dimension. Thus, in this manner, sustainability citizenship includes but goes beyond environmental citizenship.

One of the potential problems of environmental citizenship is how it may unnecessarily narrow the remit of political and citizen action to solely environmental issues, and how therefore it can easily be usurped and co-opted by organizations and institutions in a manner that hollows out its transformative, oppositional, and radical political dimensions. This is discussed in more detail below. It is important to note that the connection I am assuming between active sustainability citizenship leading to or being constituted by lifestyle changes as well as public/political changes—while passive environmental citizenship does not have this same spillover effect—can in the end only be determined empirically.

Of course, one can be either an environmental or a sustainability citizen without joining particular environmental/green groups. We can probably all think of individuals who fall into one or another of these categories. Citizenship in general can be viewed as a continuum from minimalist, liberal notions of passive citizenship to full-fledged civic republican ones of active and participative citizenship. Likewise, green citizenship can be viewed as a continuum from passive environmental to active sustainability citizenship. It is to one understanding of active citizenship—namely, a republican conception—that we turn next.

Republican Sources for the Greening of Citizenship

One of the reasons for seeking to explore the civic republican tradition of citizenship, apart from its enduring interest, especially in terms of connecting solidarity, commitment, and democracy to citizenship, is to help our discussions about the greening of citizenship. While there are obvious dangers in passive (state or corporate-based) forms of environmental citizenship (some of which come close to green consumerism), equally there are dangers or questions about the active, republican form of sustainability citizenship.

An obvious one concerns the assumption or perception that the heavily duty-based conception of green citizenship would be too burdensome, reducing the many other possible identities, interests, and activities individuals have to a dominant or master identity.[4] Here, one could think of the criticism often made of longtime and committed political activists: they are in danger of denying themselves nonpolitical opportunities and life experiences (as parents, lovers, caregivers, workers, artists, etc.), which can damage their chances of becoming fully rounded individuals. In short, limiting oneself to a narrow range of interests and life experiences can lead to the development of one-sided characters and identities. Despite this criticism, however, what is interesting and valuable about republican citizenship is its explicit commitment to freedom as nondomination, and a consequent plurality in ways of life and views of the good. Thus, while republicanism certainly emphasizes the importance of active citizens doing their duty, participating and defending the collective way of life of their free community (especially from external threat), it does not require that there be one commonly held view of the good life. Republicanism does not demand that private views of the good conform to some standard or master conceptualization, and it is compatible with a variety of views of the good, so long as they do not threaten or undermine the freedoms and practices of the common public/political life of the community.

Another related problem with republican notions of citizenship is the danger that this mode of self-understanding and identity is viewed as the best or ideal character, and associated virtues and activities toward which individuals should strive. Such views of republican citizenship stretch back to Aristotelian notions that elevated the public/political life of the citizen above the sphere of privation, as the Greeks characterized the domestic/private realm.[5] However, this need not necessarily be the case with modern reinterpretations of republican citizenship, given that the private sphere is no longer (necessarily) a sphere of privation, and indeed there are citizenly and sustainability virtues and practices to be found within the private/domestic sphere (Barry 1999, 2003c; Dobson 2003).

Civic republicanism is often viewed as a stern and austere notion of citizenship—centrally concerned with doing, acting, and performing duties and public acts, and in which one's identity is both constituted by this notion of active citizenship and connected to a view of the good life in which citizen action for the common/public good is key. The civic republican notion of citizenship contains a realistic view in that it is clear that citizens are made not born, and that there is the ever-present danger that citizens can forget, become soft, and be lured by the attractions of a fully private life of consumption. As Marquand puts it, "The soil in which citizenship grows often becomes barren. And one of the most insidious threats to its fertility is the possessive hedonism which lies at the heart of the free-market model of man and society and perhaps the liberal-individualist conception of citizenship itself" (1997, 47).

The self-discipline, constant vigilance, and militaristic origins and echoes within civic republicanism cannot be denied, and in particular classic city-state republicanism has a thoroughly militaristic notion of the citizen-solider, disciplined, fiercely loyal to his city-state, willing to dutifully fulfill his service to the community, and if need be, willing to die for the common good, his city-state, and in defense of its—and his—

freedom. There is no reason why this should continue to define twenty-first-century interpretations of republican citizenship, however.[6] Indeed, as pointed out below in the analysis of critical or resistance green citizenship, many of these (and other) republican virtues can also be found in green political activism, such as the levels of discipline, dedication, commitment to a cause or principles, solidarity, and steadfastness in the face of opposition (from state, corporate, or fellow citizens).

It is not my intention here to conduct a comprehensive critical analysis of civic republicanism. Rather, my aim is more limited: to see if there is anything we can learn from the republican tradition of citizenship in thinking about new models of citizenship explicitly motivated by ecological concerns. A key issue I wish to highlight regarding environmental and sustainability citizenship that connects with the republican tradition is the idea that for republicans, citizenship is something that has to be learned rather than something that comes naturally to members of society. Just as citizenship can be learned and therefore needs to be taught or encouraged, it can also be forgotten.[7]

In terms of vulnerability, which I take to be a key organizing idea/principle of sustainability and green politics (Barry 1999), the republican conception of politics and citizenship is explicit in recognizing the ever-present temptation for citizens to forget their duty or lapse into self-regarding interests and pursuits at the expense of fulfilling their individual contribution to collective action and vigilance for the common good. And the point here, of course, is that contributing to such collective enterprises and efforts is in the enlightened self-interest of individuals as well—individuals are not, under the conception of republican sustainability citizenship outlined here, expected to sacrifice their interests for the common good.[8] The attractiveness of such notions of citizenship lies, in part, in the Rousseauian aim of encouraging people to do what they both need to do in order to fulfill their obligations to secure the common good, and would assent to doing but for the temptation of private/selfish enjoyments and interests, the danger (or vice) of what the Greeks called *akrasia* or weakness of will, or indeed ignorance and forgetfulness.

In other words, a republican view of citizenship and the state can be defended on the grounds that it is consistent with cherishing and promoting individual liberty and also constitutive of the fulfilling of individual and collective long-term interests, values, and goals. Taking the concern with promoting liberty as nondomination as the key issue for republicans—that is, to enable people to "live in the presence of people but at the mercy of none" (Pettit 1997, 80)—opens up the possibility for the role of the state in promoting and encouraging modes and practices of citizenship in the name of liberty (and sustainability), in ways that are legitimate and in keeping with the wishes and interests of citizens.[9]

The moot issue animating this move toward more directive and state-backed notions of active, republican forms of sustainability citizenship is the lack of progress on sustainability throughout the Western world. Despite three decades of green politics and a global environmental movement, coupled with growing public awareness of ecological problems and their causes, we are, despite some improvements in some areas, still no further along the road to genuine sustainability.[10] Given that appeals to voluntary action and behavioral changes on behalf of democratic citizens do not seem to have worked, the appeal of compulsory alterations in behavior and action is understandable (though of course controversial). Since the provision of knowledge and information about the ecological crisis has failed to encourage sufficient numbers of individuals to become environmental (never mind sustainable) citizens and alter their behavior accordingly, a republican view would be that what is needed is the creation or cultivation of such citizenly virtues and behavioral changes. The state needs to step in and create the conditions for green citizenship.

Practices of Green Republicanism: Compulsory Sustainability Service?

In this section, I wish to flesh out in more detail what a republican notion of sustainability citizenship might look like, and to explore some practices of green republicanism that are bound to be controversial.[11] My aim is not to recommend exclusively republican notions or practices of green citizenship but to scrutinize the controversial notion of compulsory service/work for the achievement of sustainability (sustainability service) to see what it may tell us about the types of conceptions and practices of citizenship that the greening of citizenship may or may not involve.

The potential green republican practice of sustainability service—that is, forms of compulsory service (enforced by the state) for sustainable (including but not limited to ecological or environmental) goals—is similar in form to the national service we find in many states today (or in Britain up until the 1950s). This service could take the form of all citizens having to give up some proportion of their time to engage in a range of sustainability activities—these activities could include cleaning up a polluted beach or river, working in community-based recycling schemes, working in socially deprived areas, assisting campaigns to decrease social inequality and social exclusion, participating in public information initiatives about sustainability or environmental education, working on community farms or community wind farms, becoming a development worker or human rights activist overseas, and so on. The amount of time given to sustainability service could range from one year (posteducation) in the service of the common good to a couple of hours each week over a longer period.

Of course, such talk of compulsory and state-enforced work will send shivers down the spines of most green thinkers and activists, associated as it is with conservative, right-wing, militarist, misogynist, and state-centric thinking. Green boot camps or compulsory labor for state-directed ecological ends are not policies or practices that most greens would see as consistent with the libertarian, non- or antistatist ethos and principles of green politics.[12] On the face of it, nothing could be further from the core ethical and normative political principles of green politics. Although I share many of these concerns—and as stated above, I am not advocating this conception or practice of green citizenship—there is nothing to be gained from simply ignoring or rejecting the idea of sustainability service on the perfunctory grounds that prima facie it seems to violate certain green principles and as such we should not even explore it in more detail.

The republican overtones of compulsory sustainability service are obvious and one could relate them to the military (and thus male) character of classical republican conceptions of citizenship. The republican citizen was typically someone (a man) who was willing and able to bear arms and fight in defense of the republic of free citizens. This patriotism—defending the city-state along with its way of life, land, and people—is something one finds in civic republican thought. Equally, one might view it in terms of Karl Marx's notion of "socially necessary labor:" labor that has to be done in order for society to flourish, and provide the goods and services that constitute the wherewithal/resources for fulfilling individual and collective needs, wants, and views of the good. One could therefore call sustainability service a form of "sustainability necessary work": work or action that needs to be done in order to achieve a sustainable development path that provides the human/social and natural resources for fulfilling individual and collective needs, wants, and views of the good.[13]

In many ways, this suggestion for sustainability service or "sustainability necessary work" argues for making compulsory what already goes on voluntarily.[14] There is already a tremendous amount of voluntary work done for environmental and other social and political causes. The aim is that by making it compulsory, the positive effects and benefits associated with these practices that constitute forms of "public service for the common good" will be increased (because more people will be engaged in them), thus making the achievement of sustainability or the lessening of unsustainability more likely. Nevertheless, it is possible that the positive democratic, social, and ecological effects of sustainability service can of course be achieved through a system of voluntary rather than compulsory service (Dagger 2001).

As Dagger notes (2001, 14), it is also interesting that no less a liberal than John Stuart Mill did not see any necessary contradiction between liberty and certain forms of compulsory behavior. For example, in his *On Liberty,* Mill states that there "are also many positive acts for the benefit of others, which [the individual] may rightfully be *compelled* to perform; such as, to give evidence in a court of justice; *to bear his fair share in the common defence; and to perform certain acts of individual beneficence . . . ,* things which, whenever it is obviously a man's duty to do, he may rightfully be made responsible to society for not doing" (1859, 14; emphasis added).

The idea of compulsory sustainability service exhibits an obvious state-focused conception of green citizenship that is perfectly in keeping with the republican tradition, which classically is very state centric (or rather city-state centered).[15] More important, any positive connotations or potentials of such controversial, obligation-based/compulsory citizenship practices seem to depend in part on whether the state that demands and enforces such obligatory work/time is a green or greening one or not.

On the face of it, it is less objectionable (though of course not without other grounds for objection) if such compulsory forms of green citizenship are authorized by a green state that is working toward sustainability. For example, being obliged to work a couple of hours a week in a community city garden or allotments, formed in partnership between a green local authority and the local community, is quite different from being obliged to spend time on some environmental project on behalf of a state that has little or no interest in achieving sustainability.

Equally, one of the (many) objections to compulsory sustainability service is that in a grossly unequal society, the operation of such schemes would result in the unemployed, the poor, and the marginalized being the ones who do the bulk of this compulsory work. One has only to look at how in societies with compulsory military service, the rich and the powerful can evade their obligations—George W. Bush's posting to Texas rather than Vietnam during the Vietnam War springs to mind. It seems that compulsory public service for sustainability ends requires a more equal society. That is, a precondition for such practices of citizenship is equality, which is not only in keeping with the egalitarian ethos of republicanism but also a constitutive aspect of democratic citizenship itself.

There are imaginative ways in which notions of public service can be articulated, however. For example, one could imagine schemes whereby graduates could have their fees waived (of course, dependent on the continuation of fees) or greatly reduced if they participated in some form of sustainability service (as I believe is the case in the United States regarding participation in foreign development work). Or decreases in one's income tax in proportion to the sustainability service one gives, or perhaps ideally, that the more unsustainable one's lifestyle is (such as the ownership of Sports Utility Vehicles, for example, or air miles per year, or shares in fossil fuel corporations), the more one should pay for this through either higher green taxes or more sustainability service. The point is that there are ways in which incentives could be developed to make ideas of sustainability service less authoritarian, though of course such overtones may still persist. But despite the legitimate concerns around the authoritarian potentials, we must ask ourselves whether an obligation to pay one's way (either through taxes or forms of public service) is as liberty denying as critics make out.[16] And think of the possible social and educative benefits of corporate and financial highfliers (or green academics) having to help the unemployed or get their hands dirty digging on a community farm one day a week.

I would suggest that sustainability service can also be interpreted as meaning that there is an obligation within sustainability citizenship—that is, those who seek to implement the "full spectrum" of sustainable development rather than narrowly focusing on the environmental agenda—to engage in political and other forms of resistance, and struggle against the underlying structural causes of environmental degradation and the nonenvironmental components of unsustainable development. In other words, one can think of the necessary work that is a constitutive aspect of sustainability citizenship as including "resistance work" and not simply equatable with "compliance." Arguing for a conception of sustainability necessary resistance work trades on the same argument used in debates about injustice: that one of the demands of justice in the face of prevailing injustices is to seek to both recognize these injustices and remedy then through appropriate political action. That is, just as we can say that the first demand of justice is to fight against injustice as well as comply with the demands of maintaining a system of justice, equally we can say that the first demand of sustainable development is to fight against unsustainable development as well as comply with the demands of sustainable development. Justice, politically speaking, arises as a central issue precisely because the prevailing political and socioeconomic organization is "unjust" (either completely or in part); that is why justice is the main and dominant ethical-political language and discourse within almost all societies. But equally, to speak and deploy the language of justice demands action to address, challenge, and change unjust social relations.

In a similar manner, therefore, sustainability citizenship, as I understand it, is a form of "resistance citizenship" that exists in the midst of unsustainable development, and comprises practices and "work" that not only includes "maintenance"—sustainability service as indicated above—but also is a corrective to unsustainable development, thereby requiring "corrective" or "oppositional" work in the form of resistance and challenging the underlying causes of that unsustainable development.[17]

Resistance Is Fertile: Civil Society–based Conceptions of Sustainability Citizenship

It seems that if we are to have such republican conceptions or practices of green citizenship centered on public service, we need to have less unequal societies and greener states. Thus, we come to the argument that in order for such state-based notions of green citizenship to be justified, we need to cultivate civil society–based notions and practices of green republican citizenship. These civil society practices of green citizenship focus on nonstate authorized notions of the common good/sustainability where action toward sustainability requires criticism and transformation of state structure and policy.

Such resistance- or civil society–based notions of sustainability citizenship, while clearly constituted by the use of various rights that critical citizens and groups have, are also constituted by notions of duty and obligation. Critical sustainability citizenship (as opposed to what might be called regulatory, compliance, or state-based notions) employ environmental rights such as those articulated by the Aarhus Convention, various constitutional environmental rights (Hayward 2005), community right-to-know laws as in the United States, or various procedural environmental rights (Eckersley 1996). Still, there is also an argument that from a sustainability perspective, critical sustainability citizenship requires that citizens challenge dominant state and economic actors, processes, and institutions, since without such resistance and pressure, it is unlikely that anything approximating a sustainable development path will be realized. Greener states and economies will not come about independent of critical, collective political action by citizens and civil society actors.

In this sense, if one accepts the argument for sustainability, one does not just have the *right* to demand changes to create a more sustainable society but one also has the *obligation* to do so—as suggested in the last section. Just as in the absence of justice one has the right and duty to resist and seek to challenge injustice, equally in the absence of sustainability, one has the right and duty to challenge unsustainability. Duties-based as much as rights-based reasoning can be potentially radical, and not just oriented around the compliance and cooperation of citizens in the achievement and maintenance of collective goods and ends such as sustainable development.

Just as one can argue that we (in the West) have the moral obligation to help the poor in the developing world, as long as by so doing we do not harm important interests we have, so too the well-off, the comfortable classes, and the powerful are the most responsible for the unsustainability of modern societies, and have an ethical obligation to help create a more sustainable society, even if this results in decreases in their economic standard of living. We have an obligation to both help those who are suffering and rectify injustices that we have done/are doing that cause that suffering. This is in keeping with the standard green moral argument concerning our obligations to help other vulnerable groups (future generations, nonnationals, and nonhuman species). There is no obligation to impoverish ourselves for the sake of these vulnerable groups, however.

An interesting case is that of nonviolent direct action for sustainability, which can be regarded as part of an extended notion of sustainability citizenship as individuals doing their bit for the environment by recycling, having fewer children, and so on. Indeed, given the fact that states, economies, and cultures show little sign of independently becoming more sustainable without citizen action, there is a strategic argument that critical or resistance citizenship is more important to cultivate and support. It is highly unlikely, though, that state-based citizenship modules in education, workplace, or corporate notions of environmental citizenship, as discussed above, will cultivate and encourage this activist and duty-based notion of citizenship. Will nonviolent direct action tactics, the ethical and political dimensions of civil disobedience, and other dimensions and potentials for citizen activism be taught in (environmental) citizenship classes? Will the educative capacity of political struggle itself be conveyed? Will students of such citizenship classes be exposed to ethical arguments highlighting such forms of citizen action as positive for democracy? Will such forms of resistance citizenship be seen as caring for and defending democracy?[18]

It is telling that at least in the United Kingdom, government-backed initiatives about encouraging citizenship stop at finding new, more convenient ways for citizens to cast their vote in elections, by extending the places where one can vote, instituting electronic voting, or more radically, examining the case for lowering the voting age to sixteen, for example. In such understandings, citizens are reduced to voters, and by extension democracy is reduced to elections.

This resistance-based view is the more usual understanding and practice of active sustainability citizenship mentioned above—typically characterized as an environmental activist and/or someone who lives their life by the principles and practices of sustainability.[19] At the same time, this focus on equality and linking social justice as preconditions for creating a state worthy of green citizens does lead us to say that civil society–based conceptions of green citizenship require engagement with the underlying global capitalist political economy of the state, economy, and culture (Schlosberg 1999; Martinez-Alier 2002; Barry 2003b).

Some of the virtues associated with republican citizenship can be seen to typify various forms of green political activism—such as discipline, self-restraint, loyalty, courage, perseverance, and commitment as well as other virtues such as compassion, care, tolerance, knowledge, and moderation.[20]

Here, the recent work by Dryzek et al. (2003, 193) is instructive in terms of the strategic choices that have to be made by the environmental movement when engaging with or attempting to attach its ends to one of the state's core imperatives: legitimation or accumulation. Indeed, it seems that there is a need to integrate emerging green analyses of environmental citizenship (Dobson 2003; Root forthcoming) and work on theories of the green state (Eckersley 2004; Barry and Eckersley 2005).[21]

Still, there are other problems facing republican or indeed any activist-based understandings of green citizenship in which the state, while clearly implicated, is but one aspect of a wider and more challenging problem that green citizenship has to face.

Challenges Facing Republican/Green Citizenship

What are our current practices of citizenship? What are the rights and duties enacted in contemporary citizenship? It is a commonplace observation that there is a limited range of practices that constitute modern citizenship. Try listing these practices and one soon produces a short list: voting in elections, joining a political organization, paying taxes, obeying the law, and jury service. It is interesting (or telling) that this list primarily concerns more the duties than the rights we have as citizens. Rights we could include here relate to access to social welfare, health, education, and other entitlements we can claim from the state and its agencies as well as the legal system.

It is a commonplace observation that for the most part, modern citizens in Western democracies are private citizens, detached or alienated (by poverty, wealth, or choice) from politics and the public sphere, and concerned with the private spheres of employment (if they have formally paid jobs) and the family. Modern private citizens are also increasingly unequal citizens in terms of income, opportunities, and quality of life, while continuing to be equal in formal terms. Equally significant is the number of citizens who do not care about politics, most often gauged from voting turnout, membership of political parties, or viewers of political programs.

How do we explain this decline in citizenship? We are confronted with the tragic paradox of individuals and movements around the world struggling for democracy and the right to vote and participate in government side by side with a decline in voter turnout at elections in Western democracies. How are we to explain this coincidence of people in other parts of the world literally dying for the democratic rights many individuals in Western societies so casually toss aside?

While there are many issues one would have to consider to offer an explanation, Kymlicka and Norman offer a good starting point in identifying two:

> In order to explain the modern indifference to political participation, civic republicans often argue that political life today has become impoverished compared to the active citizenship of, say, ancient Greece. Political debate is no longer meaningful and people lack access to effective participation. But it is more plausible to view our attachment to private life as a result not of the impoverishment of public life but the enrichment of private life. *We no longer seek gratification in politics because our personal and social life is so much richer than the Greeks.* (1994, 362; emphasis added)

The private sphere—viewed as enabling lower or less honorable and valuable modes of life and identity by civic republicans from the ancient Greeks to Machiavelli—is no longer a sphere of privation in comparison to the public sphere as one of freedom. The private sphere of work, the home, family, and domestic life is in fact held up to be the main locus of a fulfilling view of the good life in modern society. The dominant modern view of human flourishing is not one associated with notions and practices of public service, citizen participation, loyalty to the community, and activity for the common good. While of course such examples of active citizenship are culturally and politically valued (and sometimes supported by the state), and may be integrated into a private view of the good life, such a public conception of the good for individuals is clearly accorded a lower priority or value in modern societies.

Given the reality that for the majority of individuals in modern Western society it is the private not the public/political sphere where their energies are spent and, equally important, where they are actively encouraged to find fulfillment, it would seem sensible that rethinking new models of citizenship should begin from this reality. At the same time, it is not the case that the private sphere is somehow suspect or else inferior to the public sphere of politics and active citizenship. Indeed, in terms of the expanded notion of sustainability citizenship, the private sphere can partake of ecological virtue and be a site for practicing green citizenship. That is, just as virtue-based notions of citizenship seek to integrate issues of identity and practice (by cultivating sustainability habits and citizens rather than sustainability laws and principles), faced with the dominance of private, consumption-based notions of personal fulfillment (and indeed notions of collective/national identity in which consumption is a constitutive aspect), there also needs to be a consideration of the various cultures of consumption and privatized modes of being and doing that constitute the dominant view(s) of the good.[22]

There is not just one private sphere that we can identify. Rather, there are a number of different but interrelated modes of life, of being, doing, and thinking, that together constitute what we wish to convey in talking of the private sphere. In the interests of space, however, I will focus on consumption.

Strictly speaking, consumption—by which I mean the purchasing and using of marketed commodities and services—is an activity that takes place across the domestic and formal economic spheres, but given its centrality both in terms of its contribution to environmental damage and as a major modern form of identity, it deserves to be treated on its own.

It is not my intention to simply criticize consumption and seek to replace it with citizenship, which is a common strategy one finds in green analyses, the most prominent of which is Sagoff (1988). As I have argued elsewhere, the sphere of consumption and the mode of being as a consumer can be a site for the practice of ecological virtue (Barry 1999). One of the main issues it seems to me, when faced with the issue of consumption is not simply to condemn and reject it out of hand as normatively (as well as ecologically) flawed and blameworthy. Rather, the issue is to attempt to cultivate and support mindful as opposed to mindless consumption, and to seek a balance between the extremes of excessive consumption and no consumption/poverty.

Hence, it is simply wrong, as Pennington (2001) has suggested, referring to the work of green theorists such as myself and Dryzek (1996), that what greens seek is to replace the consumer with the citizen. According to Pennington, "The emphasis can be shifted away from a narrowly instrumental conception of rationality and the notion of the individual as consumer towards the socially more empowering notion of citizenship. This may in turn help to develop the holistic sensibility deemed appropriate to the anatomy of the environmental crisis" (174).

It is not in virtue of some holistic sensibility (in epistemological terms—which seems to be the main focus of Pennington's article) that green politics seeks to emphasize sustainability citizenship. Rather, it is that sustainability citizenship requires engagement with the political struggle against market and state-based forms of inequality, injustice, and ecological unsustainability. Consumer activity, such as boycotts and so on, do have a part to play in the struggle for sustainability, and as indicated above consumption can be a site of ecologically virtuous activity. Yet consumer behavior considered solely as market actors or property owners, unconnected with a wider political economy of struggle and sustainability citizenship, will not by themselves create a more sustainable society.

The point is not to reject consumption and the consumer identity in favor of a citizen one, as indicated above. Such simplistic dualisms do not capture the full range of possibilities open to green citizenship. Put simply, there are ecological virtues available as consumer, parent/householder, and producer/worker. Ecological virtues are not exclusively associated with what is conventionally understood as the political dimensions or practices of sustainability citizenship; one can be a good sustainability citizen as a consumer, parent, worker, or investor. And consumption can be a site of political resistance. Indeed, one of the most powerful and radical political acts an individual or group can do in modern, consumption-oriented societies is to refuse to consume.[23]

Conclusion

Work on green citizenship needs to be linked to work on developing new green theories of the state as well as insights into the greening of the state and the characteristics of a green state. Equally, green citizenship is not exclusively attached to the state and also needs to be located within civil society, and to be especially cognizant of resistance forms of green citizenship, which as suggested above, are absolutely central to the creation of greener states.

Green states are made by green citizens gathered within civil society forcing states to change. States will not become green by themselves, or at least not in the full sense of green—perhaps the most we can expect of endogenous state transformation is some form of weak ecological modernization (Barry and Paterson 2003). There is also the important issue (as raised in the discussion of green republican conceptions of sustainability citizenship) of the extent to which green citizens require green states in order to remind them of their duty, and to help and encourage them to cultivate those habits and practices that are constitutive of sustainability citizenship an the collective political project of achieving sustainability.

At the same time, cultivating sustainability citizenship from a resistance perspective is as much about duty, courage, and discipline as more compliance- or state-based notions of environmental citizenship can be. Indeed, in terms of cultivating sustainability citizenship, it is critical that greens push for the radicalization of these programs beyond either employment-based or formal education curriculum-based environmental citizenship that do narrow, contain, and constrain the transformative potentials of active citizenship. Just as Sagoff (1988), although wrongly, drew the distinction between citizen and consumer, of equal importance is to begin the work on fleshing out notions of sustainability citizenship that cannot be reduced to voter and taxpayer. And here, the republican tradition has a lot to offer in terms of the coming political, economic, and cultural battles in the 21st century involving states, corporations, and civil society. Resistance is not only fertile for the cultivation of the virtues of sustainability citizenship and the emergence of greener states; it is increasingly a necessary obligation. To exaggerate, in the struggle for more sustainable, just, and democratic societies, we need civil disobedience before obedience, and more than ever, we need critical citizens and not just law-abiding ones.

Notes

1. I would like to thank Derek Bell for his insightful comments on an earlier draft of this chapter.

2. As such, one could imagine these limited views of environmental citizenship fitting within a *Factor Four* (von Weizacker, Lovins, and Lovins 1998) or weak ecological modernization, resource-based policy approach to sustainability. Thus, one could say that the political economy underlying such limited conceptions of environmental citizenship is (neoclassic) environmental economics. For an overview and critique of the political economy and politics of ecological modernization, see Barry (2003a).

3. This distinction between environmental and sustainability citizenship echoes the one that O'Riordan makes between green politics and sustainability politics. Issuing a warning to green parties, he notes, "The future of sustainability politics in Europe lies in new forms of governing—much of which will be outside of formal political institutions and international relations. Sustainability politics increasingly will involve many centers of power and decision-making, connected by public-private partnerships and civil society coalitions reaching out across space and time to connect global to local and here and now to the distant future. Here is where sustainability science can become a key catalyst in the new politics of engagement. Supported by civil inclusion and new forms of financing and local political responsibility, sustainability science can create visioning of possible future scenarios. By so doing, it can help guide adaptive responsiveness in which society both monitors and modulates changing needs and aspirations. Green parties may well fade and die unless they resonate with the new political mood" (2002, 2).

4. Dobson (2003) follows standard thinking in this association of duties and republicanism by distinguishing between liberal and republican citizenship on the basis that the former is rights based while the latter is duties based.

5. As Kymlicka and Norman note of civic republicanism, "Political life is superior to the merely private pleasures of family, neighborhood, and profession and so should occupy the centre of peoples lives. Failure to participate in politics makes one a radically incomplete and stunted being" (1994, 362).

6. Dobson in his critical analysis of republicanism rightly points out the gender bias of the classic republican focus on military and manly virtues, as noted by many feminist writers, but is surely correct in contending that we need to "leave open the possibility of an unarmed civic virtue, unless and until it becomes clear that civic virtue in all times and in all places just has to be masculine in this particular way" (2003, 60). In many ways, this is the same argument that given the thoroughly undemocratic historical origins and aims (from most modern conceptions of democracy) of democracy in ancient Greece, all conceptions of democracy are always and everywhere condemned to be gender unequal, xenophobic, and based on property ownership (as was the case in ancient Athenian democracy). Yet Dobson is, in my view, incorrect in rejecting republicanism as a basis for green/sustainability citizenship (what he calls ecological citizenship) on the grounds that "for civic republicanism, virtue attaches to the relationship between the citizen and the constituted political authority: citizenship virtue here is aimed at saving cities" (61–62), and later he notes that "both liberal and civic republican citizenships focus on the relationship between the citizen and the constituted political authority—a vertical relationship if you will" (74). While this vertical/hierarchical relationship is a part of republicanism, it is premised on strong ties of social solidarity, and horizontal relationships practices, and virtues between citizens themselves, who after all from a republican point of view, themselves constitute the political authority in and through which they govern their common life. Republican citizenship, based as it is on the republican notion of freedom as nondomination, is premised first on citizen-citizen and only second on citizen-state/political authority relations. Equally, although I do not have the space to go into it here, I think Dobson offers an incomplete picture of republicanism in the sense that republican citizenship for him is territorially confined (67–68) in a manner inconsistent with the demands of a green political response to the realities of a postcosmopolitan, ecological world of flows of people, energy, resources, pollution, and so on. It seems to me that the republican conception of freedom as nondomination can be translated into the language of ecological harm via the ecological footprint idea discussed in Dobson's book as the way to conceptualize ecological or metabolic relations of justice between citizens of different territories and states (97–117). Indeed, I would go so far as to say that Dobson's notion of postcosmopolitan ecological citizenship is not as sharply distinguished from a republican notion as it first seems—something that can be discerned in that ecological citizenship shares more features with republican than with liberal conceptions and goes with the grain of republican rather than liberal conceptions of citizenship.

7. This focus on the need to educate citizens is not unique to republicanism. Liberals, like Rawls, are also committed to citizenship education. Nevertheless, perhaps a distinction can be drawn between education and training, between republican and nonrepublican political socialization. For a discussion of the environmental implications of liberal citizenship education, see Bell (2004).

8. This linking of individual interests and individual contributions to collective, citizen activity and projects has been one of the key themes emerging from

third-way thinking in the United Kingdom and elsewhere. A typical example of this is the work of Bentley and Halpern (2003) on twenty-first-century citizenship. They start from the position that "there is no shortage of challenges requiring collective solutions. The problem is that politics needs new tools with which to bring together disparate constituencies and persuade them to behave in ways which make collective solutions possible" (97). Bentley and Halpern go on to offer a variety of policy and political responses to this—ranging from a stress on political leadership that enables rather than dictates behavioral change, the importance of social capital and trust between citizens who live in an increasingly plural moral, ethnic, and cultural society, to policy and institutional innovation. Underpinning all of these suggestions, however, is the idea that the engagement of individuals in collective enterprises will depend on the aims and means (institutions) of these enterprises being responsive to individual needs and aspirations. As they put it, "People will only be persuaded to enact their individual rights in responsible ways if they are offered membership of organisations whose routines and priorities are actively responsive to their own changing identities, needs and patterns of engagement" (123). This responsiveness of institutions to individual needs is related to the issue of "creating a sense of shared responsibility to motivate certain kinds of behaviour and to generate causes and identities with which people are willing to engage" (97). It is clear that sustainability and sustainable development have the capacity to be such a cause or ethically based overarching narrative that can be shared by a diverse set of moral perspectives (115–116).

9. For a discussion of how a republican conception of citizenship and politics is consistent with promoting liberty (understood as freedom from nondomination as opposed to the liberal conception of freedom as freedom from interference), see Dagger (2001); Pettit (1997). For an application of republican political theory to global environmental issues, see Slaughter (2005). It is also the case that there are liberal arguments that can be employed to support some version of public service. For example, in the liberal tradition as Dagger (2001, 13–16) points out, theorists as different as Mill to Rawls (1971, 380) have defended conscription and other forms of citizen/civic service.

10. For an excellent analysis of one of the reasons for this—namely, the normalization of the environmental crisis—see Bruell (2002); Barry (2004). For other analyses concerning the domestication and de-radicalization of environmentalism, see Wissenburg and Levy (2004).

11. For a thoughtful argument that shares some similarities to the one outlined here for civic service from a republican point of view, see Dagger (2001).

12. Such notions of sustainability service are wide open, of course, to a critical analysis from a Foucauldian governmentality perspective about microlevels of eco-governmentality, seeking to discipline and order individuals. For a more macrolevel Foucauldian analysis of governmentality, see Neale (1997); Luke (1999).

13. There is an interesting link here between right-wing libertarian views of taxation as compulsory slavery and sustainability service. Given that much of the public policy debate about sustainable development revolves around green taxes, time-based notions of green citizenship might be usefully explicated based on

time-dollar schemes or alternative time-based notions of currency—where currency is shorthand for or an approximation of publicly valuing someone's contribution. Equally, when one thinks about it, citizenship education is also, as part of the state education curriculum more generally, compulsory. Apart from some exceptions such as homeschooling, primary and postprimary education is compulsory for our children. Therefore, any move to green the curriculum by introducing an environmental dimension to citizenship studies is also compulsory. An interesting issue here concerns whether a parent or guardian (or child themself) has the right to opt out of citizenship studies, just as one is permitted to exempt children from compulsory religious studies.

14. It is interesting to note that one of the twenty-four Scottish Executive indicators of sustainable development includes "volunteering." The rationale for this is that "sustainable communities are ones in which every person both contributes to, and benefits from, the community in which they live. A high level of volunteering is a useful indicator of sustainable communities" (Scottish Executive 2004). It is perhaps in support of this that a voluntary rather than a compulsory sustainability service policy be advanced.

15. Thus, another potential link between republicanism and green thinking concerns the local state focus of green citizenship, which is of course in keeping with the long-standing green principle of decentralization, and connects with the Agenda 21 process as well as theoretical work on municipal forms of green politics (Mellor 1995; Bookchin 1992).

16. In contrast to right-wing libertarians, I do not think that the compulsory payment of taxes is liberty denying (or rather, is not *unjustly* liberty denying) insofar as such taxes are required by justice and a commitment to egalitarianism. In the same manner, I do not think this is true of forms of public service. A moot question is, "Apart from the educative effects (which might be enough), is there any reason for preferring public service to taxation? Wouldn't taxation be more efficient?" (Derek Bell, personal correspondence). If, however, one adopts a green political economy position that is critical of the orthodox economic growth model and the emphasis on formally paid employment (from which income taxation is raised), and instead embraces the need to shift from an exclusive focus on employment to work (understood as taking place outside the formal economy—such as child rearing, caring, etc.), then public service is preferable to taxation. Yet I do accept Bell's point that "it is worth emphasizing that if public service and taxation are to be alternative ways of doing one's duty, economic equality is essential if we don't want to force the poor into public service." (personal correspondence). Indeed, one could say that shifting from taxation (based on employment and the growth economy, which is inherently unequal) to public service within a less growth-oriented economy may be a better way of achieving and maintaining equality (Barry and Doherty 2002; Jacobs 1996).

17. There is also an argument here, which I don't have space to develop, concerning the relationship between justice and sustainable development. If we accept the claim that the demands of justice include action and often oppositional action to rectify injustice, then a strong connection can be made between

justifying resistance citizenship in the cause of sustainable development. This is the case if we view sustainable development as denoting justice between generations, between fellow citizens, and between different parts of the world—intergenerational, social, and global justice, respectively. In this case, expressing the demands of sustainable development in the language of justice strengthens the case for resistance forms of citizen action to create a less unjust and unsustainable society both locally and globally. Although more contentious, there is also the argument that we can include relations between humans and animals within the remit of justice, and this is certainly the prevailing rationale among sections of the animal rights/welfare movement. My own view, however, is that the language of justice is not the appropriate moral or political idiom for dealing with human-nonhuman relations (Barry 1999).

18. There is an interesting argument here connecting caring with citizenship in relation to the welfare state. The welfare state supports (albeit often inadequately) individuals as caregivers who have a responsibility for the vulnerable members of their family. One possible interpretation of the resistance form of citizenship articulated above is citizenship as a form of caregiver for democracy. Now, if the state (on behalf of society) supports and publicly values the work of caregivers for the vulnerable, there seems to be no reason why it should not support caregivers for democracy. This is one of the reasons why a long-standing green economic policy is for a universal citizen's income to be paid to all citizens. In some states, such as Germany, there is direct state funding for political parties, while in most states there is support for political parties once elected, yet there is not the same levels of support and funding for citizens. The idea of citizenship as caregivers for or defenders of democracy can be easily connected to republican notions that conceive of citizenship in this mode of defending and being vigilant in the maintenance of *their* democracy as well as *their* democratic rights and freedoms. Collective ownership of and responsibility for democracy is at the heart of republican notions of citizenship. Nevertheless, Bell has asked, "Would a citizen's income, which is paid to a carer for democracy, be equally dependent on the citizen *doing* his job of caring for democracy? Does the analogy suggest a necessary connection between a citizen's income and some version of compulsory sustainability service?" (personal correspondence). Here I tend to agree, and suggest the importance of a link between being a carer for democracy (and being paid for it, in part by a citizen's income) and actually being a carer and doing public service. An interesting example of some of these issues was the manner in which the right-wing press in the United Kingdom was surprisingly (but in a qualified way) complimentary about the antiroads protester "Swampy," lauding him as an example of a "good citizen," and identifying his sincerely held beliefs and willingness and courage to act on them as presenting a good role model for other young people. For a critical analysis, see Paterson (2000).

19. Like in compliance-based notions of sustainability citizenship, resistance or critical sustainability citizenship can also partake of virtues. That is, just as moderation, prudence, and self-reflection and knowledge are constitutive of sustainability citizenship across the various spheres and identities one has, virtues of

courage, fortitude, and the willingness to be open to alternative views, among others, can be said to be virtues of resistance forms of sustainability citizenship. Here, Welch's discussion of fear and courage in an ecological context (1991, chapter 8) can be linked to work on direct action, civil disobedience, and other forms of critical sustainability citizenship (Seel et al. 2000). Just as direct action environmental action has been connected to green views of democracy (that such extraparliamentary, politically motivated action is good rather than bad for democracy), equally it needs to be connected to ideals of sustainability citizenship.

20. While of course not all green political activists display these virtues, such virtues are commonly found to characterize those involved in radical forms of green politics. For case studies of direct action environmentalism, see Seel (1997); Seel et al. (2002); Doherty (2002); Wall (1999); Begg (2000). For an argument for compassion to be considered as a political virtue that can be related to green activism, see Whitebrook (2002).

21. For an overview of recent work on theories of the green state as well as green theories of the state, see Barry (2003b).

22. As Keat (1994) has ably pointed out in his critique of Sagoff's (1988) simplistic opposition between citizen and consumer, consumption is not simply a private act but also an identity-forming act for collective identity. For a discussion of this, see Barry (1999).

23. In some ways, we could distinguish citizen and consumer as *sites* of action (which might be better done in terms of formal politics, market, civil society, home, etc.) from citizen and consumer as *motivational or value orientations* (which might be better done in terms of justice, community interest, nationalism, self-interest, etc.). I owe this point to Derek Bell.

References

Barry, John. 2004. From Environmental Politics to the Politics of the Environment: The Pacification and Normalisation of Environmentalism? In *Liberal Democracy and Environmentalism: The End of Environmentalism?*, ed. Yoram Levy. and Marcel Wissenburg. London: Routledge.

Barry, John. 2003c. Vulnerability and Virtue: Democracy, Dependency, and Ecological Stewardship. In *Democracy and the Claims of Nature,* ed. Ben Minteer and Bob Pepperman-Taylor. Lanham: Rowman and Littlefield.

Barry, John. 2003b. Holding Tender Views in Tough Ways: Political Economy and Strategies of Resistance in Green Politics. *British Journal of Politics and International Relations* 5, no. 4:614–625.

Barry, John. 2003a. Ecological Modernisation. In *Environmental Thought,* ed. Edward Page and John Proops. Cheltenham, UK: Edward Elgar.

Barry, John. 1999. *Rethinking Green Politics*. London: Sage.

Barry, John, and Brian Doherty. 2002. The Greens and Social Policy: Movements, Politics, and Practice? *Social Policy and Administration* 35, no. 5:587–607.

Barry, John, and Robyn Eckersley, eds. 2005. *The Global Ecological Crisis and the Nation-State.* Cambridge: MIT Press.

Barry, John, and Matthew Paterson. 2003. The British State and the Environment: New Labours Ecological Modernisation Strategy. *International Journal of Environment and Sustainable Development* 2, no. 3:237–249.

Begg, Alex. 2000. *Empowering the Earth: Strategies for Social Change.* Totnes: Green Books.

Bell, Derek. 2004. Creating Green Citizens? Political Liberalism and Environmental Education. *Journal of Philosophy of Education* 38:37–54.

Bentley, Tom, and David Halpern. 2003. Twenty-First Century Citizenship. In *Progressive Futures: Ideas for the Centre Left,* ed. Anthony Giddens *et al.* London: Policy Network.

Bookchin, Murray. 1992. Libertarian Municipalism. *Society and Nature* 1, no. 1:3–17.

Buell, Frederick. 2002. *From Apocalypse to Way of Life: Environmental Crisis in the American Century.* London: Routledge.

Dagger, Richard. 2001. Republican Virtue, Liberal Freedom, and the Problem of Civic Service. Paper presented at the annual conference of the American Political Science Association, Boston.

Dobson, Andrew. 2003. *Environmental Citizenship.* Oxford: Oxford University Press.

Doherty, Brian. 2002. *Ideas and Actions in the Green Movement.* London: Routledge.

Dryzek, John. 1996. Foundations for Environmental Political Economy: The Search for *Homo Ecologicus? New Political Economy* 1, no. 1:27–37.

Eckersley, Robyn. 1996. Liberal Democracy and the Rights of Nature: The Struggle for Inclusion. *Environmental Politics* 4, no. 4:169–199.

Eckersley, Robyn. 2004. *The Green State: Rethinking Democracy and Sovereignty.* Cambridge: MIT Press.

Hayward, Tim. 2005. Greening the Constitutional State: Environmental Rights in the European Union. In *The Global Ecological Crisis and the Nation-State,* ed. John Barry and Robyn Eckersley. Cambridge: MIT Press.

Jacobs, Michael. 1996. *The Politics of the Real World.* London: Earthscan.

Jacobs, Michael. 1999. Sustainable Development as a Contested Concept. In *Fairness and Futurity,* ed. Andrew Dobson. Oxford: Oxford University Press.

Keat, Russell. 1994. Citizens, Consumers, and the Environment: Reflections on the Economy of the Earth. *Environmental Values* 3, no. 4:333–349.

Kymlicka, Will, and W. Norman, Wayne. 1994. Return of the Citizen: A Survey of Recent Work on Citizenship Theory. *Ethics* 104, no. 1:325–381.

Luke, Tim. 1999. *Capitalism, Democracy, and Ecology.* Urbana-Champaign: University of Illinois Press.

Marquand, David. 1997. *The New Reckoning: Capitalism, States, and Citizens.* Oxford: Polity Press.

Martinez-Alier, Joan. 2002. *The Environmentalism of the Poor: A Study of Ecological Conflict and Valuation.* Cheltenham, UK: Edward Elgar.

Mellor, Mary. 1995. Materialist Communal Politics: Getting from There to Here. In *Contemporary Political Studies*, ed. Joni Lovenduski and Jeffrey Stanyer, vol. 3. Belfast: Political Studies Association.

Mill, John Stuart. 1859. *On Liberty and Other Writings.* Repr., New Haven, CT: Yale University Press, 2003.

Mills, Mike. 2001. The Duties of Being and Association. In *Sustaining Liberal Democracy*, ed. John Barry and Marcel Wissenburg. Houndsmills, UK: Palgrave.

Neale, Alan. 1997. Organising Environmental Self-Regulation: Liberal Governmentality and the Pursuit of Ecological Modernisation in Europe. *Environmental Politics* 6, no. 4:1–25.

O'Riordan, T. 2002. Green Politics and Sustainability Politics. *Environment* (April): 1–2.

Paterson, Matthew. 2000. Swampy Fever: Media Constructions and Direct Action Politics. In *Direct Action in British Environmentalism*, ed. Ben. Seel et al. London: Routledge.

Pennington, Mark. 2001. Environmental Markets vs. Environmental Deliberation: A Hayekian Critique of Green Political Economy. *New Political Economy* 6, no. 2:171–190.

Pettit, Philip. 1997. *Republicanism: A Theory of Freedom and Government.* Oxford: Clarendon Press.

Rawls, John. 1971. *A Theory of Justice.* Cambridge: Harvard University Press.

Root, Amanda. Forthcoming. *Green Citizenship: Experiments in Democracy and Environmentalism.* London: Sage.

Sagoff, Mark. 1988. *The Economy of the Earth: Philosophy, Law, and the Environment.* Cambridge: Cambridge University Press.

Schlosberg, David. 1999. *Environmentalism and the New Pluralism.* Oxford: Oxford University Press.

Scottish Executive. 2004. *Indicators of Sustainable Development for Scotland: Progress Report 2004.* February. Paper 2004/3. Available at <http://www.scotland.gov.uk/library5/ environment/isds04–00.asp>.

Seel, Ben. 1997. Strategies of Resistance at the Pollock Free State Road Protest Camp. *Environmental Politics* 6, no. 4:108–139.

Seel, Ben., et al., eds. 2000. *Direct Action in British Environmentalism.* London: Routledge.

Slaughter, Steven. 2005. The Republican State: An Alternative Foundation for Global Environmental Governance. In *The State and the Global Ecological Crisis,* ed. John Barry and Robyn Eckerlsey. Cambridge, MA: MIT Press.

von Weizacker, Ernest , Amory Lovins, and Hunter Lovins. 1998. *Factor Four: Doubling Wealth—Halving Resource Use: A Report to the Club of Rome*. New York: Kogan Page.

Wall, Derek. 1999. *Earth First! and the Anti-Roads Movement*. London: Routledge.

Welch, Sharon. 1991. *A Feminist Ethic of Risk*. Minneapolis: Fortress Press.

Whitebrook, Maureen. 2002. Compassion as a Political Virtue. *Political Studies* 50, no. 4:529–544.

2

The Virtues of Environmental Citizenship

James Connelly

This chapter explores the idea of the green virtues and suggests that concern for these virtues be placed at the heart of green citizenship.[1] The starting point is the simple question, What are the appropriate responses to environmental problems? Clearly, externally motivated environmental actions are necessary but not sufficient. If flights are cheap, we will fly; if gas is cheap, we will drive. Some eco-citizens, already keen practitioners of environmental virtue, deliberately limit their choice of transport to what they deem environmentally sustainable; but most of us, most of the time, will act only in response to the external motivations of price, punishment, or prohibition. The use of legal or economic instruments is therefore a necessary part of the environmentally sustainable whole. Although these measures are valuable in their own way, however, they do not constitute the whole answer because they are all alike in providing a motive extrinsic to the desired goal or effect. External motivation will continue to be required for some purposes, especially to break through the deadlock of collective action problems, but legal instruments and economic incentives need to be supplemented by appropriate environmental virtues. Virtuous eco-citizens will internalize the purpose and value of good environmental practices, and their obedience will thus transcend mere compliance, going beyond it toward autonomous virtuous activity.[2]

We should nevertheless be careful. Of course, a universal shift in our "eco-consciousness" would perhaps solve all our problems, but this is not a practical goal, and therefore it is a bad platform for policymaking, which cannot wait on universal shifts in consciousness. Besides, it might be asked, Were such a shift to occur, what role would be left for policymaking?[3] In extolling the virtue of the environmental virtues, we are not committed to developing or waiting for a new form of eco-consciousness per se, as some advocates of deep ecology maintain we should. Attitudes need to change, but it does not follow that change needs to presuppose an ontology of deep ecology or the like. On the contrary, we already have the resources available and the seeds of green consciousness at hand. This can be seen in our already-existing political engagements and activities; and even if it were not, the prospect of arguing a new consciousness into existence through the ontology of deep ecology (or something similar) is an unlikely one. Our real challenge, therefore, is the practical one of nurturing the seedlings of already-existing green consciousness into new forms of ecological citizenship.

Considering Virtues

To assert the relevance of the virtues to green politics and citizenship is not in itself to endorse virtue ethics as such. Virtues might be taken to be important without this necessarily entailing a commitment to a particular claim in metaethics. The position defended here is the first-order claim that consideration of the virtues is a crucial part of green ethics and politics because exercise of the virtues is practically efficacious. On this account, virtues concerning the environment are directed outward toward the realization of environmental goods (and justified by their success in producing those goods) rather than human well-being or happiness (eudaemonia) in the Aristotelian sense. It might therefore be said that an eco-virtue ethics as presented here is impure because the virtues, traditionally understood, are situated within a conception of human flourishing and presuppose an account of what it is to be fully human. In this, a virtue is a character trait that a human being needs to achieve eudaemonia; virtues are thus teleological, the telos being internal to a conception of human flourishing. The account presented below, however, takes the telos to be primarily outwardly directed and consequential, and the account of the virtues is accordingly couched in instrumental terms. To that extent, our use of the virtues has to be justified according to their success in achieving environmental goods; the corollary is that if they fail to achieve these goods, we would have no interest in promoting them. Of course, we could always square the circle by making the bold claim that what is good for the environment is ipso facto good for human flourishing—but having to argue particular onto-logical claims prior to putting the virtues to good use is not my preferred starting point. For my purposes, then, a virtue is a character trait a human being needs to realize environmental ends; if eudaemonia is also achieved, so much the better, but that is not the direct focus. So let us accept that our use of the virtues is, in terms of virtue ethics per se, impure; but then, we *are* dealing with the "dirty" virtues. Here we can follow Mill, who suggests that virtue although "not naturally and origi-nally part of the end, is capable of becoming so; and in those who love it disinterestedly it has become so, and is desired and cherished, not as a means to happiness, but as a part of their happiness" (1949, 200). In order to use the language of virtue, we are not restricted only to the Aristotelian idiom.

Virtues go beyond their bearers; they are not private but social, and their exercise therefore requires a conception of the common good. This point was made clear by Green: "All virtues are really social; or, more properly, the distinction between social and self-regarding duties is a false one. Every virtue is self-regarding in the sense that it is a disposi-tion, or habit of will, directed to an end which the man presents to him-self as his good; every virtue is social in the sense that unless the good to which the will is directed is one in which the well-being of society in some form or other is involved, the will is not virtuous at all" (1966: §247). In the case of the eco-virtues, this common good (which I shall term "sustainable common environmental good") needs to be further developed and specified. It is also important to remember that the con-ception of the good is not a pregiven entity but something itself in the process of being defined, molded, and brought into being. One of the key virtues will thus need to be the virtue of deliberating on what the sus-tainable common environmental good itself is. In the phrase sustainable common environmental good, the word *sustainable* appears at first glance simply to be added to an already-accepted idea of a common good. But it is rather more than a mere addition: it is an emergent fea-ture arising out of a reflection on what the common good requires at this point in our history. We can be sure that if we are deliberating on the common good at all, then we will at the same time be including within it considerations of sustainability and related goals.

To summarize, because responses to the environment have to go all the way down, environmentally sensitive dispositions need to be developed and encouraged. In this we are not starting ab initio; the language of virtue is already familiar, and we can use or appropriate many old virtues. In part, therefore, we need to clarify familiar virtues; in part we need to engage in "focus extension": conceptual innovation, value reversal, and the creation of new virtues or vices (Wensveen 2000, 32). This means modifying the scope of the application of traditional virtues; engaging in conceptual innovation to bring the virtues up to date and make them relevant to environmental concerns; revaluing and perhaps reversing certain virtues and vices; and identifying or creating new virtues and vices appropriate to our current concerns. Yet in all this, we are working within a tradition because ecological virtue language is "materially innovative but formally traditional" (107): although new applications differ from the old, both old and new share the same formal structure.

The Analysis of Virtue

We need, then, to develop internally motivated, environmentally sensitive dispositions—virtues. These virtues constitute a key part of ecological citizenship. A virtue, fully formed, transcends mere compliance with law or policy, because it includes as part of itself the appropriate motivation and intentionality. Nevertheless, my focus here is primarily on consequences, not the internal features of moral character, and my claim is that environmental virtue is more practically environmentally effective than the alternatives. I am here not considering virtue as an intrinsic good but as an efficacious set of dispositions. My account is, to this extent, compatible with at least some versions of utilitarianism and is not dependent on an Aristotelian conception of virtue. I leave open the question of whether or not in the end environmental virtue has to be grounded in something like an Aristotelian account. My claim, then, is based on the intuition that virtues work; it avoids the necessity of adopting a strong view of the unity of humans and nature in human flourishing. This is because for the sake of environmental action, it is better to move forward with the resources we already know we possess, rather than wait for confirmation of stronger ethico-ontological claims around which it is harder to secure consensus.

What is a virtue? By contrast with the state of affairs in which the motivation for action does not necessarily coincide with the intention to do good, for a virtue approach motivation and intention are brought together. A virtue is a settled disposition to act in a certain sort of way. The formula for virtuous action is: I am *motivated* to do environmental good for the sake of the environment (or humanity) and I *intend* to do that environmental good. My motivation stretches back before the individual action and looks ahead beyond the action; I have a settled disposition to act in certain ways (including a disposition to consider my actions in a certain way) and this settled disposition is environmental virtue. When I act, I act intentionally, taking the environment as either the direct or indirect object of my action. Of course, not all action is explicitly intentional where "intention" implies deliberation; the whole point of a virtue is that it becomes second nature, albeit a nature that (unlike the natural world) is affected by being known, and is in principle malleable to our intellectual touch.

Virtues are not merely habits, although they include elements of the habitual. They are habits critically reflected on and reflection habituated. A virtue is also the mean between two extremes or vices. This requires judgment, which is reflective; hence, the exercise of virtue must be reflective. Virtues are therefore critical dispositions—or at least, dispositions of which we can and should become critically aware, although we shouldn't be aware of them to the detriment of action. They cannot literally *be* second nature; they have to be reason naturalized through emotion and emotion rationalized through reason. Virtues cannot be acquired once for all. They are (and have to be) in constant flux; they exist only in use and there is no virtue at an instant. Over time, even the same disposition, which in one sense never alters, is nevertheless undergoing constant change as the agent deals with different problems in unique circumstances of judgment. Virtues are character traits, dispositions of character, but more than just dispositions—they are excellences of character.

The virtues require practical wisdom for their completion in the sense that one might "possess" the appropriate virtues without the understanding to put them into practice. This is why virtues cannot be completely unconscious or too deeply embedded in our "second nature." As Hutchinson puts it, "Real wisdom involves knowing the right values, the things that are good or bad for man, as well as being able to put them into practice; so it is not possible to be really wise without having the moral virtues as well. Likewise, it is not possible to have a fully developed moral virtue without having practical wisdom as well" (1995, 208).

The opposite of a virtue is a vice. I would like to believe that a reflective vice is a contradiction in terms and that vices emerge from the absence of thought, not the presence of vicious thought. Yet this might be too sanguine a view resting on the heroic claim that reflection makes us moral. Although the view that vice is the product of a lack of thought is worth serious consideration, for the present it might at least be agreed that vices often emerge from thoughtlessness rather than reflection.[4] Perhaps a vice is best thought of as simply a habit without reflection. A virtue is a habit and yet more than a mere habit; a vice is just a habit; and any virtue is in danger of becoming a vice if it becomes *merely* habitual. Virtues are moderated and mediated by the metavirtues of judgment and reflection; a vice is a habit devoid of these—not so much a misjudgment as an absence of judgment. It is perhaps wise to qualify the term *vice* as it covers both the act (or type of act) and the causes of acting in a certain way. These causes differ, but broadly we can distinguish (as Aristotle does) between vice (*kakia*) and weakness of will or incontinence (*akrasia*). A vice is typically but not invariably unreflective. Thus, acting wrongly can emerge through a lack of knowledge or a lack of emotional self-control, and depending on character, it can be conscious or unconscious of itself as a wrong action. Ecological vices can be related to all three possibilities. Sometimes it is a matter of knowing but not caring; sometimes caring but not knowing; and sometimes neither knowing nor caring.

We do not have to follow Aristotle here. It is enough to note that he takes seriously the puzzle that Socrates addressed by denying that it was possible to realize what it was right to do and yet not do it. Aristotle largely agreed, but sought to explain the obvious fact that nonetheless wrong things are done in knowledge of their wrongness. His general account is that we know that certain things are right or wrong, but we don't recognize this as applying to our own circumstances because we are in the grips of a passion. We cannot apply our knowledge or grasp of the general principle, and passion is left in charge (Aristotle 1959, 1145b21–47b19); Hutchinson summarizes Aristotle's position:

A vice is a condition of the soul in which an emotion is incorrectly adjusted, and the rational part of us does not realise that anything is wrong. . . . Moral weakness is similar to vice in that our emotions are out of adjustment and cause us to do the wrong thing; it is also dissimilar to vice in that our rational part is aware that what we do is wrong. Yet we still do it, because the moral and rational side of us is weaker than the emotional side. Vice and moral weakness are different conditions, although they sometimes lead to the same results. Moral weakness is aware of itself, but vice is not; it involves regret, but vice does not. . . . Vice is thorough badness, but moral weakness is only partial badness. (Hutchinson 1995, 215; Aristotle 1959, 1146a31–b2, 1150b29–51a20).

There are important distinctions to be made between the different reasons for not engaging in environmentally virtuous activity. Some seek to be virtuous but fail through ignorance, while for others motivation is lacking or remains a problem in the face of ever-present worldly temptations. Thus, eco-vice can often result from a simple lack of understanding; but it can also result from the simple contentment of want satisfaction, or from the pull of habit or the effortless sway of dominant political structures. As Mayer Hillman suggests, we can see this in the excuses we make. In his recent manifesto, *How We Can Save the Planet,* he considers the excuses people make in justification of their inaction on climate change. Among the top-ten excuses, Hillman cites: "I blame the government or Americans" (or whoever), "it's not my problem," "there's nothing I can do about it," and "there are other more important and urgent problems to tackle" (2004, 54–62). Whatever our environmental vices or excuses, however, it should always be remembered that we are (at least in part) responsible for our character. Hence, where we are now depends on what we were before and we cannot remove ourselves from moral responsibility in the present through the shallow subterfuge of disowning our responsibility for how we got there. As Wensveen puts it, "While we may not directly choose to be vicious, insofar as we have chosen the paths that lead there, we are responsible for our vices" (2000, 104).

Virtues and Dispositions

An objection to the position advanced here might be that not all virtues (including some of the most important ones) are individual dispositions. We have already accepted that virtues have a necessary social component (as suggested by Green), the individual and the social being mutually reinforcing; but the objection made by Dobson, for example, is different. In rebutting claims made by Barry, Dobson argues that

"virtues are central" to green politics—and to ecological citizenship—but I do not think that the "dispositions of character" of which Barry speaks are the central virtues of ecological citizenship. The key virtue is, rather, justice—although I entirely agree that certain dispositions of character may be required to meet its demands . . . [S]ympathy, or other candidates such as care and compassion, might be regarded as ecological citizenship virtues *in the second instance*. This is to say that they might turn out to be important to the effective exercise of the first virtue, justice. (2003, 133)

Dobson is making a double distinction here. He wants to "distinguish both between the foundational virtue of ecological citizenship and other virtues that may be instrumentally required by it, and also between virtue as Aristotelian 'dispositions of character' and *political* virtue" (132). Justice, then, is the first virtue of ecological citizenship and other virtues are second-order virtues instrumental in realizing the primary virtue of justice. Further, although "it is very common to see accounts of ecological virtue expressed in the Aristotelian idiom . . . I do not think it works in the specifically political context of citizenship" (132); in ecological citizenship, for Dobson, we are looking for political virtues (not dispositions of character) and the primary political virtue is justice.

My response to this is to agree that justice is the primary virtue. I therefore also agree that other virtues might be instrumental in realizing justice. Yet I disagree with the sharp distinction Dobson draws between dispositions of character and political virtue. All virtues are dispositions, including the primary virtue of justice. These dispositions may be of an individual character or a corporate, societal, or institutional character, but in my view virtues are active embodiments of principles working themselves out through dispositions and not abstract principles acting as abstractly animating ideals. Dobson himself draws a crucial distinction between principles and motives for actions; virtues, whether individual dispositions of character or political virtues, combine both principles and motives. To some extent, therefore, Dobson undertheorizes the virtues. To see why, let us further examine some points emerging from the above discussion.

The first point is which virtue is the most important one; the second is whether we are primarily concerned with institutional or individual virtues. The key point is that although there can be legitimate disagreement on whether justice is paramount, there is no need for disagreement over the implied contrast between individual and institutional virtues. From Plato onward, a virtue such as justice has been analyzed both as a state of the soul and a feature of the polis, the political community. The exact form of the relationship between the two locations of virtue has been (and will continue to be) fruitfully explored, but there is no ultimate conflict between the two. A related point, however, is whether there can be *non*dispositional virtues? The reason for asking this question is that the term virtue is sometimes used to refer to a quality of an object or a system rather than an activity or a disposition.

In the term virtue as used in everyday discourse there is some seeming ambiguity. For example, we talk of the virtues of a thing where we mean its merits. This is a derivative meaning of the term in which the properties of the object either derive from concrete human activity, or are being understood solely in terms of their actual or potential contribution to human activity, with the predicates attaching to the activity being, as it were, projected onto the object. We can distinguish dispositions, excellences, and merit. A virtue is a disposition to act excellently, and this creates merit in the objects or states of affairs created through human activity.

Thus, when Rawls suggests in *A Theory of Justice* that "justice is the first virtue of social institutions, as truth is of systems of thought" (1999, 3), there is no contradiction because social institutions are constituted, maintained, and reproduced by human activity. They are that activity objectified. That is why later in the book, Rawls always characterizes virtues in terms of activity and dispositions; this follows from his comment that "being first virtues of human activities, truth and justice are uncompromising" (4). Thus, for Rawls, virtues are predicable both of social institutions and activities, and the opposition vanishes.

Virtues, then, are dispositions; these dispositions can be structural or constitutional dispositions, or individual dispositions of character. Given that my present focus is the exercise of virtues understood as individual dispositions of character, I need to say a little more about what it means for a virtue to be a disposition. Consider, for instance, what might be termed *intermittent* versus *continuous* dispositions. Intermittent dispositions are those that will issue forth when called on. They exist in the background, not constantly being exercised but ever-ready to be exercised. In this sense, a pane of glass has a disposition to be brittle. Continuous dispositions, by contrast, continually issue forth.[5] Both sorts of disposition are permanent, but one is episodic where the other is continuous—at least in respect of the outward effects. And this is our problem. First, how do we know that a certain disposition is present if it is not being exercised? And second, how are episodic dispositions incorporated into the mental and emotional economy of their bearers? This is a problem, for example, for someone who is courageous but not often called on to be brave. Such a disposition might therefore be both relatively unstable and relatively uncertain. Further, we might not even know that it is present prior to its external display. Exercise of the virtues requires more than conceptual analysis and its application; it requires a deep knowledge of what that exercise means in practical psychological terms. The eco-virtues we develop and promote will need to be sustainable in two senses: they should be related to sustainability, and they should be in themselves sustainable.

Human Nature and the Human Good

An age-old group of questions is whether the virtues constitute a unity, whether the life of virtue constitutes a unified character, and whether there can be a unity of character in the absence of the unity of the virtues. Rather than offering a direct answer to these questions, I shall answer obliquely by stating that virtues may or may not constitute a unity, but they exist and are appreciated as well as employed as a network of virtue relations. In other words, we should think of the unity of character and the unity of the virtues as a developmental historical process, in line with our conception of the development of the appropriate environmental virtues themselves. We might suggest that we will always tend to seek unity in the theory and practice of the virtues, but that we are never likely to attain it. One reason for this is that the virtues with which we are concerned are explicitly intended to be operative in a transition between one state of society and another. They are transformative virtues and hence dynamic not static. Another reason is that the unity of the virtues rests on conceptions of human nature, well-being, and flourishing, to which I now turn.

Some might object to this general line of thought on the grounds that traditional accounts of the virtues presuppose a developed view of human nature and purpose, and that we are rather less certain than Aristotle was that we can provide or agree on such a strong conception of the human good. This prompts the worry that if virtues require agreement on ends, and the ends are themselves contested, we are erecting our virtues on the sand of contestability rather than the rock of agreement. Our response starts with the observation that we should root our discussion of virtue in what we can agree on, not in what we cannot, and that virtue does not collapse simply because there might be some disagreement on ends. Further, we might not be able to agree on a strong conception of the human good, but we might plausibly be able to agree on at least some of the necessary preconditions for human existence, within which individuals and societies freely develop their own conceptions of the good. Thus, other things being equal, to provide people with the essential conditions of life and to maintain or enhance the choices available to them must be a good thing, and to do the opposite is a bad thing. So, for example, if it is accepted that world climate change is a major concern, and that it adversely affects the conditions of life in both predictable and unpredictable ways, it follows that we should do what we can to mitigate its effects and so far as possible remove its causes. In considering those whose ecological footprint is somewhat lighter than ours, we might remark that what is good enough for us is good enough for them, and that if we do not think that what is good enough for them is good enough for us, we should cast a self-critical eye on our lifestyles and use of the earth's resources. It also follows that there should be equal concern for basic needs and opportunities: the starting point is a presumption of equality of rights to a share of the world's resources and an equal obligation to uphold those rights. Departures from equality require justification; they cannot be accepted simply through historical presumption. First come, first served is a good description of our patterns of resource use, but it is a bad recipe for social, economic, and environmental justice.

There is of course the thorny issue of whether we have obligations to future generations and why. One answer is simply to argue that care for future generations follows from the overlap of generations here in the present. This generation cares for the next generation, which will in turn care for generations yet to come. This argument is sound, so far as it goes, but it is an empirical observation rather than a justification and it leaves two vital questions unanswered. The first is whether (and why) we in this generation have obligations to generations further removed from us in time; the second is what do we do to ensure justice for future generations and what principles do we employ? It seems reasonable to assume that future generations will want to inhabit an inhabitable world and will not thank us for restricting their choices, including the variety and wonder of the natural world available to them, but we should be careful in assuming that we know what exactly it is that they might want. Obvious life necessities aside, there is a real sense in which we simply cannot know what they will want, because to know what they will want would be to predict future states of knowledge and belief. If we already knew these, they would be present realities, not future possibilities. If we are seeking to ensure conditions of fairness, though, we can at least appeal to the same notions of fairness as we have in dealing with distributive matters in the present and then ask whether they can be extended to consideration of future states of affairs insofar as we can realistically anticipate what those might be.[6] Thus, in order to maintain the integrity of the natural world, we appeal to the interests of future generations in inheriting a natural world as rich and diverse as the one we inherited.[7] We have to have some way of proceeding and this is as reasonable as any immediately available alternative. Out of these considerations is generated the environmental concern out of which springs environmental virtues and the obligations of ecological citizenship. An eco-virtue is ecological thoughtfulness plus the disposition to pursue appropriate internally motivated action.

Some view of human nature (even if only a negative one) is necessary to our understanding of virtues because virtues are normally characterized by contrast with their corresponding vices, to the temptations into which we are likely to fall. So a negative conception of human motivation is the minimum requirement for consideration of the virtues. This is why Foot suggests that virtues are corrective of feelings or tendencies in human nature. We therefore need to identify the tendencies in human nature that work against environmental ends and encourage the related virtues because virtues, according to Foot, "are corrective, each one standing at a point at which there is some temptation to be resisted or deficiency of motivation to be made good. As Aristotle put it, virtues are about what is difficult for men" (1978, 8).

A directly related point is the extent to which a conception of the virtues rests on a conception of the good life. We have already touched on this. We might add that at a minimum, we have to include a consideration of the conditions for the existence of any conception or realization of the good life, and that we might go a lot further in claiming that human well-being is dependent on and inseparable from the well-being of other species and the natural environment in general. The desirability of sustainability seems to be easy to agree on—but even here we must be careful because sustainability itself stands in a to-be-explicated relationship with the human good and happiness. Obviously, sustainability is required for the sake of life, but if it is required for the sake of the *good* life (to paraphrase Aristotle), are we going to be able to agree on what sort of good life to aspire to? But let us not grasp pessimism too readily. The absence of complete agreement need not signify the complete absence of agreement. We already possess the resources to float an eco-virtue approach without undue leakage and with some sense of an appropriate destination; we need to have a vision even if the details are to be filled in en route rather than in advance. Eco-ethics and eco-politics are both nonvoluntary adventures; we are going somewhere and we might as well have an intuition of where that is.

So how do the eco-virtues cohere with the aims of life? Is the aim of life happiness? If it is, where and how does nature fit in? Is it a by-product? Is there a necessary or contingent relation between happiness and our care for nature? Is healthy nature a necessary condition for happiness? Clearly, in the environmental context as in others, vision shapes virtue. If there were no vision of environmental excellence held up as an ideal then there would be no possibility of the environmental virtues flourishing. Flourishing virtue leads to human flourishing and human flourishing is expressed in the life of virtue. But there must be an external telos or purpose as well as an internal *ergon* or function. Virtues require a telos. We might argue that a plausible telos is sustainability. Yet how do we specify sustainability so as to make it a suitable telos for the green virtues? Does it need to be specified in terms of human or environmental needs? Can it be an immanent telos? An immanent ideal? We could assert of course that the telos is to be found through inspection of and alteration to the ideals and principles informing our worldview as expressed and developed in actually existing societies. And indeed this was true for Aristotle. The telos was given and virtues in a sense became a matter of accommodating the individual to that society. Still, this might not apply to the eco-virtues. The eco-virtues are not about accommodation to an already-existing society but rather about bringing about a different form of society. This is a sine qua non: our starting point is that our society, our present way of living, is not sustainable. But this might seem to open up a gap between the "is" and the "ought," to create a problem of motivation and run the risk of rooting eco-virtues in a never-never land. The solution is to recognize, first, that the norms, virtues, and principles characteristic of any society or civilization contain both normative and descriptive elements in the sense that they are already in some degree what they aspire to be. Second, any civilization is historically rooted and therefore always already in flux—there is no place where we can locate a unified, coherent, and changeless ready-made theory and practice. Third, any future state of society must originate in its present, and thus we should seek to enhance the coherence of our norms, principles, and virtues as our contribution to the process of transition and transformation.

Can we agree on a minimum specification of human nature and flourishing from which we can derive the duties and virtues of eco-citizenship? Perhaps something akin to a minimum content of natural law might be produced covering the right to survival and existence—but this is only the *precondition,* not the *condition* for the realization of the human good. Can we derive more than this? Yes we can, if we reflect on the idea of a common environmental good. This relates us back to our conception of human nature. Whatever our human nature is, it at least allows us the possibility of self-reflective deliberation and consideration of human goods.

The Duties of Ecological Citizenship

Ecological citizenship is characterized not by rights but by the self-imposed duties of the citizen. Duties are commitments that require the free exercise of the virtues to identify and perform them. Liberal theories of citizenship tend to focus on the granting and maintaining of rights; civic republican views focus on a deeper reciprocity between rights and duties. Ecological citizenship is different from the former in focusing its concern on duties, not rights, and it is different from the latter in being nonterritorial. This claim can be challenged on the grounds that citizenship is necessarily territorial, thereby making a nonterritorial citizenship a contradiction in terms. This is a powerful point. Nevertheless, we have to act *as if* (at the very least) we have global citizenship responsibilities for the simple reason that environmental problems are not locally containable. And we can go further by suggesting that if our responsibilities extend as far as the bounds of our community, and if our community is increasingly globalized both politically and commercially, then the claim that citizenship is nonterritorial in the traditional sense seems a reasonable one to make. Ecological citizenship thus conceived embraces duties that are not limited in scope to time or place, and that are voluntarily self-imposed. The source of the duties is not the product of a reciprocal, contractual, social set of arrangements. Rather, it is the outcome of a recognition of the fact that we are already affecting (or have affected) others. The leading proponent of the view just articulated, Dobson, suggests that "while this is a citizenship with international and intergenerational dimensions, its responsibilities are asymmetrical. Its obligations fall on those, precisely, with the capacity to 'always already' act on others" (2003, 49–50). Those affected, that is, feel the heavy tread of others' ecological footprint; relationships thus arise with those on whom it impacts. These impacts will be asymmetrical because of the differential size of ecological footprints. As Dobson notes, "The relevant cleavage is that between 'globalizing' and 'globalized' individuals, where the former is taken to refer to those whose action can 'impact at a distance,' and the latter to those whose actions cannot" (115).

In short, ecological citizenship is not so much about rights as about obligations. But can there be self-imposed duties without corresponding rights? That depends. Duties and rights are not necessarily symmetrical. In this they differ from reciprocally defined concepts such as *winner* and *loser* and *winning* and *losing*, each of which implies the other. Of course it is true that if I have a right, someone else (or some agency) has a corresponding duty; and again, if I, as a citizen, have rights, we might expect that I will be required to assume the duties of citizenship (this view would be typical of a civic republican perspective). But if I have a duty, it does not necessarily follow that there is a corresponding right. There is no difficulty in saying that we have duties toward people, animals, or things where we don't suppose that they have a corresponding right, merely that they are the object of our dutiful concern. In eco-citizenship, then, it might be said that we have duties to other people; they in turn have corresponding rights. But should we understand this literally or rhetorically? Everyone, as claimed above, has an equal right to an equal share of environmental goods. It seems reasonable to proceed to the conclusion that everyone therefore has an equal duty to maintain those rights or at least not to act so as to knowingly violate them. This position could, however, leave us with moral demands that are impossible to fulfill if it is taken to imply that we should always be acting positively so as to maintain rights, and it is wise to avoid making unreasonable and excessive demands. It might be that not a great deal is lost if we adopt the position that we have duties toward those who have had less than their share of the world's environmental goods—a duty that does not require reciprocity. But this is a moot point: to deny the applicability of rights in such a context might be taken to imply the relative lack of importance of the duties thus specified.

On a related point, consider the nonhuman natural world. I suggest that we have a duty toward it, but that it has no rights per se—rights being conceptually difficult to ascribe to beings incapable, even in principle, of being part of a rights-making and rights-maintaining community.

Is this duty direct or indirect? Some might argue that it is *direct*. This is certainly an intelligible position: I have already argued that there can be direct duties without corresponding rights. Nevertheless, it is politically more prudent to adopt the view that our duty to it is derived *indirectly* via a recognition of what we owe to human beings who have an equal entitlement to share and enjoy the fruits of the earth. We can generate the political agreement we need for eco-citizenship more easily without the need to make the claim that we have a direct duty toward the non-human natural world. As we don't *need* to make this claim, on the principle of Occam's razor, we should avoid making it. If indirect obligations to the natural world are sufficient, let us rest content; after all, nothing precludes individuals assuming for themselves additional direct duties should they so wish. Here, the contrast might be (in a Rawlsian sense) between a moral duty that is part of someone's comprehensive doctrine and an indirect duty that is (in Rawlsian terms) a political duty.

Ecological Citizenship

The world's commitment to sustainability has been developed and expressed in national policy, European Union policy, and international laws and protocols. Standard policy instruments and economic incentives are not in themselves sufficient to achieve sustainability. We also need to change environmental dispositions and habits. No polity can maintain its own health and vitality without citizens displaying the appropriate public and private virtues; this is equally true for the environmental polity. Ecological citizenship goes beyond citizenship as ordinarily understood. It covers different forms of political engagement in different parts of the public and private spheres. It also draws on different sources—sources that are already present in our society.

Ecological citizenship comprises the ecological duties together with the virtues appropriate to their fulfillment. This includes the duty of deliberating on duties: we have a duty to ask what our duty is. And even where our duty seems obvious—for example, to reduce the size of our environmental footprint—we should still question this and ask exactly how it might be translated into specific actions. Here, we should perhaps distinguish between duties as general goals or aspirations and specific duties appropriate to particular occasions. The latter cannot be determined in advance even where the general features are known. A concrete duty only becomes actual at the moment of acting, and the content of that duty at that point is a combination of the circumstances, ideals, principles, character, and virtues of the actor.[8]

An eco-virtue is an internally motivated ecological thoughtfulness leading to action. The virtue of rational deliberation, avoiding the twin vices of insufficient thoughtfulness and too much thought at the expense of action, is essential to the proper formulation and understanding of our eco-duties. For example, the general duty to reduce the size of our eco-footprint is refined both by investigating expedient practical responses, and through reflection on our place in the world and differential use of its resources. An eco-duty is derived from an assessment of the size of our eco-footprint and the extent of our departure from equality in the way we tread the earth. Ecological duties are therefore not equal; they vary between individuals and between groups and nations. Those who have already consumed (and continue to consume) most have correspondingly greater duties.

Agency and Action: Promoting Virtue?

To what extent is it possible to promote the life of eco-virtue? What role can the state have in this? Or are we forced to conclude that (virtue being voluntary) it cannot be promoted by the state and that attempts to promote the voluntary through the means available to the state are by their very nature self-stultifying?

The exercise of the virtues, even at its most developed, does not imply that we cease to need rules and regulation: they cannot be dispensed with, but neither are they primary. To merely live by rule is no virtue; but without rules there can be no virtues. Rules are refreshed by active virtuous action and reflection, and a framework of supporting legislation is desirable as a reminder to those who ought to develop the virtues, as a guide to those who are developing the virtues, or as a coherent and reliable underpinning and support for the actions of the already virtuous. Although virtues are private responsibilities, their possession is a public good, and their development and reinforcement is a public as well as private duty.

How are people to be drawn into the practice of environmental virtue? One answer might lie in designing deliberative institutions. But deliberative and other intellectualist approaches are not enough. They need to be part of something bigger in which people are drawn in by doing. The idea of "enabling environmental practice" explored by Weston (1994) is relevant here. This includes but goes beyond tax and charge paying (although this is important in not only changing behavior but also encouraging people to reflect on their behavior). Practical participation can induce virtuous action; when reflected on, the virtue thus induced can become conscious of itself as such. *Being virtuous precedes virtuous being.* Virtue cannot be theorized into being; one must participate in a practice to discover its internal goods and goals.

It should be remembered, however, that we are not looking for moral perfection but merely virtue enough to achieve our environmental ends. We need sufficient virtue, not perfect virtue, and here we reopen the question of the state's role. A virtue-centered approach must include a consideration of both agency and motive. In the case of prohibition, the agent is the state compelling action through the threat of external compulsion. In the case of economic incentives, agency is shared in that the state facilitates action through external incentive rather than internal motivation. And in the case of duty or virtuous action, the action is internally motivated and the state cannot directly promote this; but can it be promoted *indirectly*?

Everyone must make their character for themselves. State action cannot directly make a person moral because acts done under compulsion tend to lose their character as moral acts. For this reason, as Green argued, "the effectual action of the state . . . for the promotion of habits of true citizenship . . . [is] confined to the removal of obstacles" (1890, §209), or as Bosanquet put it, to "the hindrance of hindrances" (1923, 180). The state has at its disposal (broadly) sanctions, incentives, and education. We are looking to generate intrinsic motivation on the part of citizens. How can the state move from sanctions to incentives to indirectly promoting environmental virtue and duty? The state can perhaps indirectly promote this through education, but can the other two means be used indirectly to promote the virtues or do they tend to destroy the possibility of freely motivated virtuous action? There are reasons (some of which have already been given) to think that they can both secure the minimum necessary level of environmental compliance while at the same time making a contribution to the nurturing of citizen virtue. Participation in certain sorts of activity encourages the development of appropriate ways of thinking and doing, and the state can encourage this. Again, the existence of a sense of approval or disapproval toward certain actions and ends as expressed in policy statements, legislation, differential taxation, charges, and appropriate intervention (for example, facilitating recycling through the provision of separate bins and collections) is influential in encouraging people to act in ways that become habitual and might become virtuous.

There is a distinction between being virtuous and being a spectator of the virtues, but this is not an absolute separation. If the spectator can recognize the moral significance of what they observe, spectating lies on a spectrum with activity at one end and passivity at the other. Thus Green's remark: "What is called 'moral sentiment' is merely a weaker form of that interest in social well-being which, when wrought into a man's habits and strong enough to determine action, we call virtue" (1966, §250). Of course, passivity sometimes just *is* passivity, and yet the possibility of induction into the life of active eco-citizenship lies open for those able to respond.

From Velleity to Virtue

Drawing the threads together, the main thrust of this chapter can be summarized as follows. We all have our velleities—that is, we all have desires too small to be acted on. Many people's environmental desires are velleities. It may not be that people are opposed to environmentally sensitive activity, merely that their desire is too weak to motivate them to action. One response is to employ external forms of incentives for good action and punishment for bad action. But as already argued, this approach has its limitations: we are looking to stimulate internal motivation. One answer is therefore to take our cue from Green and Bosanquet, and consider how we might hinder the hindrances to environmentally sensitive action. In general, people have to be inducted into action. One way of doing this, appropriate to governmental action at the local level, is by making it easier to do certain things such as recycling that otherwise might not be done. We are looking to convert velleity into virtue by removing the hindrances to action, thereby tilting the agent toward action. An unreflective velleity becomes a vice where there are compelling moral reasons for performing the action that there is so little motivation to perform.

The encouragement of voluntary action, through encouragement and facilitation, is therefore vital. The principle shades into a form of induction. Through action, participation, and engagement, people become inducted into a way of living and doing that begins to settle into a virtuous groove. In the first instance, it perhaps matters little what the motive was; the point is that actions having been embarked on have a way of becoming the focus of reflection and thought. This can then lead (just as action according to incentives can) to other environmentally virtuous actions. The difference with action based on economic incentives is that the gap between external and internal motivation is always stronger than the encouragement of any form of voluntary action will be. Environmental virtues can be encouraged, but this encouragement is not a straightforward matter, and it requires a range of subtle responses to people's circumstances as well as an appreciation of their already-existing dispositions and motivations. But there is every reason to believe that success is possible: after all, if people were always already perfect specimens of the self-interested utility maximizer assumed in the rational choice literature, we would never be able to account even for the levels of voluntary environmental activity that we see around us day to day. What we have to do is to build on and extend this predisposition to environmental virtue so that it reaches those who don't at present recognize or act on their own predispositions. Predispositions become dispositions of character through acting, especially acting with others in common projects, and thereby generate the environmental virtues central to the argument of this chapter.

There is a saying attributed to St. Francis: "Preach the gospel always and when necessary use words." In our language, exhibiting and encapsulating the virtues is as vital as talking the virtues; both are required in the life of the virtuous individual. But what (to pick up the theme from above) of virtue and the problem of collective action? Can we create a virtuous society from virtuous individuals? We know that "thou shalt not follow a multitude to do evil" (Exod. 23:2). This raises no problem for traditional virtue ethics, but it does for the position maintained here. What if others do not do what needs to be done, thereby (it would seem) rendering one's own actions purposeless? For traditional virtue ethics, the value of the virtues lies in the well-being of the moral agent, and the life of virtue is its own justification, whereas I have argued that a virtue approach in environmental policy and ethics is justified largely by its beneficial consequences. But if we are concerned primarily with consequences, why should an agent be virtuous if others are not? What would be the point? Does the logic of the free rider destroy the value of virtue? Do we have to wait for everyone to be virtuous before any individual is virtuous? As noted above, however, we have to account for the facts, and the facts are that virtuous action can and does exist, and that it does and can beget virtuous action in others. We should not overlook the practical value of exercising the virtue of encouraging others to act virtuously for the sake of the consequences of virtue.

Conclusion: Some Eco-virtues

Up to this point I have discussed virtues in general, but few in particular. Perhaps I should give some clues as to which virtues are the eco-virtues? Faith, hope, and charity seem appropriate to any list of virtues, as do the four cardinal virtues of courage, wisdom, justice, and moderation. If justice is the key virtue, the others will be subordinate to it, but it is not part of my present purpose to establish a hierarchy of environmental virtues, merely to indicate what some of them might be.

Frugality might be considered a candidate as a cardinal environmental virtue, with care, patience, righteous indignation, accountability, asceticism, commitment, compassion, concern, and cooperation making up the numbers. Of course, not all these virtues are specifically environmental—but we acknowledged earlier that environmental and nonenvironmental virtues would overlap, with old ones typically being put to new uses, and extending their scope and reference. This follows from the fact that we are seeking to generate a practical conception of a sustainable common environmental good, which is a modification of the old common good, not an entirely new aspiration unrelated to all our previous goals and ideals. It might be suggested that not all these virtues are citizenship virtues, that some are private not public virtues. But this objection is invalid because one important difference flowing from the character of the eco-virtues is precisely that in the environmental context, the distinction between public and private virtues (and the related issue of what are often referred to as masculine and feminine virtues) has to be reconsidered. Feminine virtues are typically those associated with domesticity and the private realm, and masculine virtues with the public realm. On this understanding, many eco-virtues such as care, love, compassion, and so on, are cast as feminine virtues. This might be so, but we need to recognize that they should apply both in the public and private realms because their end lies in their contribution to sustaining and preserving the natural environment.

Whatever their precise nature, any putative list of virtues and vices could be extended a tremendously long way—for example, Wensveen identifies 189 virtues and 174 vices in the post-1970 environmental literature. If we now turn to vice, we can perhaps agree with her that hubris or pride is first on the traditional list of sins, and should also be regarded as one of the major eco-sins (Wensveen 2000, 98). It is notable how many sins translate easily into eco-sins—envy, anger, sloth, greed, and gluttony being good examples, with their avoidance obviously necessary for any sustainable future. Other eco-sins clearly include exploitation, cruelty, willful ignorance, cynicism, and despair. Yet the point of this chapter was not to provide a definitive list of virtues so much as to argue for the importance of the virtue approach within environmental citizenship. So I conclude with the comment that environmental virtues are continuous and reliable dispositions, internally motivated, but that a sustainable society will continue to require law, regulation, and economic incentives whose presence serves as a moral indicator of values and goals. The environmentally conscientious will internalize this awareness and consider how best to act on it; others won't, but at least their actions will be circumscribed by the law and public policy—and the possibility of choosing the good for its own sake remains open to them.

Virtue is about doing those things that we should all do and yet that we can easily forget to do. This might be turning off lights, switching off the car engine when waiting in a line of traffic, or minimizing our consumption of much-traveled and overly packaged out-of-season goods.[9] The virtuous are already minded to do what should be done; they remember. The potentially eco-virtuous life is characterized by a need for reminding. It is in the gap between minding and being reminded that encouraging the virtues of environmental citizenship can make an important difference.

Notes

1. I would like to thank Andrew Dobson, Derek Bell, Piers Stephens, and Eccy de Jonge for their comments on earlier drafts of this chapter. I would also like to thank participants at the various seminars at which I have presented versions of this chapter.

2. For a related discussion of virtue and self-motivated compliance, see Pellikaan and van der Veen (2002, 28–46).

3. The conclusion that a society of the ecologically enlightened would require no policymaking and enforcement does not, of course, necessarily follow; see Connelly and Smith (2003, chapter four).

4. It should also not be forgotten that a certain sort of vice could result from an excess of reflection in situations requiring immediate practical action.

5. The difference between the two is, of course, relative, not absolute.

6. What lies behind these remarks is clearly a modified version of Rawls's analysis of social justice.

7. An ingenious objection to this conclusion is that we might be valuing richness and diversity rather than naturalness as such, and hence there would be no objection to a rich and diverse world produced solely by genetic engineering. For some of the issues, see Eliot (1997). Another objection might be that just as we ourselves have accepted a certain loss in what we inherited that we accept in return for the technological gains we also inherited, so might future generations want from us not natural variety so much as technological capacity.

8. For a fuller account of this understanding of the nature of duty, see Connelly (2003).

9. For example, it is worth remembering (and acting on the knowledge) that "a kiwi fruit flown from New Zealand to Britain emits five times its own weight in greenhouse gases" (Williams 2004, 286).

References

Aristotle. 1959. *Nicomachean Ethics*. Trans. W. D. Ross. London: Oxford University Press.

Bosanquet, B. 1923. *The Philosophical Theory of the State.* 4th ed. London: Macmillan.

Connelly, J. 2003. *Metaphysics, Method, and Politics: The Political Philosophy of R. G. Collingwood.* Exeter, UK: Imprint Academic.

Connelly, J., and G. Smith. 2003. *Politics and the Environment: From Theory to Practice.* London: Routledge.

Dobson, A. 2003. *Citizenship and the Environment.* Oxford: Oxford University Press.

Eliot, R. 1997. *Faking Nature.* London: Routledge.

Foot, P. 1978. *Virtues and Vices.* Oxford: Basil Blackwell.

Green, T. H. 1890. *Prolegomena to Ethics.* Oxford: Clarendon Press.

Green, T. H. 1966. *Lectures on the Principles of Political Obligation.* London: Longmans.

Hillman, M. 2004. *How We Can Save the Planet.* London: Penguin.

Hutchinson, D. A. 1995. Ethics. In *The Cambridge Companion to Aristotle,* ed. J. Barnes. Cambridge: Cambridge University Press.

Mill, J. S. 1949. Utilitarianism. In *The English Utilitarians,* ed. J. Plamenatz. Oxford: Blackwell.

Pellikaan, H., and R. J. van der Veen. 2002. *Environmental Dilemmas and Policy Design.* Cambridge: Cambridge University Press.

Rawls, J. 1999. *A Theory of Justice.* Rev. ed. Oxford: Oxford University Press.

Wensveen, L. Van. 2000. *Dirty Virtues: The Emergence of Ecological Virtue Ethics.* New York: Humanity Books.

Weston, A. 1994. *Back to Earth: Tomorrow's Environmentalism.* Philadelphia: Temple University Press.

Williams, J. 2004. *Fifty Facts That Should Change the World.* Cambridge: Icon Books.

3

Local Landscapes and Global Belonging: Toward a Situated Citizenship of the Environment

Bronislaw Szerszynski

Since 1990, when Environment Canada, the federal ministry of the environment, reputedly coined the term, *environmental citizenship* has been slowly establishing itself as a distinctive way of linking environmental concern, the public, and the policy process. Academic exploration of environmental or ecological citizenship has lagged behind practice in this area, but it is gathering pace (e.g., Curtin 1999; Dean 2001; Dobson 2003; Jelin 2000; MacGregor 2001; Smith 1998; van Steenbergen 1994). Mark J. Smith (1998), for example, defines ecological citizenship ecocentrically, in terms of the need to displace the human subject from the center of thinking about rights and obligations. Environment Canada defines environmental citizenship more broadly: "Environmental citizenship encourages individuals, communities and organizations to think about the environmental rights and responsibilities we all have as residents of planet Earth. Environmental citizenship means caring for the Earth and caring for Canada."[1] But what is the relationship between "caring for the Earth" and "caring for Canada"? More generally, is it possible to care for a particular place in a way that is informed by a concern for the wider environment? Is it really possible to erase the tensions between concern for a particular place and concern for the globe as a whole?

In this chapter, I use findings from two research projects carried out in the United Kingdom to explore such questions. I do so by concentrating on the visual, in a number of respects. I briefly examine the importance of the visual in the practice of citizenship, before focusing on the way that citizenship involves a *transformation* of vision, one that relies on an imaginative removal of the self from immediate everyday engagement in the world. Introducing three different visual metaphors or "tropes" for that self-absenting—blindness, distance, and movement—I then look at how these tropes are used in attempts to encourage a more informed appreciation of the visual distinctiveness of local places. Drawing on the anthropologist Tim Ingold's work on how people perceive their environments (2000), I argue that there is a tension between citizenly modes of relating to place and what Ingold, following Martin Heidegger (1975), calls "dwelling": the ongoing, corporeal engagement with one's surroundings that constitutes the primary mode of human "being-in-the-world." I conclude by suggesting ways in which environmental citizenship might be reconceived to be more in tune with such human realities.

Citizenship, Seeing, and Not Seeing

There are many ways in which issues of "visuality" are relevant to the practice and experience of citizenship in modern societies. Of course, contemporary societies are large and complex entities in which many social relations take place over a distance, rather than through face-to-face interaction (Giddens 1990). Relations are also increasingly conducted in the currency of abstract, coded information, rather than through visual channels of appearance, speech, and gesture. In modern society, the importance of the visual in relations between citizen and state, and between citizen and citizen, has thus become as much a grounding metaphor as a literal reality. Nevertheless, there are key ways in which both the modern citizen and the sense of a polity of which he or she is a member are brought to presence through seeing and being seen. Before applying these ideas to specifically *environmental* citizenship, let me briefly discuss some of these visual dimensions of citizenship.

First, then, citizenship implies relations of mutual visibility between citizen and citizen. From its emergence in the Greek city-state, citizenship was understood as a mode of human interaction in which individuals could appear to each other, face-to-face, in a public theater dedicated to the performance and remembering of exemplary, virtuous action (Arendt 1958). This understanding and practice of citizenship enjoyed a revival in eighteenth-century Europe with the emergence of new social spaces, such as the coffeehouse and the salon, in which the new bourgeoisie could assemble as free, equal individuals to discuss the political and social matters of the day (Habermas 1989). Codes of dress, speech, and gesture emerged—as did conventions for understanding them—that enabled the development of an urban public sphere where strangers could be understood and what was said was separated from who said it (Sennett 1986).

Second, modern citizenship depends on relations of mutual visibility between the citizen and the state. In medieval and early modern societies, it was the theatrical, copresent visibility of the monarch to their court that was central to the maintenance of society's symbolic order. The ritual procession or "progress" of the king or queen around their kingdom further served to constitute their wider subjects as a community of watchers. With the emergence of modern societies, this economy of visibility between citizen and state has altered in a number of distinct ways (cf. Thompson 1995, chapter 4). Modern citizens have become constituted not just as watchers of royal spectacle but as objects of state surveillance and monitoring (Foucault 1977). In liberal democracies, there is an increased demand on public authorities for more rationalized, open, and accountable forms of behavior and visibility. But at the same time, this has stimulated the emergence of new forms of "impression management" by public individuals and organizations in reaction to the increased visibility brought about by mass media (Meyrowitz 1985).

Third, visual symbols are frequently used in totemic fashion to signify membership of a civic or political community (Franklin 2001). These emblems or "badges" can differ along a number of dimensions. Some are official and formal (flags, coats of arms); others are unofficial and arise informally (graffiti, bumper stickers, modes of dress). Some are mobile and carried around on the person (lapel badges, passports, coins); others are fixed, and are to be visited, represented, or imagined (monuments, battlegrounds). Some refer purely by convention (flags, logos); others pictorially refer to a common territory, object, or practice. Finally, some are ascribed, signifying "communities of fate" into which we are born (nations, faiths); others are elective, signifying "communities of choice" that we decide to join (clubs, movements, brands).

Fourth, being a member of an audience, a community of cowatchers, can still be an important element in a person's sense of themselves as being a citizen among other citizens. This sense of "communion" can be evoked through

• routine, daily events—the reading of daily newspapers, for example, played a critical role in the emergence of a sense of nationhood (Anderson 1983, 39);

• extraordinary, planned events, such as sports events or presidential inaugurations, that are seen as required viewing (Dayan and Katz 1992);

• extraordinary, *unplanned* events, such as revolutions, disasters, rescues, or deaths, that displace normal broadcast schedules with rolling coverage (e.g., the fall of the Berlin wall or the death of Princess Diana— see Richards, Wilson, and Woodhead 1999).

Through such processes, relations of mutual visibility and totemic marking have long been significant mechanisms for the generation of a sense of collective solidarity and individual self-presence, and the different forms that citizenship has taken over the centuries have deployed these mechanisms in various ways.

If the visual and its metaphoric extensions remain a important element within contemporary forms of citizenship, however, there are also ways in which citizenship has always involved something like the *privation* of vision. For citizenship is a *distinctive* mode of belonging to a greater collectivity. From the emergence of the public realm in the Greek polis as a space beyond the private *oikos* or household, citizenship has always involved a certain self-absenting from the quotidian social world with its identities, interests, and perspectives. To act as a citizen—whether in relation to the environment or some other domain—is to think of the good of society in the abstract, and thus in some sense to leave behind one's private identity and interests; and this self-absenting is itself often conceived of through a visual metaphor. In the next three sections, I will explore three interrelated visual metaphors for the self-absenting demanded by citizenship: blindness, distance, and movement, discussing in turn how each of them might inform our understanding of environmental citizenship.

Blindness

An important component of environmental citizenship is the demand for environmental justice. To be a "resident of planet Earth," as Environment

Canada puts it, one must act in a just way—a way that treats one's own environmental interests proportionately in relation to those of others. In Kristin Shrader-Frechette's discussion of the environmental justice movement, which she defines as "the attempt to equalise the burdens of pollution, noxious development, and resource depletion" (2002, 6), she articulates the moral instincts animating the movement in terms of a "principle of *prima facie* political equality." For Shrader-Frechette, this principle has two components: distributive justice, which involves equality of both treatment and opportunity, and participative justice, which requires that all individuals have an equal opportunity to participate in decision making and that their deliberation be given equal weight. To be enfranchised as an environmental citizen is to be granted these equalities by the state; to act as an environmental citizen is to ensure that one's actions are informed by reference to them.

John Rawls's (1973) notion of the "veil of ignorance" uses a visual metaphor to capture this aspect of citizenship; to think justly is to *not* be able to see where we are, to be blinded like the traditional statue of justice, to imagine a veil drawn across our perspectival vision.[2] Rawls asks us to imagine that we do not know as whom we are to be born, at what station in society we are to be positioned, and thus what interest we will have, and to design society accordingly. He argues that from this "original position," any rational person would design a society organized according to certain basic principles of justice: that each person has the equal right to the most extensive system of basic liberties compatible with similar liberties for all; and that social and economic inequalities should be arranged so that they are to the greatest benefit to the least advantaged, and attached to offices and positions open to all under conditions of fair equality of opportunity.

Pursuing this metaphor of blindness further, to think as an environmental citizen would be to imagine that we did not know where we were to live, and to make arrangements concerning environmental "goods" and "bads" accordingly. Andrew Dobson (2003), for example, argues for a postcosmopolitan citizenship in which those who place disproportionately large demands on the environment have obligations to those who are ecologically poor. Such obligations could be interpreted differently. One kind of response is substantive: to equalize—and one hopes, improve—the environmental quality enjoyed by people in different places,

by different races and classes; another might concentrate on putting procedures in place whereby environmental "bads" might be traded or com-
pensated for in some way. Either way, environmental justice is blind. It
assumes equality; "only different or unequal treatment requires justification" (Shrader-Frechette 2002, 27).

Yet at the same time, the environmental citizen is expected to appreciate and care for their local environment. Recall that Environment
Canada insisted that "environmental citizenship means caring for the
Earth and caring for Canada." What is it to care for the earth *and* to care
for where one happens to live? Are these two separate tasks, possibly at
times in tension with each other, or are they somehow one and the same?
If the environmental citizen is blind, why should they care for Canada
any more than Botswana or Kazakhstan? Perhaps blindness has its limits as a metaphor for environmental citizenship; perhaps we need to look
for another metaphor for the transformation of vision required if one is
to be a resident and citizen of the earth.

Distance

One other such way of thinking about environmental citizenship is in
terms of elevation—not closing one's eyes but seeing from a vantage
point that transcends particular locations and narrow horizons. Such a
perspective seems to be offered by a global view—one that views not
locality or nation as the primary area of identification but the world as
a whole.[3] In December 1968, as Apollo 8 completed the first manned cir-
cuit around the far side of the moon, astronaut William Anders took a
photograph of the distant Earth that came to symbolize the leveling
effects of distance on ethical perception. NASA image AS08–14–2383,
commonly referred to as "Earthrise," was not the first full-Earth image,
but it was startlingly clear, and received a huge amount of attention
when the 70 mm film was brought back and developed. Anders says that
he prefers to hang the picture as he experienced it—as if he were once
again coming around the side of the moon, with vertiginous infinite
blackness "below" him, and catching a welcoming sight of Earth again.[4]
Yet "Earthrise" is usually reproduced as a conventional nocturnal landscape with a half moon, except for the reversal of landscape and celestial

object—all color is in the celestial orb, not the landscape—and the lack of any stars in the image, which seems to emphasize the isolation of terrestrial life (Cosgrove 1994, 275).

The image quickly enjoyed a massive circulation. A few weeks after the flight, Apollo 8 Commander Frank Borman received a telegram that just said, "You saved 1968." The image was used as a backdrop for news and current affairs programs, and on the cover of *The Whole Earth Catalogue*. It has been widely cited as playing a key role in inspiring the first Earth Day, held in 1970, and in galvanizing the then still-emergent environmental movement (Goldberg 1991, 57).[5] Denis Cosgrove (1994) quotes at length the essay by the U.S. poet Archibald MacLeish that appeared in the *New York Times* on Christmas Day in 1968.[6] It was reprinted alongside "Earthrise" in the May 1969 issue of *National Geographic*. "For the first time in all of time," MacLeish wrote, "men have seen [the Earth] not as continents or oceans from the little distance of a hundred miles or two or three, but seen it from the depth of space; seen it whole and round and beautiful and small. . . . To see the Earth as it truly is, small and blue and beautiful in that eternal silence where it floats, is to see ourselves as riders on the Earth together, brothers on that bright loveliness in the eternal cold—brothers who know now that they are truly brothers" (1968). Here, for once, we seemed to have the perfect icon for the "unlimited finitude" of the earth, and for the "panhumanity" that dwells on it (Franklin, Stacey, and Lury 2000).

Between 1996 and 1999, I and others at Lancaster University carried out a study of the production, circulation, and reception of such global images.[7] Using interviews with communications professionals, a survey of broadcast television output, and a series of focus group discussions, we sought to understand the dynamics through which global imagery, narratives, and appeals are produced and circulated within the mass media, and the effect this might be having on people's senses of themselves as bearers of environmental rights and responsibilities in an increasingly globalized world (for a summary, see Szerszynski, Urry, and Myers 2000). One way of describing what we were doing in the project was trying to identify the cultural conditions for a putative postnational, global, or cosmopolitan citizenship (Bauman 1993; Beck 2000; Tomlinson 1999, chapter 6). In relation to the emergence in earlier centuries of *national* citizenship, Benedict Anderson (1983) has brought attention to the crucial "cultural work" that needed to be done before people could begin to feel themselves to be part of such large political and civic units. Printed books and newspapers, radio and public service television, flags and civic rituals all played important roles in this process—not just by making possible the circulation of information about the life of the nation but also by providing ways in which individuals could feel part of an "imagined community" made up of people they would never meet, in places they would never visit. (Anderson 1983). We argued that the formation of anything like global citizenship in the twenty-first century would require a comparable amount of cultural work, and hypothesized that this global imagery might be functioning as a vehicle for such work.

We found numerous examples of "global" images over a twenty-four hour period of broadcast content, and suggested that global imagery was starting to constitute an unremarked, all-pervasive background to people's lives—one with the potential to reshape their sense of belonging.[8] Michael Billig (1995) had argued that perhaps the most important symbols of national belonging are those of what he calls "banal nationalism"—the almost unnoticed symbols of nationhood that pepper our everyday lives, from coins and maps to the very use of the word *we*. In a similar way, we maintained that televisual images and narratives were developing a global equivalent, a "banal globalism." Such imagery, we proposed, might be helping to create a sensibility conducive to the cosmopolitan rights and duties of being a "global citizen," by generating a greater sense of global interconnectedness and belonging, and thus of a common destiny (Szerszynski and Toogood 2000).

Yet the elevated vantage point has also been criticized for its association with power. The imperial, cartographic gaze is one that surveys a tract of land from a privileged vantage point outside and above the quotidian world (Harley 1992). Might the image of the world from space have embedded within it similar encodings of alienation and power? Ingold (2000, chapter 12; also published as Ingold 1993) argues that images of the world as a globe always bear subtle meanings of technological mastery over nature. He distinguishes two ways of conceiving of the environment—in terms of *globes* (perceived from without) and *spheres* (experienced and engaged with from within)—and suggests that "the movement from spherical to global imagery is also one in which 'the world,' as we are taught it exists, is drawn ever further from the matrix of our lived experience" (2000, 211). Ingold describes the shift from the premodern to the modern as one from sphere to globe, from cosmology to technology, from practical, sensory engagement to detachment and control (216). Although Ingold does not talk in detail about the photographs from space, he implies that such images must necessarily distort our relationship with nature, positioning us outside a world conceived as pure, passive matter, on the outer surface of which meaning is actively inscribed by the perceiver (213). Cosgrove (1994) is more sanguine, but notes that representations of the globe have always played a role in the iconography of worldly power—in terms of monarchical rule, bourgeois intellectual and worldly ambition, and the commercial ambitions of corporations today. He suggests that images such as "Earthrise" served a similar function in U.S. iconography, underscoring a distinctively U.S. ideal of global harmony, building on the conventions of missionary cartography with its roots in the idea of universal Christendom. If Ingold is right, then perhaps environmental citizenship, if it is conceived in terms of taking a global perspective on the world, positions us outside the world, and alienates us from it (cf. Sachs 1993).

Movement

A third way to conceive of the transformation of vision required by environmental citizenship is in terms of mobility. Instead of vertical displacement *out* of the world, real or imagined movement *within* the world can be both a source and expression of commitments that transcend the local and the particular. Of course, physical travel often involves serious physical impacts on the environment—impacts that have to be set against any beneficial changes in ideas or attitudes that it might also engender. But a defining feature of what Zygmunt Bauman (2000) calls "liquid modernity" is an accelerated movement of people, images, ideas, products, and information across local and national borders—a movement that is not only materially but also culturally important for the way it alters the nature of place (see Lash and Urry 1994). Three kinds of "travel" are particularly significant here: physical, bodily travel, which has become a "way of life" for many in Western societies; imaginative travel, to be transported elsewhere through the images of places and peoples encountered in the media; and virtual travel, transcending geographic and often social distance through information and communications technology (Urry 2000, chapter 3).

The experience of particular places can be radically transformed by new technologies of travel. John Barrell (1972) describes how in the early nineteenth century, the mobility of the British upper class throughout Europe provided extensive cultural capital for developing a capacity to imagine what other places were like visually. He argues that "the aristocracy and gentry . . . had experience of more landscapes than one, in more geographical regions than one; and even if they did not travel much they were accustomed, by their culture, to the *notion* of mobility, and could easily imagine other landscapes" (63). Through physical and then imaginative travel, the British upper class expanded its repertoire of landscapes for visual delight and consumption. Similarly, Henry Thoreau (1927) in his return to "nature" on the banks of Walden Pond in the mid-nineteenth century did not complain about the sound of the passing railway. It made him feel connected rather than insular, able to well imagine the many distant places that the railway was coming from and going to. He found himself "refreshed and expanded when the freight train rattles past me, and I smell the stores which go dispensing their odors all the way from Long Wharf to Lake Champlain, reminding me of foreign parts . . . and the extent of the globe. I feel more like a citizen of the world" (103).

Likewise, imaginative travel via the television can expand visual repertoires. Dick Hebdige suggests that many people are "world travelers" through the television: "It is part of being 'taken for a ride' in and through late-twentieth-century consumer culture. In the 1990s everybody [at least in the 'West'] is more or less cosmopolitan" (1990, 20). This experience is rooted in what Raymond Williams (1974) calls "televisual flow"—viewers are thrown into the extraordinary, flowing visual world that lies beyond the domestic regime, an instantaneous mirror reflecting much of the rest of the world into people's homes. Sensations of other places, especially facilitated through channel hopping and programs that simulate channel hopping, thus create an awareness of extraordinary, fluid interdependence. By consuming in and through the media, one can experience oneself to be part of a dispersed, global world, united by the sense that one is simultaneously watching with millions of dispersed others. As well as the ubiquitous television (one billion worldwide), personal computers and planes, cell phones and modems, enable people to straddle the globe, circling it with bodies, messages, bits of information, and images that travel over and beyond once-distant horizons (see Franklin, Stacey, and Lury 2000). Television and travel, the cell phone and the modem, seem to be producing a global village, blurring what is present and what is absent, what is public and what is private, what is front stage and what is backstage, what is near and what is far (Meyrowitz 1985).

Environmental Citizenship and the Transformation of Vision

How might these three tropes—blindness, distance, and mobility—shape the perception of particular things? And how might that transformation of perception foster the kind of enlarged thinking demanded by environmental citizenship? One striking feature of the televisual content that we identified in our survey as denoting or connoting the global was that it did not only consist of mimetic images of the blue earth. Globality was also evoked in a number of other ways. The moral equivalence of all humanity was suggested through images of the "family of man" sharing a global product. The distanced view of the earth as an interconnected whole was connoted through long, often aerial images of generic "global" environments such as a desert, an ice cap, or a rain forest, or through images of particular wildlife species that symbolized or indexed the overall state of the environment. The experience of mobility and comparison was implied by images of relatively exotic places that suggested the endless possibilities of global mobility, and by the very experience of televisual "flow" itself. By no means did all of these thematize anything like a rich sense of global or environmental rights and responsibilities. Yet all of them, often in limited or commodified ways, displayed the sort of transformation of perception we might regard as necessary for environmental, global, or cosmopolitan citizenship, using particular places, humans, or nonhumans to signify synecdochically the global as a whole.[9]

What these findings indicate is that all the privations or transformations of vision discussed above are only half of their respective stories. It is in the *dialectic* between blindness and sight, between distance and proximity, between mobility and rest, that the possibility of an enlarged notion of citizenship lies. First, blindness is only one part of justice. In Rawls's mythical narrative, once the liberal polity has been designed and the veil is drawn aside, we see which station in society everyone actually occupies. From that point on, the procedures of justice and entitlement are such that blindness is no longer necessary; indeed, it is imperative to *see* in order to detect and correct any injustice. But this is a vision transformed by the moment of blindness—without the impartiality granted by justice, what would be perceived would not be injustice but mere difference. Second, the perspective gained by distance is impotent until it is applied to the particular and proximate. The image of the globe as a whole can offer a vision of unity and common interest, but it is in the local and the particular that this global apperception has to be made real and practically relevant. Third, the enlarged perception granted by mobility has to find its application in rest. It is not movement per se but the transformed consciousness it can occasion that is conducive to citizenly modes of thinking and seeing. Vision is transformed by the comparison that is made possible by the experience of different particulars.

"Caring for the Earth" and "caring for Canada" thus appear to be not two tasks but one. To be an environmental citizen is to have one's perceptions and actions in a local context transformed by an awareness of that locality's connections with and nesting within a wider, ultimately global context. However we envisage it—as the impartiality of blindness, as the sense of unity given by distance, as the capacity to compare granted by mobility—it consists finally in a transformation of perception. As an environmental citizen, one no longer sees places and other things as isolated, unique, sui generis; instead, one sees them as available for judgments of moral equivalence, as parts of a wider whole, or as members of wider classes of particulars that can be compared and contrasted in specific ways. As such, the local becomes experienced in a different way, one in which a certain abstraction informs the very perception of the particular—an abstraction that makes possible the critical judgment necessary to citizenship.

Yet is this abstraction fully compatible with dwelling in a locality? Could it be that the development of a more cosmopolitan, citizenly perception of place is at the expense of other modes of appreciating and caring for local environments? In the rest of this chapter, I want to focus more specifically on the more literally *visual* aspects of environmental citizenship: the capacity to appreciate and the obligation to protect the distinctive visual characteristics of one's local place. By doing this, and particularly when informed by Ingold's ideas about how people "dwell" in the environment, we can see more starkly some of the dilemmas implied by the abstraction from the particularities of place that is involved in the transformation of vision explored above.

Environmental Citizenship and Local Landscape Character

In another research project, we explored perceptions of local landscape character among different social groups in the coastal plain of West Cumbria in northern England. As well as trying to determine local residents' attitudes toward possible extensions of woodland in the area, and testing the Internet as a medium for consultation, the project was also intended to study the extent to which residents recognized West Cumbria as an area of coherent landscape character. To examine these questions, we held two sets of three focus groups in towns and villages across the area, and held an Internet-based public consultation on landscape character that was made available on public terminals in the area and on the wider Internet.[10]

The West Cumbrian coastal plain, a thin strip of low-lying land stretching from Maryport on the Solway Firth to Barrow-in-Furness on Morecambe Bay, had been identified as a coherent "character area" on the Joint Character Map produced by the government agencies English Nature and the Countryside Commission. This mapping exercise had originally been piloted in southwestern England (Countryside Commission 1994), but had then been extended to the whole of the country. Each square kilometer of the country had been assigned an attribute from each of twelve national data sets, ranging from topography, geology, and ecology, through farm types and settlement patterns, to archaeological and industrial history. These were aggregated into 181 character areas— "broad tracts of countryside exhibiting a cohesive character" (Countryside Commission 1998, 11)—which were then published as a map (Countryside Commission and English Nature 1996) with accompanying descriptions of each character area.

For the Countryside Commission, the object of the mapping exercise was twofold. It was intended that the character map play a role in "focusing national policies," allowing them to be rendered more sensitive to "local needs and priorities." But the map was also supposed to "give national meaning to local action," encouraging people to "recognize and strengthen local distinctiveness," helping them to be aware of how the distinctive character of their own local area contributes to the character of England as a whole (Countryside Commission 1998, 11–12). As such, the exercise was intended to encourage people to become environmental citizens in relation to the visual qualities of the landscape, in ways that can be related to the metaphors of blindness, distance, and mobility developed above. Firstly, the Joint Character Map was designed to encourage a perception of "aesthetic equivalence" among the different places that make up England, dispersing the environmental sacred across the landscape rather than seeing environmental value as "piled up" in certain auratic places, leaving the remainder as environmentally profane (see Szerszynski 2005). Second, the map used the cartographic convention of perceptual distance to try to nurture local awareness of how each place fits into the fabric of the country as a whole. Third, the discourse of "landscape character" was used to encourage the kind of connoisseurship of landscape comparison that is engendered by the experience of physical, imaginative, or virtual travel.

The West Cumbrian coastal plain is interesting in itself, both socially and for its place in what might be called the visual economy of northern England (see Urry 1995). It is an isolated area, hemmed in by the Irish Sea and the Cumbrian fells, that has repeatedly relied on single industries, with concomitant periods of economic hardship and social stigma. Its landscape, a historically agricultural one, is marked by traces of formerly important industries—coal mining, iron smelting, shipbuilding, and so on—leaving a landscape that is problematic in conventional landscape terms, with an intermingling of urban and rural features, and significant areas of disused land. Its status as a landscape to be appreciated in its own right is compromised by the proximity of the highly valued Lake District, and by the presence of high-tech but potentially dangerous and stigmatizing industries such as the nuclear reprocessing plant at Sellafield. Its inhabitants suffer from high average levels of social deprivation, with many social groups left underemployed by the passing of mining and heavy industry; at the same time, there are pockets of more affluent residents, often professionals who have moved to the area from outside, directly or indirectly employed by the nuclear industry.

At one level, it seems obvious that knowing the distinctiveness of a place must be to know it better, to dwell more fully in place. Yet the findings of the project illustrated a tension at the heart of such attempts to foster environmental citizenship. In order to illustrate this, I want to concentrate on two of the focus groups held in the area in February 1999. For the first, held in a small, affluent rural village close to the Lake District National Park in the central part of the coastal strip, we recruited professional, male and female residents of the village. The second focus group was held in a medium-sized, inland ex-mining village with high levels of unemployment and social deprivation, and was made up of mothers in their thirties from "underemployed" families living in social housing. As might have been expected, the first group were far more mobile in terms of distance and frequency of travel, in their history of residence as well as in work and leisure, and had experienced higher levels of education. Most had moved to West Cumbria from elsewhere in the country for employment reasons, but also cited landscape character as a reason for remaining in the area. The working-class women had almost all been born in the area, and said they remained in the village because of family reasons as well as the lack of opportunity to move. Their loyalty to their village was compromised by a sense of growing social problems, especially drugs and petty crime, resulting from inward migration to the village from larger cities in northern England.

A number of contrasts between the two focus groups are particularly relevant here. First, the two groups had quite different ways of talking about the distinctiveness of their local area. The professional group talked about landscape character in ways that were similar to those adopted by the Countryside Commission and other official bodies. When asked to imagine a photograph these professionals might take of the area, they chose characteristically "scenic" images. In a photograph-sorting exercise and in their general conversation, they readily abstracted out visual properties of landscape, talked about places by comparing and contrasting them with other places, and did so in a way that abstracted the visual appearance of a place from the people who lived there. By contrast, the imaginary photographs chosen by the working-class women were attempts to invoke personal memories and associations—for example, through an image of the steps on which they all played as children. Their village was not a point in space that happened to possess a certain combination of characteristics; it was simply their village, "home." Their comparative talk about the village was more temporal than spatial, comparing life in the village today with that of the past, using narratives of increasing mobility, loss of community, and decline of social mores.

Second, when the women did talk about their own and other localities in terms of characteristics, these were rendered more in practical than visual terms. They could compare in great detail the kind of housing that was available in different villages nearby, but made little mention of how their area compared visually with anywhere else. Their response to the sorting exercise was to classify the photographs in terms of whether the places shown would be nice locations to have a house. They conceived of the outdoors as a domestic, social space, to be judged by the character of its people and its social relations, and by the practical benefits that it did or did not offer—as a "taskscape" rather than a landscape (Ingold 2000, 195). If anything, the professional group made more use of the outdoors; but they favored activities that depended on the visual properties of the landscape, such as walking, bird watching, mountain biking, fishing, and diving. The working-class women's use of the surrounding countryside was more tightly focused on practical (dog walking, walking to school, rabbit catching) or social (camping, picnicking) activities. Their discussion of possible new woodlands made little mention of the visual properties of trees, concentrating instead on the new risks to children that wooded areas might bring. They preferred any available land to be used for new housing or sports facilities rather than woodland.

Third, the professionals naturally employed a cartographic perspective when they talked about the area. In a map-drawing exercise, they clearly conceived of West Cumbria as a continuous two-dimensional surface that had various characteristics that came and went as one moved about on it. The women in the ex-mining village, by contrast, seemed to conceive of the area in terms of radial excursions away from the village to other places, especially other villages and towns. Even though one of the women was a bus driver, and frequently traveled up and down the plain, they all had great difficulty completing the map-drawing exercise, clearly being unfamiliar with cartographic ways of thinking at that scale. In the terminology for place developed by the philosopher Edward Casey, they experience West Cumbria as a "region"—as "an area concatenated by peregrinations between the places it connects" (1996, 24; quoted in Ingold 2000, 227). In Ingold's terms, they were "wayfinders" moving around *within* a world, rather than "map-readers" moving across a surface as imagined from above.

What are we to make of these differences? It is possible to argue that they simply show the uneven distribution of the sort of cognitive capacities necessary for citizenly modes of being-in-the-world; that the economic, educational, and cultural deprivation suffered by the working-class women meant that they were unable to locate themselves and their locality in a wider context of global interconnectedness and responsibility; and that their levels of deprivation kept them focused on lower-order, survival needs, preventing them from manifesting any latent postmaterialist concerns for environmental quality and social justice (Inglehart 1981; Maslow 1970). But I think something more interesting is happening here.

It is striking how different is the understanding of local distinctiveness promoted by the Countryside Commission when compared with that of the nongovernmental organization Common Ground.[11] In the Countryside Commission approach, places are an accretion of characteristics according to abstract categories. In effect, the Countryside Commission's approach to place is that of the *citizen,* in whose experience of place there is a moment of self-absenting or abstraction, of seeing it as if from afar or outside. By contrast, Common Ground encourages the proliferation of vernacular, ideographic, and connotative descriptions of local places—place myths, stories, celebrations, personal associations. Common Ground's approach is that of the *denizen*—the person who dwells in a particular place and has come to know it through moving about *within* it.

Ingold points out that when someone is in an unfamiliar place and is asked, "Where are we?" they typically use the abstract, nonindexical language of maps and coordinates. But when traveling in a familiar country, the answer is more likely to be the name of a place, accompanied by stories, associations, and memories (Ingold 2000, 237). The language of abstract, visual landscape character is a language of mobility and comparison. It is not simply that the privileged, mobile, cosmopolitan sections of society are better at it; the language is itself an expression of a mobile, abstracted way of being (cf. Schegloff 1968). In the terms developed by Heidegger in *Being and Time* (1967), the working-class women discussed above experienced their locality in terms of its equipmentality—its offering of practical affordances. For them the world was *zuhanden,* "ready-to-hand," known through use. For the mobile, professional group, by contrast, West Cumbria was apprehended in a way that was closer to the cartographic and professional vision of landscape, for which the land is *vorhanden,* "present-at-hand," known through being looked at, conceived in terms of objects and predicates, locations and characteristics.

There is an irony here. The Joint Character Map was intended to provide ways of looking that helped residents to dwell more fully in place, by both enhancing their perception of its distinctive character and appreciating the contribution that each place makes to the character of England as a whole. But becoming an environmental citizen in the sense implied by the map requires one to look at one's own home as a visitor would. The abstraction from the particular involved in turning denizens into citizens—the transformation of someone who simply dwells in a particular place into someone who takes up an enlightened environmental responsibility to it that locates it in its wider milieu—in effect turns residents into visitors.

Recasting Environmental Citizenship

I want to argue that there are wider lessons for the future of environmental citizenship to be gained from this exploration of local distinctiveness and landscape character. In the last section, we looked at the social situatedness of the language of landscape character—its dependence on modes of imaginative self-absenting that are themselves embedded in forms of life associated with high educational achievement, physical mobility, and economic power. It may be the case that environmental citizenship in its more general sense, as it is conceived in terms of abstract rights and duties pertaining to the natural world, is similarly socially located. It is already known that forms of environmentalism that are indigenous to the developing world tend to be extremely different from that of the West, focusing on present needs and situations rather than abstract ideas of nature and human duty (Guha and Martinez-Alier 1997; see also Szerszynski 2004, chapter 7). Perhaps even within Western societies there are limits to the spread of the ideas and practices of environmental citizenship unless they can be reconceived in terms that do not pitch them directly against a widespread habitus of local dwelling.

In the project on global citizenship mentioned above, we also conducted nine focus group discussions in northwestern England to explore the different meanings that images, ideas, and experiences of global belonging and responsibility had for different social groups.[12] Few of the focus group members would count as "good environmental citizens" in terms of them allowing their consumption or travel patterns to be significantly shaped by environmental or ethical considerations. Yet the way the respondents discussed their experience and feelings of responsibility in relation to global or globally distant problems might give us clues as to what an environmental citizenship that goes with the grain of local dwelling might look like.

How do the tropes of blindness, distance, and mobility apply to these respondents? First, they rarely expressed an abstract equivalence between people and places across the globe; Rawls's veil of ignorance did not seem to be part of their normal moral vocabulary. Second, neither did most of them seem familiar with the distancing effect of the image of the globe; rather, they felt themselves to be looking out onto a complex and diverse world from a clear location—that of English or British society and culture. Third, however, the language of mobility and comparison seemed to be more familiar to them, displaying as they did a facility to contrast and compare different places and cultures. But unleavened by any strong sense of moral equivalence or organic solidarity, this was rarely translated into the language of justice or injustice.

However, in a more piecemeal way, our respondents exhibited an openness to responding to moral demands that might be presented to them in terms of distant suffering or environmental damage, such as in terms of charitable giving. But when they tried to conceive of moral action at the global scale, they always conceived it as an extension of local forms of compassionate, charitable action. They found talking about citizenship in terms of abstract principles difficult and unnatural, preferring to speak about specific figures—such as Nelson Mandela, Mother Teresa, Princess Diana, and Greenpeace—who might be able to serve as *exemplars* of global citizenship, but who signified not so much abstract rights and duties as care, compassion, and the affective (for the distinction between duty and care, see Gilligan 1982). Yet the respondents seemed to operate with an implicit division of moral labor between the extraordinary morality exhibited in many highly mediated lives and the ordinary morality of everyday, private lives. The global exemplars were overwhelmingly what Lawrence Blum calls "idealists"—people who have a mission in life, who consciously choose and affirm their ideals, and look for ways to implement them in their own life and the wider world. In their *own* lives, however, the participants felt that it was enough for them to be what Blum calls "responders"—people who although they have no clearly articulated moral vision, nevertheless try to respond to the situations that confront them in a morally appropriate way (1988, 208–209).

This conceptualization of global responsibility as an extension of local compassionate action partly reflects the virtual institutional vacuum at the transnational level. Deprived of almost any opportunity for meaningful political action outside the nation-state, people naturally reach for moralized and moralizing vocabularies. Yet our respondents' language of care and moral response also provides more positive clues for an alternative way of conceptualizing a cosmopolitan, environmental citizenship. In its practical, ongoing *phronesis,* the charitable action of our respondents is similar to what Ingold calls wayfinding. Rejecting the idea of mental maps as a model of the manner in which people and animals find their way around a region, Ingold insists that such knowledge is a form of embodied knowledge. He points out that maps were originally not seen as representations of landscape but simply as *reminders* of past journeys. Finding one's way, Ingold maintains, is not like map reading, as if we calculate our movements in advance, and then make them—it *is* our movement through the world, in a process of constant engagement and readjustment in relation to our environment (2000, 239).

Developing this line of thought, what we need is environmental-citizenship-as-wayfinding. An environmental citizenship conceived in terms of abstract ethical principles is cartographic in ambition; it conceives of knowing where one is and where one should go in the moral landscape as if one can read them off from a cartographic representation. But judgment in the ethical life is not well described as the application of abstract rules; rather, values are better seen as emergent from ongoing transactions and relationships. Moral judgment involves the slow, steady development of craft skills and tacit knowledge, rather than the learning of rules or procedures (Dreyfus and Dreyfus 1990). Iris Murdoch (1970), following Simone Weil, understands judgment as involving a form of "attention," the cultivation of which enables us to see the (moral) reality of a situation. For Murdoch, this attention is not just something we switch on at moments of moral crisis but a continuous, cumulative process whereby we fashion and hone our moral openness.

Let us recall where our particular wayfinding has taken us. We set out to explore different conceptualizations of both global and local responsibility. Recognizing the importance of the visual in the ideas and practices of citizenship, we also noted that seeing as a citizen—environmental or otherwise—seems to require a certain transformation of vision, and we examined three possible ways of thinking of that transformation: blindness, distance, and mobility. Then, taking the example of landscape character, we saw how the capacity to see in this way appeared to be located in particular social strata and forms of life, and seemed at odds with the forms of local dwelling likely to be experienced by many in society. Nevertheless, rather than concluding that environmental citizenship was incompatible with situated dwelling and care, I then suggested that in the everyday moral responses of ordinary people to global moral demands might lie clues to a different way of thinking about a global environmental citizenship.

Following Ingold again (2000, 210), I would suggest that this could be conceived as an ethic not of the globe but of the spheres—of an environment we do not gaze at from the outside, with astronomical, cartographic clarity, but inhabit from within. Like the women in the West Cumbrian mining village, we should conceive of the global moral landscape not as a maplike surface to be grasped with masculine power from above but as a region constituted through specific moral excursions. As Ingold himself says, "Our perception of the environment as a whole, in short, is forged not in the ascent from a myopic, local perspective to a panoptic, global one, but in the passage from place to place, and in histories of movement and changing horizons on the way" (227). With such a haptic, rather than visual conceptualization, projects such as the promotion of environmental citizenship might better engage with the moral lifeworlds of the wider public.

Acknowledgments

I am grateful to Sherilyn MacGregor and Mei-Fang Fan for the many wide-ranging discussions we have had over the past few years on environmental citizenship and environmental justice, respectively. Many thanks to David Archard for his helpful comments on an earlier draft of this chapter. Last but not least, I must also thank the colleagues I worked with on the two research projects that inform this chapter—John Urry, Greg Myers, and Mark Toogood (Global Citizenship and the Environment) and Sue Holden (Public Perceptions of Landscape Character in West Cumbria)—without whom the specific arguments developed here would have been unlikely to emerge.

Notes

1. Environment Canada Web site, <http://www.ec.gc.ca/water/en/info/pubs/mountain/e_intro.htm>.

2. Here, I am using *blindness* to refer to the deliberate refusal to perceive. I am aware that the physical condition of impaired vision generally goes hand in hand with enhanced perception in other modalities; these are not the sort of issues I am pursuing in this chapter.

3. For an extended discussion of the issues explored in this section, see Szerszynski (2005, chapter 10).

4. See cover image of Szerszynski (2005).

5. For a fuller NASA account of the reception of the image, see <http://nctn.hq.nasa.gov/innovation/Innovation_84/wnewview.html>.

6. The full essay is available at <http://cecelia.physics.indiana. edu/life/moon/Apollo8/122568sci-nasa-macleish.html>.

7. The Global Citizenship and the Environment project ran from November 1996 to April 1999, and was supported by the Economic and Social Research Council (award number R000236768).

8. We conducted a survey of twenty-four hours of broadcast output on four television channels available in the United Kingdom: BBC2, one of the two public service channels paid for by license fees; ITV, the network of regional UK commercial terrestrial broadcasters; Channel 4, the national terrestrial television channel, focusing on arts and public affairs programs and minority interests not provided for on ITV; and CNN, the international satellite news network, based in Atlanta, Georgia, but broadcasting throughout the world.

9. As Stacey observes (Franklin, Stancey, and Lury, (2000, 98–109), among the products of consumer culture the global is often signified by reference to the exotic otherness of particular, often third world cultures and peoples.

10. This research was funded by the Countryside Agency, Cumbria County Council, the Forestry Commission, and Lancaster University, and was conducted by Sue Holden and Bronislaw Szerszynski. The three focus groups conducted in February 1999 were chosen to be representative of the main types of settlement in the area. The three groups that met in July 1999 were chosen to exhibit differing degrees of engagement with conservation and consultation, and with the Internet as a communications medium. The Internet consultation ran for 20 weeks, and had 243 visitors over that period—over half of which went on to complete some or all of the consultation (for more information, see Szerszynski and Holden 2000).

11. See <http://www.commonground.org.uk>.

12. Each of the nine focus groups met twice for two-hour sessions. Three groups from Blackpool were chosen to explore different kinds of activity that people pursue in their leisure time (local citizenship, consuming the globe through travel, consuming the globe through the media). Three groups were convened in Manchester to look at comparable sets of options in different professional, working domains (caring for local places and people, producing the global mediascape, traveling the global corporate world). And three Preston groups were chosen to examine how notions of citizenship might play out within recognizable, existing subcultures (local businesspeople, "Old Labour" internationalism, global flows of labor) (for more information, see Szerszynski, Urry, and Myers 2000).

References

Anderson, Benedict. 1983. *Imagined Communities: Reflections on the Origin and Spread of Nationalism.* London: Verso.

Arendt, Hannah. 1958. *The Human Condition.* Chicago: University of Chicago Press.

Barrell, John. 1972. *The Idea of Landscape and the Sense of Place: 1730–1840.* Cambridge: Cambridge University Press.

Bauman, Zygmunt. 1993. *Postmodern Ethics.* Oxford: Blackwell.

Bauman, Zygmunt. 2000. *Liquid Modernity.* Cambridge: Polity Press.

Beck, Ulrich. 2000. The Cosmopolitan Perspective: On the Sociology of the Second Age of Modernity, *British Journal of Sociology* 51, no. 1:79–106.

Billig, Michael. 1995. *Banal Nationalism.* London: Sage.

Blum, Lawrence A. 1988. Moral Exemplars: Reflections on Schindler, the Trocmes, and Others. In *Midwest Studies in Philosophy, Vol. XIII—Ethical Theory: Character and Virtue,* ed. Peter A. French, Theodore E. Uehling Jr., and Howard K. Wettstein, 196–221. Notre Dame, IN: University of Notre Dame Press.

Casey, Edward S. 1996. How to Get from Space to Place in a Fairly Short Stretch of Time: Phenomenological Prolegomena. In *Senses of Place,* ed. Steven Feld and Keith H. Basso, 13–52. Santa Fe, NM: School of American Research Press.

Cosgrove, Denis. 1994. Contested Global Visions: One-World, Whole-Earth, and the Apollo Space Photographs. *Annals of the Association of American Geographers* 84, no. 2: 270–294.

Countryside Commission. 1994. *The New Map of England: A Celebration of the South Western Landscape.* Cheltenham, UK: Countryside Commission.

Countryside Commission. 1998. *Countryside Character, Vol. 2: North West.* Cheltenham, UK: Countryside Commission.

Countryside Commission and English Nature. 1996. *The Character of England: Landscape, Wildlife, and Natural Features.* Cheltenham / Peterborough, UK: Countryside Commission / English Nature.

Curtin, Deane W. 1999. *Chinnagounder's Challenge: The Question of Ecological Citizenship.* Bloomington: Indiana University Press.

Dayan, Daniel, and Elihu Katz. 1992. *Media Events: The Live Broadcasting of History.* Cambridge: Harvard University Press.

Dean, Hartley. 2001. Green Citizenship. *Social Policy and Administration* 35, no. 5: 490–505.

Dobson, Andrew. 2003. *Citizenship and the Environment.* Oxford: Oxford University Press.

Dreyfus, Hubert L., and Stuart E. Dreyfus. 1990. What Is Morality? A Phenomenological Account of the Development of Ethical Expertise. In *Universalism vs. Communitarianism: Contemporary Debates in Ethics,* ed. David M. Rasmussen, 237–264. Cambridge: MIT Press.

Foucault, Michel. 1977. *Discipline and Punish: The Birth of the Prison.* London: Allen Lane.

Franklin, Adrian. 2001. *Nature and Social Theory.* London: Sage.

Franklin, Sarah, Jackie Stacey, and Celia Lury. 2000. *Global Nature, Global Culture: Gender, Race, and Life Itself.* London: Sage.

Giddens, Anthony. 1990. *The Consequences of Modernity.* Cambridge: Polity Press.

Gilligan, Carol. 1982. *In a Different Voice: Psychological Theory and Women's Development.* Cambridge: Harvard University Press.

Goldberg, Vicky. 1991. *The Power of Photography: How Photographs Changed Our Lives.* New York: Abbeville Press.

Guha, Ramachandra, and Juan Martinez-Alier. 1997. *Varieties of Environmentalism: Essays North and South.* London: Earthscan.

Habermas, Jürgen. 1989. *The Structural Transformation of the Public Sphere: An Inquiry into a Category of Bourgeois Society.* Oxford: Polity Press.

Harley, J. B. 1992. Deconstructing the Map. In *Writing Worlds: Discourse, Text, and Metaphor in the Representation of Landscape,* ed. Trevor J. Barnes and James S. Duncan, 231–247. London: Routledge.

Hebdige, Dick. 1990. Fax to the Future. *Marxism Today* (January): 18–23.

Heidegger, Martin. 1967. *Being and Time.* Trans. Edward Robinson and John MacQuarrie. Oxford: Blackwell.

Heidegger, Martin. 1975. Building Dwelling Thinking. In *Poetry, Language, Thought,* 145–161. New York: Harper and Row.

Inglehart, Ronald. 1981. Post-Materialism in an Environment of Insecurity. *American Political Science Review* 75, no. 4: 880–900.

Ingold, Tim. 1993. Globes and Spheres: The Topology of Environment. In *Environmentalism: The View from Anthropology,* ed. Kay Milton, 31–42. London: Routledge.

Ingold, Tim. 2000. *The Perception of the Environment: Essays in Livelihood, Dwelling, and Skill.* London: Routledge.

Jelin, Elizabeth. 2000. Towards a Global Environmental Citizenship? *Citizenship Studies* 4, no. 1: 47–63.

Lash, Scott, and John Urry. 1994. *Economies of Signs and Space.* London: Sage.

MacGregor, Sherilyn. 2001. Beyond Mothering Earth: Ecological Citizenship and the Gendered Politics of Care. PhD diss., York University.

MacLeish, Archibald. 1968. Riders on Earth Together, Brothers in Eternal Cold. *New York Times,* December 25.

Maslow, Abraham H. 1970. *Motivation and Personality.* 2nd ed. New York: Harper and Row.

Meyrowitz, Joshua. 1985. *No Sense of Place: The Impact of Electronic Media on Social Behavior.* New York: Oxford University Press.

Murdoch, Iris. 1970. *The Sovereignty of Good.* London: Routledge and Kegan Paul.

Rawls, John. 1973. *A Theory of Justice.* Oxford: Oxford University Press.

Richards, Jeffrey, Scott Wilson, and Linda Woodhead, eds. 1999. *Diana: The Making of a Media Saint.* London: I. B.Tauris.

Sachs, Wolfgang. 1993. *Global Ecology: A New Arena of Political Conflict.* London: Zed Books.

Schegloff, Emanuel A. 1968. Sequencing in Conversational Openings. *American Anthropologist* 70, no. 6:1075–1095.

Sennett, Richard. 1986. *The Fall of Public Man.* London: Faber and Faber.

Shrader-Frechette, Kristin. 2002. *Environmental Justice: Creating Equality, Reclaiming Democracy.* Oxford: Oxford University Press.

Smith, Mark J. 1998. *Ecologism: Towards Ecological Citizenship.* Buckingham, UK: Open University Press.

Szerszynski, Bronislaw. 2005. *Nature, Technology, and the Sacred.* Oxford: Blackwell.

Szerszynski, Bronislaw, and Sue Holden. 2000. *Way out West: An Experiment in Public Consultation through the Internet.* Lancaster: Centre for the Study of Environmental Change, Lancaster University.

Szerszynski, Bronislaw, and Mark Toogood. 2000. Global Citizenship, the Environment, and the Media, In *Environmental Risks and the Media,* ed. Stuart Allan, Barbara Adam, and Cynthia Carter, 218–228. London: Routledge.

Szerszynski, Bronislaw, John Urry, and Greg Myers. 2000. Mediating Global Citizenship. In *The Daily Globe: Environmental Change, the Public, and the Media,* ed. Joe Smith, 97–114. London: Earthscan.

Thompson, John B. 1995. *The Media and Modernity: A Social Theory of the Media.* Cambridge: Polity Press.

Thoreau, Henry. 1927. *Walden or Life in the Woods.* London: Chapman and Hall.

Tomlinson, John. 1999. *Globalization and Culture.* Cambridge: Polity Press.

Urry, John. 1995. *Consuming Places.* London: Routledge.

Urry, John. 2000. *Sociology beyond Societies: Mobilities for the Twenty-First Century.* London: Routledge.

van Steenbergen, Bart. 1994. Towards a Global Ecological Citizen. In *The Condition of Citizenship,* ed. Bart van Steenbergen, 141–152. London: Sage.

Williams, Raymond. 1974. *Television: Technology and Cultural Form.* London: Fontana.

4

No Sustainability without Justice: A Feminist Critique of Environmental Citizenship

Sherilyn MacGregor

Public life, obviously, was possible only after the much more urgent needs were taken care of.

—Hannah Arendt, *The Portable Hannah Arendt*

How might citizenship be framed so that environmental sustainability and gender justice are taken into account in equal measure? Many have looked at citizenship through environmental or feminist lenses, but few have brought sustainability, gender, and citizenship together in a way that serves to illuminate the complex and political nature of their interconnections. Feminist theorists of citizenship have had little to say about the environment; ecofeminists are inclined to dismiss citizenship as the inherently exclusionary product of elite male minds; and green political theorists seem rarely to think about gender, approaching citizenship—as they are now keen to do—as if "we're all in this together." I think each of these scholarly camps deserves to be challenged on their respective lacunae and I have done so elsewhere (MacGregor, 2004). My purpose here is to argue that the emerging green discourse of "environmental citizenship" suffers from its lack of attention to gender relations. If it is true that "the way we define citizenship is intimately linked to the kind of society and political community we want" (Mouffe 1992, 225), then it reasonably can be inferred that few proponents of environmental citizenship have lost sleep over the persistent barriers to women's equal participation in public life, much less over how to create an inclusive and gender-friendly polis.

In what follows, I draw on long-standing feminist concerns about the masculinist bias in political theory and key critical insights of contemporary ecofeminists to problematize some of the central themes of

environmental citizenship. The most significant problem from my feminist perspective is the assumption of a generic model of citizenship that
masks realities of gender (and other forms of) inequality while depending on a division of labor that frees citizens to participate in the public
domain. In a brief introduction to feminist commentary on the politics
of citizenship, I highlight important differences between feminist and
nonfeminist (including green) approaches to citizenship. In the second
part of the chapter, I discuss some of the central problems with nonfeminist environmental citizenship as I see them. These problems include: a
paradoxical coupling of labor- and time-intensive green lifestyle changes
with increased active participation in the public sphere; silence on questions of rights and social conditions that make citizenship practice possible; and a failure to acknowledge the ways in which injunctions to
make green lifestyle changes (as expressions of good ecological
citizenship) dovetail into neoliberal efforts to download public services
to the private sphere. I conclude with the uniquely (eco)feminist argument that blindness to gender specificity and gender relations under-
mines the very promise of environmental citizenship, for a society that
has not addressed the unequal, and therefore unjust, division of responsibility for sustaining life will not be "sustainable" socially, politically, or
ecologically.[1]

Feminist Critiques of Citizenship in General

There is debate among feminists over the value of citizenship as a concept, but most are in agreement with some fairly basic criticisms. I shall
note these criticisms briefly by way of introduction; they are explained in
greater depth in my discussion of environmental citizenship in the following section.

The general feminist consensus is that masculinist biases and patriarchal dualisms, together with the related exclusion of women from the
public sphere, have shaped the meaning and practice of citizenship
throughout its history. The very notion of "the citizen" is based on a
universal individual who, until relatively recently, was an independent,
property-owning, white male. With his basic needs attended to by noncitizens, this individual was free to participate in, and devote himself to,

the affairs of the polis by engaging in face-to-face deliberation on issues of collective interest. Historically, again until recently, it was only this kind of person who was granted the status of citizen, and so citizenship—as a status and a social practice—has been imbued with the values and experiences of white affluent men. Fundamental to this citizenly identity are autonomy, self-determination, rationality, and the maintenance of a clear boundary between public and private life. Women were denied citizenship status because they were not seen as autonomous persons (i.e., they were property), because they allegedly lacked the capacity for rational thought, because their proper role was supposedly to tend to matters emotional and domestic, and because political involvement would theoretically interfere with their childbearing duty to the nation (i.e., giving birth to the next generation of workers and soldiers). Even after women in most countries around the world have successfully fought for legal citizenship status, feminists argue that structural and cultural barriers continue to exclude them from participating as full and equal citizens of their political communities.

It is not surprising that these criticisms of citizenship have led many feminists to abandon the concept altogether. Among these feminists are those who prefer to construct an alternative approach to politics that is rooted in private sphere concerns and feminine experience (Elshtain 1981; Ruddick 1989). Like the campaigners for female suffrage at the turn of the twentieth century, these feminists argue that politics will be improved by an injection of women's values. For example, as I have discussed elsewhere (MacGregor 2004), many ecofeminists embrace a vision of the good ecological society modeled not on some abstract Western notion of political identity but on women's knowledges and practices of life-sustaining work (e.g., caring for people, tending to animals and crops) at the "grassroots" level (see Mies and Shiva 1993; Salleh 1997; Mies and Bennholdt-Thomsen 2000). Those feminist political theorists who have embraced citizenship, however, want to defend it as a potentially radical ideal that can inform both theoretical analyses and practices of membership in political communities (Dietz 1998; Mouffe 1992; Pateman 1994).

For these theorists as well as for me, there is something attractive about the civic republican tradition wherein citizenship is a specific kind of universal political identity, and politics is a realm where freedom, equity, and human excellence may flourish. Citizenship is thus regarded as a promising strategy for challenging gender inequality while imagining a form of political solidarity among women that does not forever tie them to an essential capacity or innate sense of responsibility to care for others (Dietz 1985, 1998). Take, for example, Denise Riley's postessentialist feminist defense of citizenship in which she claims that although there are risks in a notion of universal citizenship that masks gender and other local specificities, "it also possesses the strength of its own idealism" (1992, 187). "Because of its claim to universality," she continues, "such an ideal can form the basis for arguments for participation by everyone, as well as for entitlements and responsibilities for all. . . . Citizenship as a theory sets out a claim and an egalitarian promise" (187).

These procitizenship feminists make the important assertion that although this ostensibly gender-neutral concept is actually deeply gendered, it is better to join rather than to eschew the conversations about rethinking citizenship that have been gaining momentum in the social sciences in recent decades (Lister 1997; Voet 1998). Many feminists, therefore, are analyzing the gendered nature of citizenship in the context of societies where capitalist globalization and a neoliberal backlash against the welfare state (also referred to in the feminine as "nanny state") have led to a decrease in social rights and an increase in individual duties (more on this below). Rather than accepting a neoliberal definition of citizenship, some feminist theorists want to reinvigorate citizenship as a political location from which to destabilize the boundaries between public and private, and to argue for the collective provision of social goods like care (see Lister 1997). It is from this position that concerns about the shape of environmental citizenship inevitably arise.

Feminist Critiques of Environmental Citizenship in Particular

A growing body of green literature on citizenship embraces the claim that the only political arrangement that will work under conditions of radical uncertainty—such as "the ecological crisis"—is a democratic one where the voices of as many citizens as possible participate in public debate. This point may be seen as part of a renewed interest in civil society as well as civic republican and cosmopolitan meanings of citizenship among contemporary left thinkers inspired, inter alia, by a conjuncture of economic globalization, the apparent (yet debatable) weakening of nation-states, increases in international migration and transnational ecological destruction, and the desperate need to reconstruct the Left itself (Clarke 1996; Lister 1997; van Gunsteren 1998). Most eco-political scholars are critical of liberal democracy and the administrative state as being root causes of the ecological crisis. They are dissatisfied with the disempowerment of citizens through representative government and the reduction of citizen participation to periodic voting (Torgerson 1999). They are also concerned by the replacement of the "citizen" by the (more self-interested) "consumer" and "taxpayer" as the dominant political identities embraced by people living in globalizing capitalist societies. These individualist approaches encouraged by the New Right, and to an increasing extent by the New Left, are part of a culture that supports unsustainable material accumulation rather than conservation, instant personal gratification rather than prudential social planning, and competition rather cooperation. Alongside their enthusiasm for participatory models of democracy, then, many green political thinkers argue for a notion of citizenship that includes the right to a clean environment and, more important, a set of green responsibilities. Although there is a range of opinions, it is fair to say that green political conceptions of citizenship generally share common notions of what the responsibilities of the "environmental citizen" should be: to protect the interests of future generations and nonhumans by actively participating in democratic political debates about sustainability, to cooperate with and take part in community environmental initiatives, and to adopt green lifestyle practices such as recycling and reducing energy consumption (see Christoff 1996; Newby 1996; Urry 2000).

In studying this literature, I think central feminist questions, following Drucila Cornell (1997), are, *What kind of subject would one have to be to fulfill the expectations of the good environmental citizen?* And what are the assumptions that underpin the construction of such an ideal subject? My attempt to answer these questions leads me to think that most green political theorists of citizenship work from a definition of citizenship that speaks volumes about their commitment to participatory democracy at the same time as it reveals their assumptions about the organization of socially necessary work. They assume a gender-neutral citizen and a gender-neutral model of citizenship practice that mask the realities and specificities of gender inequality while depending on a division of labor that frees autonomous citizens to participate in the public domain.

It may be fair to problematize and politicize mainstream eco-political thought by looking at some of the theorists who have made important marks on the developing field, and considering how their visions and theories answer the question of "how we should live." That they are predominantly white, male academics living in advanced capitalist societies are not irrelevant facts in this discussion. Those who fit the citizen mold nicely are probably less well acquainted with the complexities of being and acting as a citizen than those who do not. But it is not only about masculinist understandings of citizenship: most ecofeminist writers have observed that environmentalism, as a largely androcentric (or male-dominated) position historically, displays sexist tendencies and overlooks specificities of gender. Feminism has always had a contentious relationship with left-green politics in general, often stemming from the failure of male-dominated perspectives and social movements to acknowledge feminist concerns (Segal 1988).[2] A useful analysis of sexism in environmental movements in particular is found in Mary Mellor's *Breaking the Boundaries* (1992), in which she argues that for much of their evolution, greens have lacked a vision that adequately integrates ecological sustainability and social equality, preferring as they do to regard capitalism or productivism as the enemy.

I do not suggest that the analysis stop here, however, at the level of blaming patriarchy or men. Nor do I think the response of too many ecofeminists (i.e., to compensate for the lack of gender analysis by celebrating women's ostensibly unique capacity for "earth care") is a particularly strategic one (see, for example, Merchant 1996; Salleh 1997). I would surmise that it is precisely this tendency to privilege caring and other values associated with the private sphere that has allowed ecofeminism to be relegated to the margins of green political theory. Meeting an underemphasis on gendered locations with a response that overemphasizes gender specifics and ways of knowing (often coming close to affirming the stereotypes about women that fuel the devaluation of all things feminine) seems a wrong move. Like those feminists who want to reconceive citizenship in feminist terms, I think it is better to engage critically with the problematic assumptions and blind spots, and then to suggest ways of seeing things differently. To that end, I will address two main problems in environmental citizenship discourse from an (eco)feminist perspective.[3]

A Problematic Paradox: Doing More (Duty) with Less (Time)

First, there is a problematic paradox in environmental citizenship discourse that in my view stems from the twin emphasis on lifestyle changes in the private sphere that promote both greater self-reliance and eco-friendliness and greater participation in the green public sphere.[4] Good environmental citizens are called on to recycle, reuse, reduce, self-provision, and make green ethical consumer choices on the home front (e.g., to buy things that are organic, nongenetically modified, cruelty free, locally made, fairly traded, minimally packaged, recycled/recyclable, and so on), while making a commitment to get involved in their community and with collective decision making in an increasing number of political spaces and institutions. Proponents of environmental citizenship assume that people will accept the inevitable increases in time and effort created by green lifestyle practices, and will still have time for citizenly pursuits.[5] This reveals a lack of consideration for the politics of the private sphere, for the likelihood that these injunctions will result in an intensification of the activities that are already divided unequally between men and women.

Environmental citizenship discourse privileges active participation as central to greening the public sphere for a variety of reasons. Social ecologist Murray Bookchin (1992), who believes the environmental crisis is a social crisis, caused by social inequality, was one of the first to theorize links between active citizenship and the transformation to an ecological society. He believes that political equality will automatically be enhanced if people can just participate more and differently. John Barry (1999) advocates various examples of deliberative democracy wherein well-informed and virtuous citizens play an active role in collective ecological management. In an ecological society, "with greater free time and a reduced need for constant employment, there would indeed be greater opportunity for enhanced discussion in a green public sphere," predicts Douglas Torgerson (1999, 153).

There are many green political theorists who model their visions of environmental democracy and citizenship after the Greek polis. It is curious that few green admirers of classical democracy point out the problematic premise on which it was established. It seems painfully predictable for me to note that in Athens, citizens were freed for politics by the labor of foreigners, slaves, and women who were not granted the status of citizen. Citizenship, understood as being about active participation in the public sphere, is by definition a practice that depends on "free time"; it is thus not designed for people with multiple roles and heavy loads of responsibility for productive and reproductive work. As feminist political theorists Carole Pateman (1988) and Anne Phillips (1993) have argued, modern theories of politics fail to take into account the sexual division of labor that not only sustains democracy but also makes it extremely difficult for women (and others with time scarcity) to participate as equal members of a political community. In fact, "the more active the democratic engagement, the more likely it is to be carried by only a few" (Phillips 1993, 112). Viewing time as a resource for citizenship is integral to any feminist political theory that seeks to problematize the unfair division of labor that has constrained women from full participation as political citizens (Lister 1997).

Also central to feminist reconceptions of citizenship is an acknowledgment that as embodied human beings, all citizens are inevitably dependent on others for care and nurturance (including, for ecofeminists, nonhuman others and the natural world). In her extensive critique of liberal democracy, ecofeminist philosopher Val Plumwood (1995) contends that the liberal democratic conception of the self (and by extension, the citizen) is flawed because in embracing independence and self-determination, they are at odds with the kind of dependency relationships necessary for ecological flourishing—relationships of kinship, mutuality, empathy, and care. (Note that these qualities are very different from the autonomy, self-determination, and rationality that traditionally have defined citizenship.) What she does not consider, however, is the extent to which post- and antiliberal green visions differ from liberal ones in their assumptions about the self-reliance of individuals. On my reading, although many green theorists offer progressive revisions of democracy, when it comes to images of the self-reliant citizen they have one foot firmly planted on masculinist ground. Inspired in part by civic republicanism, the image of environmental citizens as simultaneously self-reliant and politically active is highly problematic from a feminist perspective.[6]

One indication that the interdependency of human beings has been elided in green political theory is that discussion of the domestic sphere is at best one-dimensional, as part of the problem, and at worst nonexistent. As I discuss elsewhere, the field of feminist ecological economics has emerged precisely to correct the invisibility of unpaid life-sustaining work performed by humans (disproportionately by female ones) in environmental discourse, placing it alongside natural processes at the very heart of the human economy (MacGregor 2003). When the private sphere does appear in discussions of green citizenship it seems to be regarded only as a space of consumption (as opposed to a space of *productive and reproductive work*) or it is a place where people procreate.[7] In both situations, human excess is a threat to nonhuman nature and self-discipline becomes a green public virtue; individual behavioral change—for example, curbing unsustainable consumption habits, having fewer children—seems more important than social change.[8] Household arrangements and family relationships tend not to be considered relevant to democratic public debate even though changing the practices of individuals in the private sphere is a crucial part of many visions of how to get to an ecological society.

Viewed through a feminist lens, the ability to ignore or dismiss the significance of the domestic sphere is part of a masculinist denial of dependency and bodily fragility that has roots in Western philosophical traditions.[9] Feminist political theorist Nira Yuval-Davis (1997) argues that it is precisely this neglect of the private sphere that calls for its explicit inclusion in any discussion of citizenship. Green political theorists have recognized human dependency on natural processes and the fragile state of humankind in the face of ecological crisis. Most, however, have failed to acknowledge human dependency on the caring services performed by human beings and thus have failed to value the role played by domestic life in the search for ecological sustainability. Few, even among those who have recognized human interdependence at some level, have taken this a step further to look at its implications for human labor, at how necessary labor is distributed or who is ultimately responsible for getting it done.

It may be that left to their own devices, groups of people will find socially equitable ways to distribute necessary work among themselves. Marx seemed to think this would be so when he predicted that (to paraphrase) in the ideal communist society, a person would be free to be a fisherman in the morning, a farmer in the afternoon, and a social critic in the evening. This claim left feminist Mary O'Brien (1986, 430) wondering, "Who will be minding the kids?" Bookchin the eco-anarchist is not much different from Marx the communist in his vision of the ideal society. His libertarian municipalities are to be self-reliant and self-managing while decisions are to be made through a continuous and intensive process of face-to-face democracy in town hall meetings. This preference for time-consuming democratic processes and the assumption of an unfettered ability to participate actively in the affairs of the polis flies in the face of feminist analyses of the unequal gendered division of necessary labor. Phillips writes that we might "expect male politicos to warm to a politics of continuous meetings and discussion and debate, all of them held conveniently outside the home and away from the noise of the children. But most women have been so grounded by responsibilities for children and parents and husbands and houses that they could well have settled for the less arduous democracy of casting the occasional vote" (1993, 111).

Importantly, few green political theorists have addressed the question of how necessary labor—which in my view is bound to be intensified if people are self-reliant—will be distributed in a sustainable society. Few call, as feminists have done, for the democratization of the household (Lister 1997; Phillips 1991; Plumwood 1995). In fact, the question of how green practices in the private sphere are to be initiated, distributed, and sustained is seldom, if ever, asked. Barry (1999), for example, argues that the practice of ecological citizenship should transcend public and private, yet makes little mention of the implications for those people who often have no choice but to operate at the interstices of both spheres (e.g., women, racialized and working-class people, older or disabled people). He would rather not include the democratization of the familial sphere ("by, for example, . . . the creation of communal or state-controlled child-rearing institutions" [220]) in his theory of green politics. He may well take for granted that domestic duties will be shared equally (and would undoubtedly support the goal), but by failing to address this issue explicitly he perpetuates the assumption that the division of unpaid labor is not an appropriate matter for discussion in a green theory of citizenship.[10]

Most green theorists are silent about, unless they are critical of, establishing formal collective mechanisms for meeting social needs. As I discuss below, within green political theory there is both nostalgia for the self-reliant and self-managing community and ambivalence about the merits of a rights-granting, welfare-providing nation-state. Torgerson is typical of radical democrats when he blames welfare state policies for "bolster[ing] consumer demand and promot[ing] mass acquiescence" (1999, 8) without mentioning that they also have provided the conditions (i.e., time) for many women and other marginalized people to participate more fully in most aspects of society. This oversight is consistent with a tradition in green theory of preferring mutual aid and individual responsibility for well-being over the administration of welfare by the state or market. I maintain that not only does this not necessarily have to be an either-or choice but also that the green preference for self- and community reliance has not had the benefit of critical gender analysis. For example, when Alain Lipietz (1995) envisions an "end-of-work" scenario where people's working time would be reduced to afford more time for leisurely pursuits as well as community and environmental service, he fails to recognize that work includes more than paid employment. Nor, rather tellingly, is there a discussion of the gendered distribution of leisure time where studies indicate that men use their "time off" to engage in personal hobbies and pleasures while women tend to use theirs to catch up on the housework.[11] These gender differences in work and time are two concerns that have been significant to feminist economists (see Folbre 1993; Waring 1988) as well as feminist theorists of citizenship.

Although there are many feminist critiques of the liberal welfare state for being paternalist, racist, heterosexist, and alienating, it has also been well established that the ability of (some) women to participate in the workforce and in public life has been facilitated by the state provision of necessary services such as health care and child care (Lister 1997). The model of social democracy in Northwest European (especially Scandinavian) countries is held up by many feminists as more "woman friendly" than those systems that assume private responsibility for socially necessary work (Folbre 1993; Siim 1988). Despite the weaknesses of welfare state approaches, many feminist theorists of citizenship have recognized the need for some socialization of socially necessary-yet-feminized work in order to offer women a promise of a better quality of life and a capacity to claim their place as equal citizens (Bowden 1997). Arguing for some forms of collectivization of necessary work may also be an alternative to accepting the various private solutions to privileged women's "time poverty" that sees them purchasing the labor of other women (who tend to be marginalized economically, politically, and socially) to supplement their own (Ehrenreich and Hochschild 2003). While I have not seen the case made, I think it is worth investigating the extent to which collectivized approaches to necessary labor are less resource and waste intensive, and therefore more ecologically viable, than privatized approaches.

I am not arguing against all private provisioning of care or other forms of socially necessary work. Nor am I suggesting that the establishment of organic, vegetarian neighborhood feeding centers or "state-controlled child-rearing institutions" is a path to social and ecological sustainability. I accept that there may be an ineliminably private dimension to the production and reproduction of human life, such that collectivization and state-run service delivery can only ever be part of the answer to the provision of a society's needs. What I do want to stress, however, is that whenever and wherever the private or domestic sphere is implicated in strategies for social or ecological change, consideration must be given to the unequal and deeply gendered division of labor and responsibility, costs and benefits. Taking for granted that duties will be shared and the necessary work will get done is tantamount to making "more work for mother." Therefore, I want to suggest that at the very least, public debate over who does what and under what conditions ought to be built in to the very definition of environmental citizenship.

A Dangerous Dovetail: Emphasizing Responsibilities over Rights

The second problem that my feminist interrogation uncovers is a dispro-
portionate emphasis on individual responsibility in environmental citizenship discourse. A significant proportion of the green discourse on
citizenship tends to stress citizens' moral duty to participate in the kinds
of activities that will help societies move toward sustainability (see, for
example, Attfield 1999; Smith 1998; van Steenbergen 1994). As Andrew
Dobson (2003) explains, the turn toward a Kantian-inspired cosmopolitan view that all citizens qua human beings have moral obligations to the
human community has shaped recent conceptions of environmental (and
its close relative global) citizenship. While there is some discussion of the
need for new environmental rights (e.g., to clean air and water, to participate in environmental decision making), green cosmopolitanism
places greater emphasis on the individual duty to care for nature, to
engage in behavior that allows life on the planet to flourish (Attfield
1999). Bart van Steenbergen (1994) notes that environmental citizenship
is all about our obligations to the human community and the natural
world (see also Steward 1991). It is the acceptance of this responsibility
by individuals that matters, along with the implementation of the kinds
of behavior that this acceptance demands. Moreover, many seem to
argue that curbing liberal humanist rights and expanding ecological
responsibilities are desirable goals. For example, Peter Christoff writes:
"To become ecological rather than narrowly anthropocentric citizens,
existing humans must assume responsibility for future humans and other
species, and 'represent' their rights and potential choices according to the
duties of environmental stewardship" (1996, 159).

What concerns me is that environmental citizenship as "green duty"
dovetails unintentionally with dominant political agendas that employ a
"duties discourse" (Lister 1997).[12] Since the 1980s, the equation of citizenship with responsibility has become an "escape route" for governments as they move to dismantle the welfare state. In neoliberal
discourse, citizenship is increasingly becoming conditional on the performance of duties (especially the duty to work) and synonymous with
voluntary involvement in the community. The call for a rebalancing of
rights and duties in order to meet sustainability goals (an instrumental

approach to citizenship) seems dangerously similar to the stance of the popular "modernizing left" (known in Britain as "New Labour"), which sees citizenly service as a way to meet their economic restructuring goals. For instance, the current emphasis on citizenship in Britain is seen by some analysts as part of a reassertion of the connection between entitlements and obligations in the New Labour platform (Faulks 1999). It is often noted that the Blair government has been influenced by the writings of Amitai Etzioni, who argues that the major problem facing Western democracies is that too many social rights have made people passive and dependent on the state to administer their needs. This situation might be corrected if a sense of citizen responsibility to make communities work (with minimal help from the government) could be restored and strengthened (Etzioni 1995; see also Putnam 2000). Prime Minister Tony Blair is on record as saying, soon after his first electoral victory, that at the heart of Britain's problems is an "undeveloped citizenship" and that the preferred way to change this is to nurture a sense of community wherein "the rights we enjoy reflect the duties we owe" (quoted in Benyon and Edwards 1997, 335). In other words, *"no rights without responsibilities"* (Anthony Giddens, quoted in Dobson 2003, 44).

What is important here is that citizenship has become a solution to a problem: it is regarded as a way to both enlist public participation in the management of national affairs and relieve the duty of government to provide goods and services to the population. Relevant to the case at hand, some governments have appealed to citizens' sense of ecological duty by asking people to reduce, reuse, and recycle (the three Rs), to conserve water and electricity, and to use public transit instead of private automobiles. There are many examples of the use of "stewardship" as a concept in environmental policy and governance circles, often held up as a way to increase public participation in ecological restoration projects and establish community-based administration of local services (Roseland 1998). In Canada, for example, the federal government has developed guidelines for environmental citizenship. These guidelines are put forth with an explicit recognition that the government cannot achieve its sustainability goals without the participation of the population. In fact, it is claimed that "self-regulation is better than government regulation, and that voluntary action is the most effective way to achieve enduring results" (quoted in Darier 1996).

As part of this strategy, supporters of the concept of environmental citizenship place the onus on individuals, whether as citizens or consumers, to become more educated about environmental issues, to make the necessary changes in their own outlook and behaviors, and to take nature into account in both their personal and collective decision making. Education is seen as a key tool for building the kind of society that will be able to transform human-nature relationships, and education reform has been held up as an important part of this rebuilding project. As of 2002, British children have citizenship as a compulsory subject in the national curriculum, and while this does not specifically include "education for environmental citizenship," some effort has been made to integrate values relevant to "sustainable development" (see, for example, the UK government's 2003 sustainable development action plan, available at <http://www.dfes.gov.uk/sd/docs/SDactionplan.pdf>). I contend that the underlying premises of this education for sustainability program are problematic. It makes the (erroneous) Socratic assumption that "citizens fail to act only out of ignorance" (Cruikshank 1999, 16), and suggests that it is uneducated and *irresponsible* individuals—rather than unsustainable and unjust social and economic relationships—who are the root cause of the environmental crisis.

Although there is promise in efforts to promote cultural change from this angle, education for environmental citizenship can also become a way of disciplining the population to internalize a set of rules for behavior—to become self-governing—thereby justifying minimal state intervention. Éric Darier offers a useful Foucauldian critique of the state-designed and state-promoted notion of environmental citizenship as expressed in Canada's Green Plan, which he calls environmental governmentality or "environmentality" (see also Luke 1997):

Environmental governmentality requires the use of social engineering techniques to get the attention of the population to focus on specific environmental issues and to instil—in a non-openly coercive manner—new environmental conducts. . . . If coercion is not the principal policy instrument, the only real alternative is to make the population adopt a set of new environmental values which would be the foundation of new widespread environmental ways of behaving. These new environmental values will be promoted by the establishment of an "environmental citizenship." (1996, 595)

Darier does not address the gender (or class or race) dimensions of this process, but he makes it clear that the control of information by corporations and the state makes it difficult for all citizens to develop oppositional consciousness that could lead to meaningful acts of resistance to state power. From a Foucauldian perspective, the fact that citizenship can so easily be co-oped by (or dovetailed into) state agendas makes it an undesirable ideal for guiding sociopolitical or ecological movements.

While heeding the Foucauldian warning that "everything is dangerous" in this business, the kind of (eco)feminist perspective I am attempting to develop accepts citizenship as a valuable ideal and practice at the same time that it seeks to bring its various blind spots into focus. For instance, one can agree that nurturing citizen responsibility for sustainability is important provided that it is not done at the expense of taking steps toward structural and systemic change. I agree with those critics of green duties discourse who argue that the "privatization" of responsibility tends to take the onus off the larger problems (like corporate pollution) created by the costs and by-products of capitalist production (Luke 1997). Plumwood is correct in noting that this privatization "locates the major source of responsibility in the wrong places" (1995, 143). Household bottle and can recycling is encouraged so that nations meet United Nations and European Union environmental targets while it is business as usual for the beverage manufacturing industry. One cannot help but see green citizenship as an effective way to "greenwash" neoliberal resistance to green regulation.

So what is the gender analysis here? Granted there are ecofeminists who see hope in women's greater sense of responsibility and ability to instill green values in the next generation. Women will make endless trips to the recycling center because they care, and want their kids to care, about the future of the planet. As I discuss above, however, I am interested in how appeals for citizens to be more ecologically responsible take on a gendered dimension, especially in domestic life. This point is very much related to an analysis of how women are socialized or disciplined to perform work that benefits others, "concrete" (i.e., those they know and love) as well as "generalized" (i.e., strangers, future generations) (Benhabib 1992). As feminist moral philosopher Claudia Card (1989) notes, women have a tendency to take on a greater burden of moral responsibility due to their socialization in a patriarchal culture.

There may well be a gendering of environmental duty taking place that only a few feminist commentators have acknowledged. For example, sociologist Harriet Rosenberg highlights the ways in which mothers can become targets of corporate and governmental campaigns to download environmental responsibility: "The individual mother is exhorted to accept personal responsibility for a crisis that she is said to be able to ameliorate through private practices within her household" (1995, 197).

Insofar as women are household consumers, they too become the intended audience for morally based prescriptions for greening the household (Sandilands 1993). Advertisers also know to whom they ought to target their ostensibly green products (e.g., unbleached cotton diapers, nontoxic and biodegradable cleaning supplies, organic produce). Here, the focus on individual choice confuses the meanings of citizen and consumer. Either way, when the future of their children (and of course their children's children) is used as the reason for being ecologically responsible, women are apt to feel guilty; their compulsory feminine altruism is thereby exploited for the public (and increasingly corporate) good.

What happens when citizenship becomes all about individual responsibility as if all citizens have an equal ability to accept it? For some, this raises questions of justice and the conditions under which citizenship may be meaningfully practiced. And so we must return to the issue of how and by whom socially necessary life-sustaining work is provided. Since T. H. Marshall's ([1950] 1998) famous essay "Citizenship and Social Class," it has been held by many political theorists that the ability to perform one's duty as a citizen often depends on a set of enabling conditions (see Yuval-Davis 1997). Marshall recognized that people need a minimum level of social and economic security (and the *right* "to live the life of a civilized being according to the standards prevailing in the society" [1950], 1998, 94) in order to participate equally in society, so he adds social citizenship to his two other dimensions of citizenship: the civil and the political.[13]

A focus on duty obscures this understanding of citizenship, so important to feminist aims for gender justice, wherein rights in many ways *facilitate* the performance of duties. Arguably, a feminist conception of citizenship synthesizes the best aspects of both the Marshallian liberal social rights tradition and the civic republican tradition of participatory democracy (especially the idea that—to paraphrase Arendt (1958)— appearance in public as a citizen allows us to discover "who" rather than "what" we are) (Mouffe 1992; Yeatman 1994). This "critical synthesis" approach (as Ruth Lister [1997] calls it) stems from an understanding of citizenship as both a *practice* that involves human agency and a *status* whose attainment, with the political, civil, and social rights it entails, is crucial for protecting and advancing the interests of marginalized people. Lister writes that "the case for understanding rights as constituting a mutually supportive web of the formal (civil and political) and the sub- stantive (social and economic) has been made with reference to their sta- tus as a prerequisite for the realisation of human agency" (34).

Besides overlooking or downplaying the question of social citizenship rights, many proponents of environmental citizenship fail to discuss human rights in any significant way, preferring instead to focus on duty and questions of whether rights might be extended to future generations or the nonhuman world. By contrast, in spite of their criticisms of liber- alism and the limitations of masculine rights talk, many feminists have accepted (albeit to varying degrees) an approach to citizenship that entails human rights and political entitlements that are enjoyed equally by every member of society regardless of their social, economic, or cultural status. They have argued (and fought) for the extension of rights to those to whom they have been denied and who have thereby been excluded from citizenship (e.g., slaves, children, migrant workers). They have also argued for new rights to protect disadvantaged groups from unjust treat- ment (Lister 1997). In particular, reproductive rights have been a central concern for feminists and these are especially important in light of pre- vailing ideas about population control (including those held by some eco- centric greens).[14] Civil rights that protect against systemic discrimination and hate speech, and that help to foster social equity, are of great value to feminist and other movements for social justice. Rights that protect work- ers from exploitation and unsafe conditions are increasingly important in a global market that relies on the cheap labor of women (Bakan and Stasiulus 1996; Ehrenreich and Hochschild 2003; Lister 1997).

These assertions about rights are central to most contemporary fem- inist discussions of citizenship. Feminists would be apt to agree that too many rights and not enough responsibilities are indeed causes of the ecological crisis, *providing that* there is an acknowledgment that this applies only to very specific social groups. For most people in the world the opposite is true. Human and social rights are under attack in most neoliberal capitalist places in the globalizing world, and communities, families, and the women who care for them have little choice but to shoulder the ever-greater burdens of responsibility being created. Dobson (2003) makes a similar point about the fundamentally asymmetrical nature of globalization when he argues for a postcosmopolitan conception of ecological citizenship that does not assume a common human condition. Taking these points seriously, theorists who endorse the ideal of the responsible green citizen ought to acknowledge the importance of maintaining the workable balance between responsibilities and rights that is traditionally constitutive of citizenship—a balance that makes everyday practices of citizenship sustainable.

Conclusion

By now, the differences between feminist and nonfeminist perspectives on environmental citizenship should be clear. Perhaps the overriding difference is that there is little consideration in green political theory for the kind of *citizen relations* that would promote a just and sustainable society, whereas relations among embodied, interdependent people are of central importance to feminists.[15] Some ecofeminists wish to make this point by invoking the language of care and intimacy, while the feminist theorists of citizenship on whom I draw want to find a way of politicizing these relations and making them subjects of public debate. In contrast, while green political theorists are willing to acknowledge that individual human beings are dependent on nature for survival (thus the prudential responsibility to preserve it)—which is a significant corrective to the anthropocentric approaches to citizenship—they are less willing to acknowledge the relations of dependence that are central to human well-being. In this way, they preserve the position of the powerful vis-à-vis those who do the caring and as such are unacceptable from a feminist perspective (Tronto 1993).

I am sympathetic to the hope that in a different kind of society, collective processes of mutual aid would emerge to end hierarchy and oppression, to make state administration unnecessary. Many green theorists (especially those who embrace communalism and anarchism) take such an optimistic view of the potential for human cooperation that they think it unnecessary to mention how and by whom necessary labor will be performed. The inclusion of private sphere activities like recycling and energy conservation as examples of ecological citizenship practice is a radical departure from conventional theories of citizenship that consider household activities irrelevant to politics. This is a great improvement on past understandings. Feminists too would want to include such practices in their understanding of citizenship because, like other forms of privatized and feminized caring, they have been hitherto ignored. Yet they would want to do so as long as there is sufficient attention paid to who is performing the work. There is too much evidence to suggest that the gendered division of labor will persist regardless of the adoption of new ecological values by citizens. Consequently, even in spite of some of the dangers of state control, feminists may be more inclined than greens to argue for the preservation of social rights in a democratized welfare state.

Feminist citizenship theorists note, in contrast to greens who believe in greater self-reliance or more robust civil society, that the nation-state has the potential to be a useful means of redistributive justice that can promote cultural change. As Peta Bowden contends, Scandinavian experiences show that welfare state policies have helped to counteract the naturalization and feminization of care: they "facilit[ate] the rethinking of public values that connect the marginalisation of women and their practices of care, the injustices of gendered labor arrangements, and the irresponsibility of most men with regard to our intrinsic vulnerabilities and interdependencies" (1997, 164). With years of research and analysis of the gendered division of necessary and caring labor (and its obvious imperviousness to change), feminists must be skeptical of visions that neglect to mention the conditions that make citizenship possible for a broad number of people—like social and economic rights. And they must continue to argue that where the state does not provide desirable substitutes for necessary labor in the private sphere, this labor must be shared equally (i.e., by able-bodied men and women) as a matter of justice.

As other chapters in this volume assert persuasively, the injection of green values such as environmental sustainability into political analyses of "how we ought to live" has challenged our understandings and practices of democratic citizenship in important ways. The fact that the (eco)feminist critique I have presented here reiterates many of the objections that feminists have been making for decades, however, suggests that environmental citizenship discourse has yet to take the central feminist values of gender equity and justice onboard. Environmentalists and feminists need to do better to bring their different but not uncomplementary agendas together. I therefore conclude with the inevitable question, What would a feminist environmental citizenship be? To provide a definition or list of necessary conditions would be to contradict my commitment to deliberative democratic politics. The arguments made above do suggest what it is not. Nevertheless, it is clear that putting the words *feminist* and *environmental* in front of the word *citizenship* draws attention to what has thus far been excluded from the discourse of citizenship. There is a need to value the specificity of citizenship as an intrinsically important practice at the same time that there is a need to recognize the foundational aspects of labor (provided by women and nature) that allow this specificity to flourish. While there are several currents of political theory that do the former (i.e., civic republicans and radical democrats), feminists are alone in doing the latter—although only some feminists make clear the need to de-gender and de-privatize the conditions that make citizenship possible. I am arguing that only an (eco)feminist citizenship does both, and this makes it necessary for democratic political life and gender equity—two conditions without which environmental sustainability will be impossible.

Acknowledgments

Many thanks to the following people for their helpful comments at various stages of thinking about and writing this chapter: Catriona Sandilands, Lorraine Code, Margrit Eichler, Ilan Kapoor, and Andrew Dobson. It is adapted from a chapter in my forthcoming book *Beyond Mothering Earth: Ecological Citizenship and the Gendered Politics of Care* (University of British Columbia Press). My research was supported by doctoral and postdoctoral fellowships funded by the Social Sciences and Humanities Research Council of Canada.

Notes

1. I put *eco* in parentheses to indicate that I am bringing together a particular kind of ecofeminism (that which is *critical* of essentialism, maternalism, and spirituality as a basis for politics) and a particular strand of feminist political theory (specifically, that which embraces radical democracy and the intrinsic value of politics and citizenship) to fashion a hybridized perspective that is not reducible to either label. In my view, neither body of work—ecofeminism nor feminist political thought—does the job sufficiently on its own (MacGregor 2004).

2. Just as radical feminism emerged out of the sexism and unequal gender relations within civil rights and student movement groups in the 1960s, one impetus for the birth of ecofeminist perspectives in the early 1970s was sexism within the green movement (Mellor 1992).

3. Part of the argument I wish to make in this chapter is that these feminist objections are not unique to environmental citizenship. Rather, they are applications of the long-standing contributions feminist scholars have made to debates about citizenship and democracy in general to the relatively new discourse of environmental citizenship.

4. For a discussion of the "green public sphere," see Torgerson (1999). Drawing heavily on the writings of Hannah Arendt, Torgerson argues for a green public sphere as a space for *ecologically informed public discourse*. For him, this depends on the acceptance of a shared meaning of citizenship as an end in itself—or in his words, citizenship as "radically nonstrategic and noninstrumental" (14).

5. There is admittedly scant research to support this intuitive claim. For one empirically based feminist discussion of the relationship between green practices and increased time spent on domestic work in Germany, see Schultz (1993).

6. For a discussion of other sources of inspiration for theories of environmental citizenship, see Dobson (2003).

7. For instance, John O'Neill writes that whereas the household was once a model for political economy and the good life, "in the modern economy it serves primarily as a place of consumption of goods and services" (1993, 172).

8. I note here the example of the "things *you* can do to save the planet" lists used to promote good green citizenship by environmental organizations. I recently saw a sign in the window of the Green Party office in Madison, Wisconsin, that read, "Use your bike; reduce, reuse, recycle; and plan your family size."

9. For a discussion linking this denial of dependency and bodily fragility in Western philosophy to the ecological crisis, see Plumwood (1993, 2001).

10. To his credit, Barry (1999, 262) admits that his lack of attention to materialist ecofeminist analyses is a "central weakness" of his book *Rethinking Green Politics*.

11. This was found to be the case in studies of how working-time reduction schemes have worked in France, according to Daniel Kinderman, "The Emancipatory Potential of Modernity: André Gorz and Working-Time Reduction" (paper presented at the Postmodernism and the Environment: Critical Dialogues conference, Congress of the Humanities and Social Sciences Federation of Canada, Université Laval, Québec, May 26, 2001).

12. For example, New Labour in Britain and recent administrations in the United States (Clinton, Bush) share both the philosophical influence of U.S. conservative-communitarian Amitai Eztioni and the national economic imperatives of the globalizing capitalist marketplace.

13. For a feminist critique of Marshall's focus on class to the exclusion of race and gender inequality, see Fraser and Gordon (1994).

14. David Held notes that it is problematic that reproductive rights are ignored in mainstream citizenship literature because they are "the very basis of the possibility of effective participation of women in both civil society and the polity" (quoted in Lister 1997, 18).

15. Dobson (2003), who draws on feminist theories of citizenship to develop his notion of postcosmopolitan environmental citizenship, is a welcome exception to this observation.

References

Arendt, Hannah. 1958. *The Human Condition.* Chicago: University of Chicago Press.

Attfield, Robin. 1999. *The Ethics of the Global Environment.* Edinburgh: Edinburgh University Press.

Baehr, Peter, ed. 2000. *The Portable Hannah Arendt.* New York: Penguin Books.

Bakan, Abigail B., and Daiva K. Stasiulus. 1996. Structural Adjustment, Citizenship, and Foreign Domestic Labour: The Canadian Case. In *Rethinking Restructuring: Gender and Change in Canada,* ed. Isabella Bakker, 217–242. Toronto: University of Toronto Press.

Barry, John. 1999. *Rethinking Green Politics.* London: Sage Publications.

Benhabib, Seyla. 1992. *Situating the Self: Gender, Community, and Postmodernism in Contemporary Ethics.* New York: Routledge.

Benyon, J., and A. Edwards. 1997. 1997: Crime and Public Order. In *Developments in British Politics 5,* ed. P. Dunleavy et al. Basingstoke: Macmillan.

Bookchin, Murray. 1992. *Urbanization without Cities: The Rise and Decline of Citizenship.* Montreal: Black Rose Books.

Bowden, Peta. 1997. *Caring: Gender-Sensitive Ethics.* New York: Routledge.

Card, Claudia. 1989. Gender and Moral Luck. In *Identity, Character, and Morality: Essays in Moral Psychology,* ed. O. Flanagan and A. Rorty, 199–218. Cambridge: MIT Press.

Christoff, Peter. 1996. Ecological Citizens and Ecologically Guided Democracy. In *Democracy and Green Political Thought,* ed. B. Doherty and M. de Geus, 151–169. New York: Routledge.

Clarke, Paul. 1996. *Deep Citizenship.* London: Pluto Press.

Cornell, Drucila. 1997. Gender Hierarchy, Equality, and the Possibility of Democracy. In *Feminism and the New Democracy,* ed. J. Dean, 210–221. Thousand Oaks, CA: Sage Publications.

Cruikshank, Barbara. 1999. *The Will to Empower: Democratic Citizens and Other Subjects.* Ithaca, NY: Cornell University Press.

Darier, Éric. 1996. Environmental Governmentality: The Case of Canada's Green Plan. *Environmental Politics* 5, no. 4: 585–606.

Dietz, Mary. 1985. Citizenship with a Feminist Face: The Problem with Maternal Thinking. *Political Theory* 13, no. 1 (February): 19–37.

Dietz, Mary. 1998. Context Is All: Feminism and Theories of Citizenship. In *Feminist Ethics,* ed. M. Gatens, 301–322. Dartmouth, NH: Ashgate.

Dobson, Andrew. 2003. *Citizenship and the Environment.* Oxford: Oxford University Press.

Ehrenreich, Barbara, and Arlie Russell Hochschild, eds. 2003. *Global Woman: Nannies, Maids, and Sex Workers in the New Economy.* London: Granta.

Elshtain, Jean Bethke. 1981. *Public Man, Private Woman: Women in Social and Political Thought.* Princeton, NJ: Princeton University Press.

Etzioni, Amitai. 1995. *The Spirit of Community: Rights, Responsibilities, and the Communitarian Agenda.* London: Fontana Press.

Faulks, Keith. 1999. *Citizenship in Modern Britain.* Edinburgh: Edinburgh University Press.

Folbre, Nancy. 1993. *Who Pays for the Kids? Gender and the Structures of Constraint.* New York: Routledge.

Fraser, Nancy, and Linda Gordon. 1994. A Genealogy of Dependency: Tracing a Keyword of the U.S. Welfare State. *Signs* 19, no. 2 (Winter): 309–336.

Lipietz, Alain. 1995. *Green Hopes: The Future of Political Ecology.* Cambridge: Polity Press.

Lister, Ruth. 1997. *Citizenship: Feminist Perspectives.* New York: New York University Press.

Luke, Timothy W. 1997. *Ecocritique: Contesting the Politics of Nature, Economy, and Culture.* Minneapolis: University of Minnesota Press.

MacGregor, Sherilyn. 2003. Feminist Perspectives on Sustainability. In Introduction to Sustainable Development, in *UNESCO Encyclopedia of Life Support Systems (EOLSS),* ed. D. Bell and A. Cheung. Oxford: Eolss Publishers. Available at <http://www.eolss.net>.

MacGregor, Sherilyn. 2004. From Care to Citizenship: Calling Ecofeminism Back to Politics. *Ethics and the Environment* 9, no. 1:56–84.

Marshall, T. H. [1950] 1998. Citizenship and Social Class. In *The Citizenship Debates: A Reader*, ed. G. Shafir, 93–111. Minneapolis: University of Minnesota Press.

Mellor, Mary. 1992. *Breaking the Boundaries: Towards a Feminist Green Socialism*. London: Virago Press.

Merchant, Carolyn. 1996. *Earthcare: Women and the Environment*. New York: Routledge.

Mies, Maria, and Veronika Bennholdt-Thomsen. 2000. *The Subsistence Perspective: Beyond the Globalized Economy*. London: Zed Books.

Mies, Maria, and Vandana Shiva. 1993. *Ecofeminism*. London: Zed Books.

Mouffe, Chantal. 1992. Democratic Citizenship and the Political Community. In *Dimensions of Radical Democracy: Pluralism, Citizenship, Community*, ed. C. Mouffe, 225–239. London: Verso.

Newby, Howard. 1996. Citizenship in a Green World: Global Commons and Human Stewardship. In *Citizenship Today: The Contemporary Relevance of T. H. Marshall*, ed. M. Bulmer and A. Rees, 209–221. London: UCL Press.

O'Brien, Mary. 1986. Feminism and Revolution. In *The Politics of Reproduction*, eds. R. Hamilton and M. Barrett, 424–431. Montreal: Book Centre.

O'Neill, John. 1996. *Ecology, Policy and Politics: Human Well-being and the Natural World*. New York: Routledge.

Pateman, Carole. 1988. *The Sexual Contract*. Cambridge: Polity Press.

Pateman, Carole. 1994. Feminism and Democracy. In *Citizenship: Critical Concepts*, ed. B. Turner and P. Hamilton, 17–31. London: Routledge.

Phillips, Anne. 1991. *Engendering Democracy*. Cambridge: Polity Press.

Phillips, Anne. 1993. *Democracy and Difference*. University Park: Pennsylvania State University Press.

Plumwood, Val. 1993. *Feminism and the Mastery of Nature*. New York: Routledge.

Plumwood, Val. 1995. Has Democracy Failed Ecology? An Ecofeminist Perspective. *Environmental Politics* 4, no. 4:136–169.

Plumwood, Val. 2001. *The Ecological Crisis of Reason*. New York: Routledge.

Putnam, Robert. 2000. *Bowling Alone: The Collapse and Revival of American Community*. New York: Simon and Schuster.

Riley, Denise. 1992. Citizenship and the Welfare State. In *Political and Economic Forms of Modernity*, ed. J. Allen, P. Braham, and P. Lewis, Cambridge: Polity Press.

Roseland, Mark. 1998. *Toward Sustainable Communities: Resources for Citizens and Their Governments*. Philadelphia: New Society Publishers.

Rosenberg, Harriet. 1995. From Trash to Treasure: Housewife Activists and the Environmental Justice Movement. In *Articulating Hidden Histories: Exploring the Influence of Eric Wolf*, ed. J. Schneider and R. Rapp, 190–204. Berkeley: University of California Press.

Ruddick, Sara. 1989. *Maternal Thinking: Toward a Politics of Peace*. New York: Beacon Press.

Salleh, Ariel. 1997. *Ecofeminism as Politics: Nature, Marx, and the Postmodern*. London: Zed Books.

Sandilands, Catriona. 1993. On "Green Consumerism": Environmental Privatization and "Family Values." *Canadian Women's Studies/Les Cahiers de la Femme* 13, no. 3 (Spring): 45–47.

Schultz, Irmgaard. 1993. Women and Waste. *Capitalism, Nature, Socialism* 4, no. 2:51–63.

Segal, Lynne. 1988. *Is the Future Female? Troubled Thoughts on Contemporary Feminism*. London: Virago Press.

Siim, Birthe. 1988. Towards a Feminist Rethinking of the Welfare State. In *The Political Interests of Gender*, ed. K. Jones and A. Jonasdottir, 160–186. London: Sage.

Smith, Mark J. 1998. *Ecologism: Towards Ecological Citizenship*. Milton Keynes: Open University Press.

Steward, Fred. 1991. Citizens of Planet Earth. In *Citizenship*, ed. G. Andrews, 65–75. London: Lawrence and Wishart.

Torgerson, Douglas. 1999. *The Promise of Green Politics: Environmentalism and the Public Sphere*. Durham, NC: Duke University Press.

Tronto, Joan. 1993. *Moral Boundaries: A Political Argument for an Ethic of Care*. New York: Routledge.

Urry, John. 2000. Global Flows and Global Citizenship. In *Democracy, Citizenship, and the Global City*, ed. E. Isin, 62–78. New York: Routledge.

van Gunsteren, Herman. 1998. *A Theory of Citizenship: Organizing Plurality in Contemporary Democracies*. Boulder, CO: Westview Press.

van Steenbergen, Bart. 1994. Towards a Global Ecological Citizen. In *The Condition of Citizenship*, ed. B. van Steenbergen, 62–78. London: Sage.

Voet, Rian. 1998. *Feminism and Citizenship*. London: Sage.

Waring, Marilyn. 1988. *If Women Counted: A New Feminist Economics*. New York: HarperCollins.

Yeatman, Anna. 1993. Voice and Representation in the Politics of Difference. In *Feminism and the Politics of Difference*, ed. S. Gunew and A. Yeatman. London: Allen and Unwin.

Yuval-Davis, Nira. 1997. Women, Citizenship, and Difference. *Feminist Review* 57 (Autumn): 4–27.

5

Demonstrating Environmental Citizenship? A Study of Everyday Life among Green Activists

Dave Horton

What might environmental citizenship look like, and how might such a citizenship be produced?[1] This chapter posits that across the range of their everyday practices, green political activists demonstrate a distinctive, important, and potentially replicable form of environmental citizenship. Following a brief consideration of the concept of environmental citizenship, the chapter is divided into three parts. First, activists' typical "green lifestyles," which emerge from a shared green culture, are described. Leading these green lifestyles—embodying a culturally produced awareness of environmental risks, rights, and responsibilities—activists assemble their diverse everyday practices, from the most "personal" to the most "political," into a coherent whole. Second, the chapter discusses and analyzes the role of green networks, spaces, materialities, and times in the assemblage of activists' green lifestyles; it thereby draws attention to the specific resources required for the production and reproduction of those lifestyles. Third, the chapter explores how, in the search for "sustainability," this activist-derived "elite model" of environmental citizenship might be broadened.

The Concept of Environmental Citizenship

The concept of environmental citizenship currently tends to be used in one of two main ways. In the first, it refers to the teaching of values and practices appropriate to the achievement of sustainability. Already familiar from the writings of the environmental movement, the governmental policy discourse that emerged in the wake of the first Earth Summit also tends to follow this meaning, so that, for example, householders need to be encouraged to switch off lights, insulate their homes, conserve water, and increase their recycling rates. The assumption animating such interventions is that progress toward sustainability is achievable through incremental shifts in everyday personal behaviors. Here, environmental citizenship is an individualized project, and its discourse is primarily disciplinary. Whether through governmental programs or the pronouncements of environmental organizations, people need to be made more aware of environmental problems and become environmentally responsible citizens; they need to be disciplined into "good," "green" behaviors.

In the second main contemporary use of the concept, environmental citizenship refers less to environmental responsibilities and much more to environmental rights. Specifically, the language of citizenship is used to name and critique the uneven spread of putative environmental rights. Particular groups, for example, are said to lack the right to clean air, a safe environment, or healthy working conditions (Bullard 1990; Harvey 1996). Such discussions are obviously connected to the global politics of gender, class, "race," and ethnicity. Here, environmental citizenship is a way of talking about differential risks to specific human bodies, and the ways in which governments and corporations often trample on the environmental rights of specific peoples. This, then, is primarily a discourse of (the struggle for) social justice.

This chapter thinks about the concept of environmental citizenship somewhat differently from either of the ways outlined above. It considers environmental citizenship as a nonterritorial form of citizenship, developing not in the institutions of the nation-state but within the cultural and political spaces of contemporary environmentalism. Such a citizenship is in many ways consistent with the "postcosmopolitan ecological citizenship" articulated by Andrew Dobson (2003). In the context of a deeply unequal world with sustainability as a key objective, Dobson claims that responsibility for action is asymmetrical. Consequently, for Dobson, citizenship ought to be rooted in "identifiable relations of actual harm" (81), thus limiting nonreciprocal and unilateral obligations to those implicit in those harmful relations. Correspondingly, privileged groups in the most affluent societies bear the greatest responsibility for taking action to combat the negative effects of their unsustainable lifestyles. Contemporary environmentalism is, perhaps, producing citizens appropriate to the task that Dobson sets. Through attempts to transform their own "private" everyday practices in ways consistent with sustainability (see Dobson 2003, 51–56, 135–139), environmental activists demonstrate awareness of their own (asymmetrical) citizenship obligations. And through identification and political targeting of unsustainable institutions and practices, activists also strive to inform others—individuals, groups, governments, and corporations—of their own asymmetrical obligations.

Accordingly, a key cultural and political space for the practice of environmental citizenship is produced by the groups and networks constituting contemporary environmentalism. If as Alexis de Tocqueville claimed the virtues required of citizenship are built through voluntary association, the virtues required of environmental citizenship are perhaps best built through voluntary association in environmental groups, campaigns, and organizations. Historically, social movements have been crucial actors in the fight for citizenships (Turner 1986), and the environmental movement can be seen as continuing this tradition (van Steenbergen 1994). Pursuing this approach to the study of environmental citizenship, then, such citizenship is being promoted and organized by big international environmental organizations such as Friends of the Earth and Greenpeace, green political parties, and increasingly visible transnational networks of resistance, which converge sporadically and temporarily for "People's Summits," "Social Forums," and "Days of Action" (for one recent overview of the remarkable diversity constituting this "global anticapitalist movement," see Notes from Nowhere 2003). In this chapter, environmental citizenship is approached neither as a disciplinary project of the state nor as about the extension of environmental rights to those deemed currently to be excluded from them, but as the practice of groups and networks of the environmentally concerned and committed.

Everyday Life among Green Activists

This activist-oriented concept of environmental citizenship is based on the study of a specific green cultural world. Ethnographic research into the everyday lives of green activists, centered on the city of Lancaster in northwestern England, was conducted between 1998 and 2002. Those researched included local Green Party and Friends of the Earth activists, people involved in looser collectives emerging around specific direct actions, and those campaigning against proposed developments such as local road- and house-building projects. In contrast to many studies of new social movements, the primary aim of the research was not to analyze the most obviously "political" practices of green activists but instead to examine and understand their more mundane, ordinary practices. So exploration of the ways in which activists live from day to day, and the distinctive characteristics of their lifestyles, took precedence over specific political campaigns and protests. Of particular interest, for example, were activists' shopping practices, leisure activities, social relationships, and travel patterns. Besides participant observation, this ethnographic research comprised a set of focus groups and a series of individual interviews.

What does everyday life among green activists look like? Environmentalism is an embodied politics (Lichterman 1996), and activists tend to incorporate their environmental concerns and commitments into everyday cultural practices; they seek consistency between their "political" positions and "personal" preferences, pursuing practices compatible with the visions they strive collectively to create (Melucci 1989). One particularly striking effect of the personalized style of politics practiced by green activists is a tendency to be incredibly concerned about consumption. What toothpaste one uses, where one shops, and how one moves around both locally and farther afield are *things that really matter.* Some types of products, such as meat, cars, cosmetics, and package holidays, are generally avoided altogether. For other objects of consumption, such as financial services, food, and household cleaning products, "ethical" versions are consistently favored over the "ethically suspect." Typically, where they do not grow it themselves, activists buy "organic" food. Activists also tend to be enthusiastic, even obsessive, recyclers; indeed, a key characteristic of the green networks to which they belong and contribute is the passing on and sharing of all manner of ordinary and extraordinary goods, with the purpose of maintaining them as actively useful things for as long as possible.

Activists tend also to lead remarkably local lives. Moving around on foot or bicycle, their everyday geographies stay near to home. Favoring residential locations relatively close to central shops and services, their paths tend regularly to cross the paths of other activists, promoting the sense that they are always bumping into people they know. Local activists also patronize the same shops, socialize in the same cafés and pubs, and attend the same kinds of meetings and events. The outcome is a constantly reproduced and locally occurring green world, comprised of individuals involved to varying extents in green politics and lifestyles. Some of these activists—through the friendships that tend to develop from shared values, common interests, and collective political action—are linked by what, in social network analyses (for example, Diani 1995), are known as "strong ties." But it is the predominance of "weak ties" that is more significant to the production and reproduction of the local green world. These weak ties are built and maintained through visibly shared habits (in styles of dress, movement, diet, and leisure) as well as joint participation in key festivals and protests that occasionally bring the broad green world into intense moments of copresent sociality. Weak ties enable people to recognize and be recognized by one another as belonging to the same political community, and are the basis of political solidarity (on the importance of weak ties, see Granovetter 1973).

Demonstrating Environmental Citizenship?

Green activists see themselves as activists, not citizens; they do not use, and are unlikely to adopt, the language of citizenship to describe their practices. So why suggest they are demonstrating environmental citizenship? If we are serious about social and political change in the direction of sustainability, any practice worthy of the name environmental citizenship surely needs to entail shifts in currently dominant practices, and this inevitably requires conflict. Unless so-called ordinary everyday practices are scrutinized, critiqued, and challenged, and unless more sustainable alternatives are developed to replace them, the dominant unsustainable order will not be transformed. Beyond overt political campaigns, through a whole range of oppositional practices—bicycling not driving, boycotting "unethical" foods and shops, innovating methods of recycling consumer "durables"—green activists are a key group generating conflict. It is currently the case that these "good environmental citizens" define themselves—and are defined—as activists. But in contexts of struggle, it is precisely those meanings of good citizen and activist that are constantly contested and renegotiated (Isin 2002); we need only think of the political biography of Nelson Mandela to recognize how dominant interpretations of "the same person" shift across time and space.

The model of environmental citizenship provided by contemporary green activists living in a city in northwestern England represents only one among many possible such models. Yet there are two good reasons for exploring and increasing our understanding of the lifestyles of these activists. First, they are elective; activists *choose* to learn about and respond to growing environmental risks, *choose* to take the environmental rights of human and nonhuman others into account in their personal/political actions, and *choose* to pursue environmentally responsible lifestyles.[2] And second, these activists tangibly demonstrate one *actually existing* model of a way of life that strives to take seriously these environmental risks, rights, and responsibilities.

So this chapter takes green activists to be demonstrating one form of environmental citizenship. This is not to say they are perfectly or puritanically green, leading some ideal or idealized sustainable lifestyle, but simply that they provide a potentially useful model. Green activists represent a relatively small group of people, but it is precisely because they are an elite that they merit special interest. Through better understanding *the conditions* for their style of environmental citizenship, there is a chance that those conditions can be more widely instituted, for the sake of the planet and its people. More precisely, because green activists represent a minority that is doing good environmental citizenship, what we need to know is just *how* this minority of green activists is able to do good environmental citizenship. As such, we need to look at the specific set of conditions that produce their admirable environmental citizenship. Then we need to set about expanding those conditions, so more people can enact similar kinds of environmental citizenship (to that extent green activists are role models, but they are not role models who can straightforwardly, unproblematically be emulated; instead, we have to learn *how* their example might be emulated). The central argument of this chapter is, therefore, that the project of environmental citizenship would be effectively promoted through an expansion of those conditions required for the practices of good environmental citizenship currently being demonstrated by a small and unrepresentative sample of green political activists. It is, correspondingly, those conditions on which I want to concentrate.

Overall, then, this chapter aims to contribute to the debates on environmental citizenship by setting out the distinctive lifestyles of green activists, examining how these lifestyles are produced and reproduced, and suggesting how the conditions for these green lifestyles might be broadened for the sake of environmental citizenship. The main body of the chapter is devoted to exploring the production of activists' distinctively green lifestyles. The lives of green activists are approached in turn through four concepts: networks, spaces, materialities, and times. In uncovering the ways in which the distinctive lifestyles of green activists are culturally produced, the analysis aims convincingly to demonstrate that the wider uptake of those lifestyles cannot straightforwardly depend on the role modeling of appropriate green virtues, the power of persuasion, or information and education alone. The final section then reflects on the everyday lives of green activists in light of the assumed need for a wider project of environmental citizenship, and suggests how such citizenship might successfully be broadened. The promotion of the kind of environmental citizenship green activists are modeling requires, I argue, the promotion of the green culture from which activists' ordinary everyday practices emerge. The chapter concludes that the promotion of this green culture crucially depends on the development of a *green architecture*.

The Production of Environmental Citizenship

Green Networks
Would-be green activists must enter and negotiate an initially strange cultural world. Involvement in the diverse groups and campaigns that comprise green networks, and especially face-to-face interaction with fellow network members, exposes an individual to the slowly shifting meanings of contemporary environmentalism. Only through such involvement do people gradually learn how to act, developing competence in culturally specific behaviors and understandings. Participation in green networks, then, is powerfully productive of green performances, ensuring that an individual's talk and practice comes to conform closely to

green cultural codes (on cultural codes, see Melucci 1996; on performance according to such codes, producing green identities, see Horton
2003). Through participation in green networks, there is over time a
convergence between a person's talk and practice and the (never-static
and often-contested) norms of the cultural world with which they are
engaging and striving to belong. In other words, ongoing and elective
involvement in green groups disciplines one into the range of appropriate green cultural performances.

What forms does such cultural participation take? Green networks are
constituted out of three main kinds of intermingling. The first kind of intermingling is the green meetings of local networks. During green meetings,
ordinarily dispersed but geographically proximate activists temporarily
converge to center their green identities.[3] Green meetings obviously include
the most formal, planned, and regular meetings of specific environmental
groups and campaigns; people often first enter green networks through
participation in these relatively open and accessible meetings. But green
meetings also include the many informal interactions surrounding and
separating these organized times: chats in the bar afterward; more private
get-togethers to accomplish specific tasks with one or two other activists;
wider social and political events of particular appeal to green activists,
including protests, video evenings, parties, and "public" meetings; and
chance encounters with activist friends and acquaintances while, for example, shopping in the whole food co-op or relaxing in the vegetarian café.

A second kind of intermingling constitutive of green networks is the
green gathering. The green gathering sees the temporal and spatial convergence of geographically dispersed network members. Assorted conferences,
workshops, courses, festivals, and protest events provide opportunities for
ordinarily far-flung activists to dwell in, replenish, and reaffirm their elective and collective green identities. And a third kind of intermingling
is increasingly important to both green meetings and green gatherings.
Interactions mediated by information and communication technologies,
and particularly e-mail, are gaining significance in promoting and sustaining the whole range of face-to-face green socialities (see Horton 2004).

Besides these kinds of intermingling, the formation of friendships among
fellow cultural members means participation in green networks extends
well beyond conventional understandings of political participation.

Among friends sharing green commitments and enthusiasms, network participation also commonly encompasses much informal social interaction, including extralocal activities such as group bicycle rides, walks, and "green holidays." One result is the development among green network members of close-knit normative reference groups, sharing and sustaining similar values, tastes, and practices (on reference groups, see Merton 1957).

How do the varied socialities of local, dispersed, and virtual green networks contribute to the greening of activists' lifestyles? In these green socialities, people orient to, perform, and develop their green identities, learning to be "authentic" environmentalists. Within the multiple socialities of green networks, the primary orientation of talk is obviously to green issues. Shared environmental interests bring activists together and provide the basis, at least initially, for their interactions. Green identities are privileged and performed. It is the performance of these identities across broader expanses of everyday life that leads to the greening of diverse cultural practices and the assemblage of green lifestyles.[4] Of course, these socialities, crucial to the performance of activists' identities and the production of their green lifestyles, are also spaced.

Green Spaces

Certain sites constitute settings for the green meetings, the face-to-face socialities of local green networks, noted above. Here activists most frequently meet, center, and perform their green identities, and so develop their green lifestyles. The two most important places for the intermingling of Lancaster's green network members are a vegetarian café, the Whale Tail, and an arts and community center, the Gregson. With "private" meeting rooms, a large hall, a "public" bar, and long opening hours, the Gregson is the main venue for the regular planned meetings of local environmental groups. The Whale Tail, situated above both a whole food workers' co-op and a green activist office, forms part of a green complex; located in the city center and as Lancaster's chief vegetarian eating place, it is more popular for informal meetings during the day. But both venues are sites of a wide variety of face-to-face interactions, from chance encounters, to planned meetings, to get-togethers of green friendship groups.

Green places such as the Whale Tail and the Gregson are "spaces of interruption" in two ways. The first is in their role as sites affording both the articulation of alternative discourses and the performance of oppositional identities; they promote, in other words, interruptions to dominant cultural narratives. The second is because, within them, it is generally acceptable and appropriate to interrupt the socialities-in-progress of others. It is worth briefly elaborating on these two meanings of interruption.

The Whale Tail and the Gregson are stylistically similar. They share a taste for bare wood and a distaste for plastic, have similar bulletin boards displaying similar messages, have comparable kinds of artwork adorning the walls, and—via the use of deep warm colors and blackboard menus—they achieve a similarly distinctive aesthetic. Both places provide left-leaning newspapers, play certain styles of music, and have toys for use by customers' children. The signals sent by these places, and the reputations they develop, attract members of green networks, facilitate face-to-face interaction between them, and contribute to the performance of green identities, and so the maintenance of local green culture. The Whale Tail and the Gregson, in other words, provide sites for the performance of elsewhere marginal(ized) identities. A generation ago, Ronald Inglehart noted that "the conventions and institutions of western countries are based on materialist assumptions. To have a post-materialist worldview means that one is apt to be out of harmony with the type of society in which one lives" (1977, 365). Embodying such postmaterialist worldviews, green activists and their lifestyles find a home in green social spaces such as the Gregson and the Whale Tail, where one can comfortably perform a "greenness" that other places tend to suppress.

Beyond affording interruptions to dominant discourses, Lancaster's green places also provide sites where interrupting socialities-in-progress is legitimate, as briefly mentioned above. It is in the places most central to local green networks that activists are particularly likely to bump into one another—so much so that people often visit these places alone, confident they will find others with whom to socialize. The Gregson and the Whale Tail provide activists with "public" places where they feel "at home." Neither so public that people moving through them are rendered anonymous, nor so private that within them people meet only those they already know well, these places constitute what Ray Oldenburg (1989) calls "third places." They facilitate the maintenance of weak ties, and therefore help sustain myriad relationships based on acquaintance that are especially significant to the reproduction and continued vitality of local social networks.[5]

Why is it acceptable to interrupt and join the socialities of others in these green places? There are four main reasons. First, there is an implicit cultural awareness that places like the Whale Tail and the Gregson function, at least in part, as sites of chance encounter. To some extent, however, this is an effect more than a cause of the legitimacy of interruption; as a distinctive cultural pattern of "normal interaction" builds up, its continuation becomes increasingly routinized. Second, people are limited in the number of friendships they can service at any one time (Allan 1989). Most acquaintanceships struck through participation in local environmental groups must therefore remain at that level of familiarity. Yet people typically want to sustain their weak ties, even if in a way that will not lead to them becoming stronger. Certain places, in permitting a generous (because ephemeral) orientation to spontaneous face-to-face socialities, keep one "tied into the scene."[6] Third, participation in a shared green culture comprised predominantly of acquaintances requires the performance of culturally appropriate identities. The chance encounters afforded by the interruptions of those with whom one has weak ties thus keeps one within the flows (of gossip, mobilization attempts, or important events) of local and dispersed green networks. These encounters tend also to encourage the performance of, and so consolidate, the most significant and uncontested green cultural codes. Fourth, people approach these places already oriented to their green identities. These identities are cultural and public, in the sense that they both result from (and depend on) continued interaction with others and are directed to the search for sustainability, an important component of which is widely recognized as increased levels of reciprocity and conviviality.

The two ways in which green places like the Whale Tail and the Gregson provide spaces of interruption conjoin. These places, which interrupt dominant cultural narratives and facilitate experimentation with alternative environmental discourses, are central to the everyday lives of green activists. And the norms of social interaction governing these places ensure the performance of face-to-face socialities across the breadth of local green networks. Together, then, these two kinds of interruption enable the development of a sense of community among individuals exploring and performing alternative green identities; they provide a spatial infrastructure where individuals with identities that are elsewhere marginalized can meet, publicly (if not overtly politically) center their elective identities, and feel themselves to belong.

Green Materialities

As well as being socially and spatially organized, green lifestyles are also materially organized. Indeed, the distinctive materialities of activists' green lifestyles are continuously produced and reproduced through the strongly spatialized socialities of green networks. Everyday life is powerfully shaped by material objects, and this section considers the effects of both material presence and absence on the development of green lifestyles. By producing and reproducing participation in the distinctive socialities, spatialities, and temporalities of green networks, specific material objects facilitate the greening of lifestyle; examples include bicycles, organic food, and walking boots, but it is the increasingly important computer, along with the Internet and e-mail, that is briefly focused on below. Other objects hinder the greening of lifestyle, and so it is their absence that is important. Two significant absences in the everyday lives of green activists are noted in this section; the car and the television.

The computer is now central to everyday life among green activists. Word processing packages are vital to many activist tasks, such as composing press releases, compiling and updating membership lists, drafting and editing responses to government consultations, producing newsletters and flyers, and writing letters and articles. But beyond the computer's significance for writing and managing data, the arrival of the Internet, and especially e-mail, has revolutionized the ways in which activists communicate. Over a four-year period of research into the lifestyles of green activists, the growing popularity of e-mail resulted in dramatic increases in both the volume and frequency of communication among activists at the local level. More generally, the computer has been embraced by green activists as a technological assemblage that facilitates the pursuit of a green lifestyle, especially at the local level. One activist summarized the current situation: "How," she wondered, "did people manage to be politically active before computers came along?" (field notes, March 2000). Today, the computer is activists' key political tool.[7]

If the computer is increasingly present, the car and the television are remarkably absent from the everyday lives of green activists. The degree to which these objects are missing obviously varies, but there are two general characteristics of activists' relationships with the car and the television. First, activists are highly critical of both these material goods; although in their talk and practice activists can also sometimes demonstrate ambivalence toward both objects, they never display unbridled enthusiasm for and acceptance of either. Second, the exclusion from everyday life of either object, but especially of both together, provides a key indicator to other network members of a green lifestyle. At a wider social level, life without either a car or a television (and especially both) marks a person or a household out as either poor or (at least) slightly eccentric, but within green culture their active avoidance signals good, green living.

Among the most involved and committed green activists, the car is almost completely missing from everyday life. These activists move around by bicycle and foot, and for longer journeys by train and sometimes bus. The car's absence is particularly consequential for activists' everyday spatialities. Without a car, the geographies, and thus the socialities, of green activists tend to shrink toward the local. Carlessness produces compact lives, with the spatial ranges afforded by the practices of walking and bicycling configuring the very contours of this local. Lacking the flexibility enabled by the private car, extralocal mobilities need to be planned in advance. Living without a car tends also to result in the ethical and aesthetic elevation of the local, the cultivation of an intimate, embodied relationship to the immediate environment, and the development of a sense of place worth fighting for. So against ever-more dispersed, car-dependent, and greenfield housing, activists advocate the kind of spatially dense development that facilitates their own green lifestyles. Against new roads and the motorized traffic such roads generate, activists call for greater measures to promote their own favored mobility practices of walking and cycling. Against new supermarkets and out-of-town developments, activists argue for others, like them, to support centrally located small shops and businesses.

If most green homes have no car parked outside, inside a television set is also often "missing." In a few green homes, an old, small, black-and-white portable can be found tucked into an inconspicuous corner or hidden from view (from where it emerges on rare and special occasions) entirely. One activist, for example, kept a small portable television in the bathroom cabinet, "away from the license inspectors, and one of the few spare spaces in the house" (field notes, August 2002). Among the most important effects of the television's absence from everyday life is the way in which it releases leisure time to be spent in alternative ways. In *Bowling Alone,* Robert Putnam persuasively argues television's role in eroding civic life; he claims that television is "lethal to community involvement" (2000, 192), and "privatizes leisure time. . . . TV watching comes at the expense of nearly every social activity outside the home, especially social gatherings and informal conversations" (236–237). Conversely, among green activists the television's absence provides a significant incentive to participation in the green public sphere.

Green Times
We have seen that green culture in general and green lifestyles in particular are networked, spaced, and materialized. They are also timed. As with networks, spaces, and materialities, certain times are compatible with and productive of green lifestyles, and other times are not. Times affording orientation to green identity along with the production and reproduction of green lifestyles include green meetings, green festivals, green holidays, and environmental protest events. Protest events, and other public performances of green identity such as running city center stalls and canvasing for elections, are particularly powerful times for the constitution of green identities because here people are announcing that identity to the wider society, to those potentially hostile others beyond the boundaries of the green cultural world.

Time spent in local, dispersed, and virtual green networks results in the acquisition and performance of culturally appropriate knowledge, awareness, and understandings, and the ongoing reorganization of everyday life according to green cultural codes. Diverse aspects of daily life are converted into conformity with green cultural codes, resulting in the assemblage of a green lifestyle—a lifestyle recognized, affirmed, and reaffirmed by other green activists. For a time, environmental politics and the greening of everyday life constitute a "project" (Castells 1997; Giddens 1991) or "central life interest" (Dubin 1992). During this period, activists develop "green routines." In a focus group comprised of Green Party activists, for example, one person commented, "I don't even think about not eating meat or not driving a car; I haven't done them for so long they just don't occur to me." A life without a car and a television, centered on places like the Whale Tail and the Gregson, and organized around green meetings, becomes familiar. It likewise becomes normal to choose (and pay a premium for) all manner of green goods, from "green toothpaste" and "green detergent" to organic, fair-trade foods and recycled paper. It becomes second nature to take the train, walk, or bicycle. At this point, a green lifestyle is lived, as ordinary, and we might perhaps say that the activist is a model environmental citizen.

But green lifestyles are themselves timed. Most activists can highlight times when they were at their "most radical," when the intensity of their attachments to green cultural codes was at its peak. This is their green period. Although green lifestyles are temporally more durable than the period of particularly public activism that often strongly contributes to their assemblage, they are prone to processes of unraveling and de-routinization. This does not mean that the pursuit of a green lifestyle is a passing fad but that for many people the phase of group-based political activism that forcefully contributes to the greening of lifestyle is limited. Other commitments, typical of the movement across the life course, can get in the way of activism. So what happens to green lifestyles? Where do they go, and when?

In general, through their phase of greatest activism, people are neither working full-time nor active parents. Most green lifestyles are therefore assembled during a relatively time-rich period of the life course. For such a lifestyle to continue in more or less the same form, personal circumstances need to remain relatively stable. Activists know this, and some choose and struggle to prevent their lives, and thus their green lifestyles, from changing in dramatic ways. Specifically, these activists might avoid taking on full-time work or elect not to have children. Many activists strive to reduce their dependence on paid work and to find more "freedom" to develop personal projects, engage in politics, and become increasingly "self-sufficient."

For other activists, potentially de-greening effects such as active parenthood and career cannot easily be separated from, and treated independently of, their present values, tastes, and practices. Here, activists strive to pursue work and parenthood according to preexisting commitments (see also Klatch 2000; Lichterman 1996, esp. Ch. 5). In the narratives of some (ex-)green activists, life events such as the birth of a child or the need to earn a living are experienced less as ruptures than as pivots around which values, tastes, and practices rotate. The person's past accompanies them into the present and shapes their future. Green lifestyles change, but they do not disappear.

One way in which a person's green commitments are carried into the future is via the process of professionalization. Here, activist capacities, skills, and knowledge are transferred into relevant paid work. So, for example, a Friends of the Earth activist finds employment in the organization's London office, and a transport activist secures a county council post dedicated to promoting bus use. While this route to becoming a "professional green" is open only to some, the vast majority of (ex-) activists manage to avoid work that seriously conflicts with their green values and express strong resistance to the idea of taking "unsustainable" jobs. Following the environmentalist challenge that "if you're not part of the solution, you're part of the problem," activists strive to find "good work" and to follow "right livelihoods" (see Schumacher 1979; on similar patterns among green activists elsewhere, see Berglund 1998; Cox 1999; Lichterman 1996).

There is no doubt, however, that for many people full-time work and the onset of active parenthood impinge on their ability to sustain levels of participation in the networks, spaces, materialities, and times sufficient to the maintenance of a strong green identity. The care of young children and/or the demands of full-time work make attendance at evening meetings difficult, and produce new responsibilities that compete with preexisting green concerns and commitments. The consequent movement out from the important identity-constituting social times and spaces of green networks leads to a reduction in the disciplinary force of green cultural codes on subjectivity, and thus facilitates the breaking of those codes, widening a developing cultural gap and leading to still further lifestyle change. An erosion of green convictions and falling involvement in the green cultural world follow each other in a slowly de-greening spiral. Here, in short, lapsed participation in green networks produces a decline in performances of green identity and the gradual disassembly of a green lifestyle.[8] With insufficient structures to hold a person in their green place, it is easy to fall out of the green world. And as with green lifestyles, so for environmental citizenship; the final section therefore argues that such citizenship requires the production of green structures in order to facilitate the exercise of green agency.

Broadening Environmental Citizenship

How can the above analysis of the production of green activists' distinctive lifestyles inform our understandings of environmental citizenship? My contention is that green activists practice a kind of environmental citizenship, one that is produced through their ongoing participation in a cultural world comprised of green networks, spaces, materialities, and times. Green performances emerge and build into a green identity as a result of intermingling with green others, dwelling in green places, surrounding oneself with and using green materialities, and spending green time. For as long as people are immersed in this green cultural world, green performances are ordinary and taken for granted; conversely, nongreen performances are extraordinary and tend to produce feelings of guilt, and to render one accountable to other cultural members. During the period of their lives when the commitment to green politics and lifestyle is at its highest, the everyday routines of green activists are effectively governed by the force of green cultural codes.

But how sustainable are the lifestyles developed among green activists? Most behavior-forming structures in contemporary societies are still far from green. Thus, sooner or later, life events push many activists out from the green structures coloring their lives and into de-greening environments. Although people can and do adapt their green lifestyles, and continue to live their ethico-political commitments as a project, green infrastructures remain insufficiently developed to make the living out of green projects a wider goal. Only the most concerned and committed currently stay green. Green activists might be pioneers of a new kind of environmental citizenship, but as yet there are no clear paths along which to follow them. The behaviors they are modeling are unattainable to the majority because the structures on which they depend are insufficiently developed; and the alternative route to such green behaviors requires an exceptional leap in agency that although perhaps possible, could never be generalizable. A crucial question therefore seems to be this: How do we make more mainstream, more a part of the dominant culture, those varied resources that are currently indispensable to the production and reproduction of the political subculture of green lifestyles and activism?

If green activists demonstrate a form of environmental citizenship, they do so voluntarily. Yet broader adoption of such environmental citizenship, it might be argued, will inevitably require institutional and legal structures to promote and enforce "right conduct." But in thinking about how to broaden the kind of environmental citizenship portrayed here, is there an alternative to an elective/imposed dichotomy? An understanding of the production of activists' green lifestyles can, I suggest, enable fresh and potentially productive questions. How can appropriately green practices be facilitated? How might conditions of practice be transformed in order to afford the wider emergence of desirable green behaviors among more than an elite of mainly white, educated, middle-class adults? How could access be broadened to the networks, spaces, materialities, and times that among green activists form the basis for a recognition of environmental risks, the declaration of environmental rights, and the performance of environmental responsibilities?

A common response to such questions is education and the provision of information. People might be taught to be good, green citizens. Given sufficient details about the consequences of their actions, and strategies for taking action, it is assumed that people will alter their behaviors. Yet the kind of environmental citizenship practiced by activists is not learned through formal teaching. Rather, it becomes steadily embodied through participation in green networks, spaces, material assemblages, and times. Environmental citizenship of the kind outlined here emerges, in other words, through practice rather than pedagogy. Elements of it can of course be taught; the environmental movement is highly literate, and participants rely heavily on multiple sources of information and continuously emerging new green knowledge. But it is, above all, a citizenship that is *performed*. We know that regular, repeated performance is necessary to the constitution of identities and practices (Butler 1990). And activists' performances of environmental citizenship are produced and reproduced by a specific green infrastructure or architecture.

Put slightly differently, rather than specific behaviors, I am arguing that *it is the culture from which specific behaviors emerge that ought to be promoted*. The expansion of an environmental citizenship rooted in the cultural practices of environmentalists themselves thus requires the further development of what I call, for want of a better term, a green architecture. Such an architecture is neither wholly concrete nor purely metaphoric; following my analysis, it comprises green groups, green spaces, green materialities, and green times.

What, more specifically, might this green architecture look like? To some extent, it already exists. In the United Kingdom, there are a number of important green sites, such as the Centre for Alternative Technology in mid-Wales, the Eden Project in southwestern England, and the Earth Centre in Yorkshire.[9] Regular temporary sites, in the form of "green festivals" such as the Big Green Gathering and regional green gatherings, also already exist. But unlike places such as the Whale Tail café and the Gregson community center, such spaces are geographically dispersed, and are distant from the everyday worlds of the vast majority of people. Rather, it is local green cafés, community centers, and festivals that most effectively promote the routinized performance of the practices that build into green identities, and that might be recognized as "doing good environmental citizenship." Correspondingly, if we want more good environmental citizens, such sites ought to be urgently promoted.

Similarly, ever-more cafés provide vegetarian options, a growing number of shops stock organic and fair-trade goods, local councils increasingly provide residents with facilities for recycling, and towns and cities across Europe are beginning to experiment with low-cost, easily accessible bicycle rental schemes.[10] So a growing range of material affordances enable people in societies such as the United Kingdom to enact aspects of good environmental citizenship. But this gradual greening of a nongreen culture still requires an agent to choose to be green; to know about, find, and select, for example, the more expensive organic version from among the countless varieties on offer. In contrast, the importance of "green contexts" is the way in which, by structuring the setting, they dilute the relevance of individual agency; they do not merely invite but crucially structure and produce green performances. The significance of a vegetarian café, for example, is that one is unable freely to eat meat there without breaking a cultural taboo and must instead eat food that is meat-free. Likewise, shopping in a whole food vegetarian co-op prevents the purchase of goods that clash with green cultural codes. Again, the expansion of such sites might therefore produce an expansion in the green performances conducive to good environmental citizenship.

Social change in a particular direction is inevitably highly uneven, occurring in some groups, times, and places before others, and obviously a green architecture would not act in a homogeneous way. Many people are highly unlikely to frequent a vegetarian café or attend a green festival. The kind of green architecture I am envisaging and attempting to sketch is unlikely to be peopled by all, or even some, all of the time. But importantly, a green architecture might provide times, places, and favorable material conditions for supportive and sympathetic people who have yet to be enabled to act out their green concerns, convictions, and commitments to increasingly do so. There are surely many people who would be willing to act as good environmental citizens if conditions were only made more conducive for such actions. In this way, the development of a green architecture might gradually push out the boundaries of green culture, and thus bring ever-more green performances into being. Such an architecture might enable, in other words, a steady trickling out of the performances of environmental citizenship.

This model of social change in pursuit of sustainability obviously accepts a gradual permeation of green performances into the wider social body above any more drastic cultural shift. From a movement-building perspective, it suggests a strategy not only of recruiting ever-more green activists but also of expanding the groups, places, material culture, and times of the green movement. From the perspective of proponents of environmental citizenship, it suggests not strategies aimed at the direct making of environmental citizens so much as strategies aimed at increasing the range of places, times, and groups where environmental citizenship practices can be enacted—a project, in other words, of reinvigorating and greening "the public sphere" as a prior condition to its peopling. Citizenship is less a quality of individuals than of the architecture that produces and reproduces that citizenship. What is needed, then, are groups, places, materialities, and times where people can perform environmental concerns and commitments into a place of greater centrality in their lives.

Notes

1. Early versions of this chapter were presented to an Institute for Environment, Philosophy, and Public Policy "sandwich seminar" at Lancaster University, and the Citizenship and the Environment workshop organized by Derek Bell and Andrew Dobson and held at the University of Newcastle. Many thanks to everybody who participated in those events. For their helpful comments and suggestions, I owe particular thanks to Anne Chapman, Andrew Dobson, Sue Holden, Bronislaw Szerszynski, and John Urry. A serious debt is, of course, also owed to Lancaster's many wonderful environmental activists.

2. Of course, choice is inevitably to some extent determined by the range of predispositions appropriate to one's habitus (see Bourdieu 1984). Thus, a person's sociostructural location effects the chances of their being drawn to green culture and green activism.

3. People have multiple identities, and are variously enabled and disabled from performing them across time and space. It is situational context that determines which of a person's multiple identities is centered, and which are backgrounded as less relevant or irrelevant. Specifically green contexts, such as green meetings, thus enable a person's green identity to come to the fore. Individual subjectivity is opened most powerfully to the force of green cultural codes; the gradual internalization of these codes produces a progressive greening of lifestyle.

4. By performance, I mean not the occasional and ephemeral staging of an ordinarily hidden identity but rather the ongoing, repeated, and routinized enactment of the green cultural codes promoted by the discourses of contemporary environmentalism and centered within green network socialities, which brings forth a distinctive way of life. Activists' green identities are, in other words, performed throughout everyday life.

5. Of course, through the clues provided to potential interrupters in a range of subtle signs and gestures, participants can achieve different levels of privacy within these public places (on hybrids of public and private, see Sheller and Urry 2003).

6. Specific culturally popular times provide particularly good opportunities to participate in the convergence of locally proximate, but ordinarily dispersed

green networks. During these times, in green meeting places, people tend to feel a heightened sense of belonging to the broad green community.

7. The computer's significance as a political tool does not guarantee its straightforward incorporation into all activists' everyday lives. Having become indispensable to contemporary environmentalism, activists are now problematizing computer technologies and their own relationships with those technologies. In other words, there are signs that at least as a complex material assemblage, the computer is currently undergoing processes of politicization. Activists are asking where computer components come from, exploring the social and environmental consequences of those components, and questioning where the world's computers will end up, and with what effects. Correspondingly, current cultural work strives to ensure computer technologies fit better with preexisting green cultural codes. Many activists, for example, support alternative operating systems such as Linux, acquire equipment secondhand, and either develop or support local structures through which unwanted gear can be recycled.

8. To use the example of the car, removal from those green socialities that continuously produce the car as a polluting object combines with a less time-rich and more spatially stretched lifestyle to increase the car's appeal. On departing central locations in green networks, (ex-)activists initially search out compromise positions between their previously complete renunciation of the car and their drift toward absolutely nongreen car ownership, so as the structuring force of the green cultural codes operative within green networks successively diminishes, people become more inclined to borrow or rent cars, to organize a car pool, or to buy a (small, secondhand, fuel-efficient) car and then—perhaps in a final salve to their green conscience—convert it to run on liquefied petroleum gas; such ownership typically begins with a resolution to use the car only occasionally, for allegedly essential journeys. As the car becomes a greater polluting presence in their lives, the ability and desire to maintain participation in green networks diminishes. The car's entry into a green lifestyle tends also to undermine the everyday spatialities that keep activists tied into local green networks and their socialities. Its arrival can lead to the dispersal of a person's mobilities and social networks, and so hasten the erosion in the force of green cultural codes on subjectivity.

9. For more information on these sites, see <http://www.cat.org.uk>, <http://www.edenproject.com>, and <http://www.earthcentre.org.uk>.

10. For details on one such scheme, Budgie Bikes in Lancaster, see <http://www.budgietransport.co.uk>.

References

Allan, Graham. 1989. *Friendship: Developing a Sociological Perspective*. Hemel Hempstead, UK: Harvester Wheatsheaf.

Berglund, Eeva K. 1998. *Knowing Nature, Knowing Science: An Ethnography of Environmental Activism*. Cambridge, UK: White Horse Press.

Bourdieu, Pierre. 1984. *Distinction: A Social Critique of the Judgement of Taste.* London: Routledge and Kegan Paul.

Bullard, Robert. 1990. *Dumping in Dixie: Race, Class, and Environmental Quality.* Boulder, CO: Westview Press.

Butler, Judith. 1990. *Gender Trouble: Feminism and the Subversion of Identity.* London: Routledge.

Castells, Manuel. 1997. *The Power of Identity.* Vol. 2 of *The Information Age: Economy, Society, and Culture.* Oxford: Blackwell.

Cox, Laurence. 1999. Power, Politics, and Everyday Life: The Local Rationalities of Social Movement Milieux. In *Transforming Politics: Power and Resistance,* ed. Paul Bagguley and Jeff Hearn 46–66. Basingstoke, UK: Macmillan.

Diani, Mario. 1995. *Green Networks: A Structural Analysis of the Italian Environmental Movement.* Edinburgh: Edinburgh University Press.

Dobson, Andrew. 2003. *Citizenship and the Environment.* Oxford: Oxford University Press.

Dubin, Robert. 1992. *Central Life Interests: Creative Individualism in a Complex World.* New Brunswick, NJ: Transaction.

Giddens, Anthony. 1991. *Modernity and Self-Identity: Self and Society in the Late Modern Age.* Cambridge: Polity.

Granovetter, Mark S. 1973. The Strength of Weak Ties: A Network Theory Revisited. *American Journal of Sociology* 78:1360–1380.

Harvey, David. 1996. *Justice, Nature, and the Geography of Difference.* Oxford: Blackwell.

Horton, Dave. 2003. Green Distinctions: The Performance of Identity among Environmental Activists. In *Nature Performed: Environment, Culture, Performance,* ed. Bronislaw, Szerszynski, Wallace Heim, and Claire Waterton, 63–77. Oxford: Blackwell.

Horton, Dave. 2004. Local Environmentalism and the Internet. *Environmental Politics* 13:735–754.

Inglehart, Ronald. 1977. *The Silent Revolution: Changing Values and Political Styles among Western Publics.* Princeton, NJ: Princeton University Press.

Isin, Engin F. 2002. *Being Political: Genealogies of Citizenship.* Minneapolis: University of Minnesota Press.

Klatch, Rebecca E. 2000. The Contradictory Effects of Work and Family on Political Activism. *Qualitative Sociology* 23:505–519.

Lichterman, Paul. 1996. *The Search for Political Community: American Activists Reinventing Commitment.* Cambridge: Cambridge University Press.

Melucci, Alberto. 1989. *Nomads of the Present: Social Movements and Individual Needs in Contemporary Society.* London: Hutchinson Radius.

Melucci, Alberto. 1996. *Challenging Codes: Collective Action in the Information Age.* Cambridge: Cambridge University Press.

Merton, Robert K. 1957. *Social Theory and Social Structure*. Glencoe, IL: Free Press.

Notes from Nowhere, ed. 2003. *We Are Everywhere: The Irresistible Rise of Global Anticapitalism*. London: Verso.

Oldenburg, Ray. 1989. *The Great Good Places: Cafes, Coffee Shops, Community Centers, Beauty Parlors, General Stores, Bars, Hangouts, and How They Get You through the Day*. New York: Paragon House.

Putnam, Robert D. 2000. *Bowling Alone: The Collapse and Revival of American Community*. New York: Simon and Schuster.

Schumacher, Ernst F. 1979. *Good Work*. London: Jonathan Cape.

Sheller, Mimi, and John Urry, 2003. Mobile Transformations of "Public" and "Private" Life. *Theory, Culture, and Society* 20:107–126.

Turner, Bryan. 1986. *Citizenship and Capitalism: The Debate over Reformism*. London: Allen and Unwin.

van Steenbergen, Bart. 1994. Towards a Global Ecological Citizen. In *The Condition of Citizenship*, ed. Bart van Steenbergen, 141–152. London: Sage.

II

Obstacles and Opportunities

6

Overcoming Obstacles to Ecological Citizenship: The Dominant Social Paradigm and Local Environmentalism

Nicholas Nash and Alan Lewis

This chapter approaches ecological citizenship from an empirical and psychological perspective. We will show that a potentially significant barrier to fruitful citizenship in Western industrial societies lies in the contradictory nature of environmental opinion and material expectations. By this we mean the generally positive levels of support for environmental protection accompanied by the expectation that individual material wealth and consumption will continue to increase in the future. We build on previous research that points to a set of cultural values, which we suggest may ideologically influence attitudes, which in turn impact on participation in proenvironmental behavior. In contrast to a great deal of psychological research that has sought to identify individual characteristics that correlate with proenvironmental behavior, we examine the model of the Dominant Social Paradigm (DSP) (Kilbourne, Beckmann, Lewis, and Van Dam 2001; Kilbourne, Beckmann, and Thelen 2002). In accordance with their theory, attitudes that can be linked to ecological citizenship are determined to greater or lesser degrees by the cultural values of the society pertaining to technological, economic, and political institutions. More specifically, these three classes of attitudes pertain to faith in the application of technology, unregulated economic markets, and liberal democracy as the optimal means of resolving current and future ecological issues. Conversely, Kilbourne and his colleagues (2001, 2002) propose that adherence to these DSP values contributes to the furtherance of environmental problems. Their model demonstrates a negative relationship between DSP adherence and environmental concern, which in turn leads to a lower perceived need to act. This occurs because the ideological message of the DSP assures citizens that the aforementioned institutions will overcome any problem, thereby reducing concerns about their seriousness. This ends in the conclusion that personal action is unnecessary.

Our own empirical research tests this relationship with a less restricted public sample. In addition, we expand the DSP model to examine and compare its relationship with both *general* and *local* environmental issues. Our results confirm the negative relationship between DSP adherence and general environmental attitudes. This pattern, however, is not replicated in terms of locally grounded environmental attitudes. From these findings, we go on to extrapolate the importance of their meaning in the context of ecological citizenship initiatives and suggest recommendations by which Western industrial societies might begin to reorient themselves toward sustainability. We acknowledge that notions of what constitutes a more desirable future will vary considerably and is beyond the remit of this chapter.

We instead focus on the first steps needed to start us in the right general direction. The resounding message of this chapter is that citizens must become more politically active through greater ecological awareness, responsibility, and commitment to ecological principles in order to begin to challenge the existing paradigm. To go about this, we recommend that ecological citizenship initiatives should be concentrated at the local level, where the influence of the DSP is relatively weak. With regard to ecological citizenship theory, neither liberal nor civic republican forms stand to effectively achieve enough. As Dobson (2003) remarks, these traditional citizenship forms imply a reciprocal contract between citizen and state. Yet the core interests of the state remain incommensurate with ecology, owing to the way in which industrial interests continue to dominate policymaking. Moreover, both citizenships govern only the public realm, as the liberal tendency is to remain value neutral toward citizens' private preferences. A new model of citizenship is required—one that transcends the state contract and incorporates the private realm. We also assert that the nature of democracy requires reform, as political decision-making mechanisms enable dominant groups to exert greater influence over outcomes and marginalize other stakeholders (Opotow and Weiss 2000). In addition, liberal democracy is accused of promoting individualism (Carter 2001). Consequently, to empower local, politically active citizens, the liberal democratic system needs to be partially decentralized to remove power from the dominant groups close to government.

Cultural Obstacles to Ecological Citizenship

A substantial volume of psychological research over recent decades has been devoted to understanding relationships between people and their environments (Eagly and Kulesa 1997). Much of this has been driven by a popularization of environmental issues stemming from alleged eco-crises. The pollution of life-sustaining resources including air and water along with large-scale threats such as climate change have led some scholars to question humankind's prospects for the twenty-first century (Oskamp 1995). High-profile international conferences such as Brundtland in 1987 and Rio in 1992 have aimed to address global issues including the resource imbalance between the North and the South, and to identify inclusive strategies to implement sustainability. These summit meetings have popularized the message of sustainable development and the need to "think globally and act locally." This has sparked participatory initiatives such as Local Agenda 21, aimed at increasing citizen involvement in local environmental decision making (Selman and Parker 1999). Clearly, many citizens are fairly supportive of ecological policies in principle. High levels of support for environmental protection have been documented in recent years (Dunlap and Scarce 1991; Finger 1994; Department of Environment, Food and Rural Affairs 2002). Nevertheless, a much-anticipated transformation of behavior has not yet followed, in spite of continued publicity about serious ecological threats and generally better awareness (Kollmuss and Agyeman 2002).

Psychological theories geared at changing the behavior of the individual have often neglected the societal context and have obviously not been completely successful in their aims. For example, Foxall (1994) adopts a behaviorist approach, and focuses on the need to reward favorable actions and punish undesirable ones. These include financial incentives such as energy saving measures and disincentives such as congestion charging in the city of London, making drivers pay to enter the city. What interventions like this share is that the desired outcomes will only continue for as long as behavior is reinforced, lacking any deeper sense of ecological commitment. Additionally, some behaviors—for example, car use—are extremely difficult to change in this way because of their symbolic significance. As Du Nann Winter comments, "Our daily behavior is accompanied by beliefs and attitudes that make business as usual seem sensible, even though we know that business as usual is jeopardizing the future survival of [hu]mankind" (2000, 516).

Shetzer, Stackman, and Moore (1991) observed that a sample of business students believed that corporations should both bear greater responsibility for environmental protection and align themselves more with nature. Yet these beliefs were inversely proportional to a measure of belief of whether economic growth should be limited. Gigliotti (1992) describes how U.S. college students were not only more materialist than their counterparts of twenty years before but were also less likely to accept incurring personal sacrifices for the sake of the environment. In a follow-up study, Gigliotti (1994) documented that in tandem with the flowering of environmentalism within the U.S. social consciousness, most citizens failed to appreciate the contradiction between ecological values and economic primacy. Conversely, there are many citizens who appear to exhibit what might be called an "ecological conscience" (Leopold 1970). These individuals will choose to engage in behaviors that transcend narrow self-interest, without tangible material rewards and even incurring personal costs into the bargain. A sense of commitment is arguably a crucial factor that must underpin ecological citizenship if a social project such as this is to eventually succeed. Twine (1994) explains that a "greener future" resides in recognizing that our day-to-day lifestyles are seriously damaging ecological systems in a multitude of ways.

Given existing levels of ecological awareness in Western societies and the lack of individual action, it is apparent that we must do more to achieve greater commitment. In other words, bridging the attitude-behavior gap lies beyond the assumption that the problem is mainly due to a kind of information deficit (Kollmuss and Agyeman 2002). We share with Dobson (2003) the belief that our conception of citizenship has to evolve beyond the limiting assumptions of liberal (rights-based) and civic republican (obligation-based) traditions. First, Dobson points out that the role of the state in both forms of citizenship presents a particular obstacle. Each tradition is based on the idea of a contractual arrangement between citizens and the state. The obstacle lies within the entrenched ideology of the state itself—an ideology that prioritizes industrial interests. Hence, the nature of the citizenship contract will undoubtedly exist to accommodate ecological considerations within a broader economic framework. Second, traditional forms of citizenship fail to extend to the private sphere, lessening the likelihood that the ecological impact of lifestyle behaviors will be effectively comprehended. Essentially, the administrative structure of state policymaking comprises a core of economic institutions and corporations that lobby government for arguably narrow interests (Barnes, Auburn, and Lea 2004). Carter (2001) points to three dimensions of power by which such interest groups are able to dominate decision making. The first dimension is through their privileged positions close to the heart of government. This assumes that power is diffuse and that at some point in the future ecological interest groups may be better placed to lobby more successfully, displacing economic interests and forcing their own issues onto the agenda. Two further dimensions of power oppose this conjecture, however. The second dimension of power refers to the potential for dominant groups to use their position to engage in non-decision making. This means that ecological interests that might threaten the interests of those dominant groups are marginalized and prevented from ever reaching government agendas. The third dimension of power highlights the ideological foundation of power, where dominant groups are able to sustain their positions of privilege by shaping the cultural values of a society so that individual preferences are aligned with the dominant group. Soysal (2000) remarks that the "top-down" attributes of citizenship such as the nature of the contract itself should not be overemphasized to the detriment of the "bottom-up" attributes of confrontation, debate, and discussion. It is this latter aspect of ecological citizenship that Soysal maintains is needed to create the necessary impetus to question the values of the status quo.

A similar argument extends to the realm of democratic governance. To espouse an argument in favor of greater democracy would be to underestimate the way in which the power is structured within political decision-making mechanisms to accord with dominant group interests. Greater democracy may be no guarantee that the environment will profit. Within the current liberal democratic context, environmental decisions are typically subject to the public inquiry process. But often, the outcomes of these inquiries are alleged to favor those groups with the most lobbying power, better resources, and technical expertise at their disposal (Opotow and Weiss 2000). This results in the marginalization of less powerful groups (Davies 2001). Despite a close alliance between the principles of ecology and democracy, some ecologists call for more authoritarian forms of governance that altogether dispense with the democratic system. Goodin (1992) articulates the belief that even within an ecologically aware and enlightened society, no democratic decision-making system could ensure that decisions would always result in the most ecologically beneficial outcomes at every occasion. A benevolent ecological dictator is likely to be met with revulsion by the majority of the population within a liberal democracy, including many environmentalists. Yet as Carter writes, a liberal democracy "nurtures an atomised, individualistic focus on the private sphere, which makes it a poor breeding ground for the ecological consciousness and responsible citizenship needed to bring about a sustainable society" (2001, 53). Thus, in addition to the criticisms of traditional forms of citizenship, liberal democracy will not aid us in altering cultural values or effectively encourage citizens to defer their own interests to those of the collective good. In contrast, Carter (2001) raises the possibility of a more participatory style of democracy and a partial decentralization of government. This would have two effects. First, it would empower citizens at the local level with a real stake in their own lives and communities, thereby encouraging greater political involvement (Daly and Cobb 1990). Second, it would wrest power from the economic elites. Carter (2001) is careful not to call for a complete decentralization of government as the scale of some ecological issues is large enough to necessitate coordinated action on a national or even international scale. Of particular importance with reference to obstacles to citizenship is the influence of deeply held cultural values, as already touched on. And it is to a particular facet of this ideology that we now turn.

Dominant Social Paradigm

Central to our discussion of ecological citizenship is a specific set of cultural values that have been empirically demonstrated to discourage individual environmental action. These values serve to assure citizens that currently dominant industrial institutions will address ecological problems on behalf of society. This leads to the acceptance that ecological issues do not pose serious threats, and that there is little need for citizens to change their lifestyles. The values are known collectively as the DSP. Paradigms are "epistemological systems for interpreting reality that ground their pictures of 'reality' in their own construction" (Milbrath 1995, p. 106). The concept derives from Kuhn's (1970) work on scientific "revolution," in which established ways of seeing the world slowly give way to novel perceptions through the gradual accumulation of new knowledge that supersedes the old paradigm. Paradigms consist of a society's commonsense beliefs about the world, rooted in culture and history. Citizens adopt ideological values as they become socialized in their environments—values that become so ingrained they are taken as reflecting objective reality. As a result, the ideological values of a society are seldom questioned and exceedingly difficult to challenge from within that society (Clark 1995). Johnston (1996) remarks that it would be virtually impossible to achieve an ecological shift in cultural values through existing political mechanisms because they construct the reality that they describe. Therefore, only limited measures in line with the values of the DSP of the society are likely to be taken up.

Pirages and Ehrlich (1974) were some of the first researchers to propose the concept of the DSP, but its historical precursors stretch back hundreds of years to a range of sources. For example, Adam Smith reasoned that the individual accumulation of material wealth was entirely consistent with natural laws (Coates 1998). Similarly, Thomas Hobbes's work on possessive individualism was rooted in René Descartes' mechanistic universal framework, leading to the assumption that people in dark antiquity acted instinctively on calculated self-interest (Clark 1989). Likewise, John Locke's conception of private ownership viewed the accumulation of material wealth as both benefiting the individual and bolstering the strength of the nation. In Locke's time, the possibilities for expansion in the New World seemed limitless, leading to a perception in Western minds of infinite resources. These beliefs, like sedimentary deposits, accumulate over the ages and are reflected in the values of our own time. The DSP has come to signify individualism, wealth creation, earth as a store of resources for human use, and humans as dominators of nature for their own ends; "It is not dominant in the statistical sense of being held by most people, but in the sense that it is the paradigm held by dominant groups in industrial societies" (Cotgrove 1982, 27).

The Three Dimensions of the DSP

Previous research in this area relates that the environmental values of a society are significantly influenced by a tripartite of socioeconomic DSP dimensions. Undoubtedly, a diverse range of cultural values can be identified, of which the DSP is only a small subset. But it is this subset of values that has been shown to be directly related to the environmental attitudes of individuals (Kilbourne et al. 2001, 2002). It should be noted that the DSP model is not intended as a caricature, and it is not our premise that citizens adhere to such values, nor to any antithetical set of values in a rigidly stereotypical fashion. The model essentially reflects a particular construction of ideological values. Therefore, a given individual will exhibit a range of often-contrasting attitudes and opinions. We do not mean that individuals make an explicit ideological commitment to the DSP but they generally fall somewhere along a continuum of values. The importance of the DSP's influence resides in its pervasiveness and subtlety. Our task is thus to highlight an empirical relationship between the DSP and the formation of environmental attitudes, which we feel must be considered when thinking about ecological citizenship.

The DSP has three distinct dimensions: technological, economic, and political. The *technological* dimension of the DSP equates to the belief that technological progress will resolve any existing and future environmental problems. This assumption is termed the techno-fix. Tiles and Oberdiek (1995) comment that technology, by virtue of its unrivaled success in accelerating human progress, is hailed as a panacea for all ecological ills. Arguments to set moral limits on the application of technological solutions are commonly criticized and framed as counter-progressive by those enchanted by the prospect of ever-greater advances in the future. Such hubris stems from the illusion that today's technological dreams will be tomorrow's reality. New technology to discover new resources, for example, makes resource extraction more efficient and creates cleaner fuels (Kilbourne et al. 2002). Tiles and Oberdiek go on to explain that technology ignores the second thermodynamic principle relating that within a closed system such as our biosphere, technology will only be able to conceal its negative effects for a finite time.

The *economic* dimension of the DSP is characterized by continued economic growth and the promise of increased levels of material well-being. This entails increasingly improvident utilization of ever-higher levels of resources to meet the increasing consumption demands of the society (Kilbourne et al. 2001). Despite the obvious consequences of ever-more rapacious levels of consumption, adherence to the DSP encapsulates the premise that economic institutions will accommodate "irregularities" such as resource scarcity. This is achieved by the actions of rational citizens acting on self-interest in free markets. Therefore, the free market response to resource scarcity is to raise the price of that resource, lessening demand and stimulating the development of alternative resources. This means that environmental goods are best protected if they are commodified and assigned an economic value. Yet some nonexcludable resources such as air and water cannot easily be valued in economic terms, and so unscrupulous consumers are able to externalize costs or to "free ride" (Jacobs 1994).

The third dimension of the DSP is the *political* dimension, reflecting the core values of liberal political philosophy. These include the conception of freedom as freedom to consume and participate in free markets as self-interested individuals. The role of government is minimal, being mainly to assist citizens in the satisfaction of private interests, to ensure that ownership rights and contract laws are honored, and to safeguard the freedom of the market (Waldron 2000). It is the combination of these three dimensions that influences environmental attitudes, specifically attitudes toward environmental concern and the perceived need for society to change values.

Kilbourne et al. (2001) conducted a multinational study of university undergraduates from the United States, Denmark, and England to examine the effect of the DSP on environmental concern. They hypothesized that a strong adherence to the DSP would result in less concern about the existence of general environmental problems because of the faith citizens placed in technological, economic, and political solutions. This in turn was considered to lead to less perceived need for change to ameliorate general environmental problems. In all three countries, this pattern was confirmed for the three dimensions of the DSP. Subsequently, Kilbourne et al. (2002) expanded this research to include undergraduates from seven nations. The results supported the theory that the DSP and environmental concern were negatively correlated, and that environmental concern and the perceived need for change were positively correlated. Additionally, participants from nations such as the Netherlands, Spain, and Australia exhibited a weaker adherence to the DSP than the those from the United States, England, and Denmark. Statistical analysis indicated that participants from low DSP nations were significantly more concerned about general environmental issues and felt a greater need for change.

While acknowledging the argument that to some readers, the relationship between the DSP and environmental attitudes could be unsurprising and even simplistic, this is to privilege one ecological standpoint over others. For example, from a conservative or neoliberal perspective, the DSP would appear congruent with environmental protection. Many right-wing political activists feel passionate about ecological issues and sustainability, but would advocate free market environmentalism as the best way of moving forward (Anderson and Leal 1991). Market solutions differ in the way they approach ecological issues, but they do not necessarily imply ambivalence. The conclusions of Kilbourne et al. might therefore seem incompatible with environmental mitigation to many free market environmentalists who believe that environmental commodities need to be economically valued to ensure they are protected. As Evernden (1992) notes, it is not that industrialists are unsympathetic to and dismissive of ecological risks (which would appear to be a simplistic assumption). Rather, it is that within political decision making, groups differ over how best to ensure future well-being. The DSP model is therefore valuable in its identification of potential obstacles inherent in one particular approach.

Not all environmental issues can be termed general. In experiential terms, issues that affect our day-to-day lives often have a greater direct impression on our senses than issues of a general or global nature. Our research adds to the DSP model by investigating the relationship between the DSP and concern about locally framed environmental issues and the perceived need for change at a local level. Dunlap et al. relate that compared to specific (local) issues with tangible personal impacts, general issues are viewed as "more geographically dispersed, less directly observable and more ambiguous in origin" (2000, 426). Uzzell (2000) calls attention to a dichotomy within environmental attitude theory, demonstrating that more spatially distant environmental problems are perceived as more serious. Additionally, many people are more aware and concerned about global issues than local ones. This should not be taken as indicating that citizens are unconcerned about local issues. The greater prominence of general issues such as climate change is likely to contribute to this finding. Citizens did express a greater personal responsibility for local environmental issues, however, Axelrod and Lehman (1993) suggest that self-efficacy is a significant factor in determining proenvironmental action. It may therefore be that general problems are perceived as lying beyond the remit of individuals, whereas local issues are more assailable. Other studies have also found that environmental concern is context dependent and informed by an individual's experience of their immediate environment rather than broad cultural ideology (Stern et al. 1993, 1995; Blake 1999). This has been found in attitudes toward land use (De Haven Smith 1988), domestic energy use (Seligman et al. 1979), purchasing of green consumer goods (Mainieri et al. 1997), and household recycling (Oskamp et al. 1991). We are thus interested in examining the comparative differences in relationships between the DSP, on one hand local and general concern, and the need for change on the other. It is likely that building on a sense of local community responsibility will encourage citizen action more effectively, offering a means to begin mounting a challenge to the dominant state interests.

The Aims of Our Study

Our own study addresses three objectives. The first is to test the model posited by Kilbourne et al. (2001, 2002) while employing a less restricted sample. The anticipated inverse relationship between DSP adherence, environmental concern, and the need for change constitutes our first hypothesis. As well as confirming the model, our area of inquiry is expanded to incorporate people's attitudes toward local environmental issues. From previous research, general environmental issues have been perceived as more amorphous and remote (Dunlap et al. 2000), while local environmental issues are considered to be more tangible and rooted in immediate concerns (Blake 2001; Stern et al. 1993, 1995). Thus, an individual is more likely to frame their attitudes depending on perceived personal consequences, and somewhat less on broad cultural values. So we expect that increased adherence to the technological, economic, and political dimensions of the DSP will be a weaker influence on concern about the local environment and the perceived change required to address environmental problems. A third measure gauges residents' opposition to a local greenfield development proposal. It is possible that individuals who adhere more strongly to the DSP will favor development as it will enhance the local economy. Alternatively, some proponents might welcome development as the developers have declared their intention to enhance the remaining green areas and improve public access. It might also follow that individuals who adhere less strongly to DSP values in line with more mainstream ecology will be more opposed to the development. On the other hand, in line with our second hypothesis, we believe that salient local concerns will stifle the influence of the DSP.

Method

In contrast to previous DSP research by Kilbourne et al. (2001, 2002), our study utilized a general public sample drawn from residents living near a proposed greenfield development site adjacent to the southern border of Swindon, Wiltshire, in the United Kingdom. Swindon Borough Council submitted a proposal in July 2002 to build on land along the town's southern boundary colloquially termed the "Front Garden." This would involve building between 3,800 and 4,500 new homes, business areas, amenities, and recreational facilities. Existing urban areas lie to the North and the M4 motorway bounds the southern border of the site, beyond which is the outlying village of Wroughton. Figure 6.1 depicts an aerial view of the site scheduled for development. Proponents maintain that the project is crucial to addressing a chronic housing shortfall in the county, and the need to attract skilled workers to the area to meet projected countywide and local

Figure 6.1
Aerial view of the proposed Greenfield development site on the southern border of Swindon. Reproduced by kind permission of DPDS Consulting Group. Copyright reserved DPDS Consulting Group 2002

structure plan requirements. Many residents have expressed concerns about the biodiversity impacts, coalescence with outlying communities, increased traffic congestion, pollution, and the risks associated with building homes near existing floodplains. The sampling area was selected as the prospect of development provides a salient local issue for residents, in contrast to hypothetical environmental attitude measures.

Two hundred and fifty-two residents of Swindon participated in the study. Of those, 124 (49.2 percent) were male, 117 (46.4 percent) were female, and 11 (4.4 percent) did not respond. The number of participants describing their ethnic status as "White UK" was 238 (94.4 percent). Of the remainder, 6 (2.4 percent) responded "White Other," 1 (0.4 percent) responded "Black Caribbean," and 7 (2.8 percent) did not respond. The participants' ages ranged widely: 15 (6 percent) were 18–30, 67 (26.6 percent) were 31–44, 97 (38.5 percent) were 45–59, and 67 (26.6 percent) were 60 or above. Six participants (2.3 percent) gave no age details. All participation was voluntary and no incentives were offered. An opportunistic sampling procedure was adopted for the study whereby survey literature was delivered to a number of homes in residential areas bordering the proposed development site. Demographic data on household income were also collected. Respondents then left completed surveys on their doorsteps for collection.

Participants completed a written survey composed of attitude statements, to which respondents selected one of five possible replies indicating their level of agreement. The items covered a range of issues.
Twelve participants completed a draft version of the survey. Item reliability analysis (Cronbach's Alpha) was then applied to each subscale.
The initial draft survey of one hundred and thirty-five items was reduced to sixty. Alpha values on all seven final subscales were around .8,
constituted as follows: adherence to the socioeconomic dimensions of
the DSP was measured on three subscales—technological (seven items),
economic (seven items), and political (seven items). These came from
similar scales used by Cotgrove (1982) and Kilbourne et al. (2001,
2002), and were worded so that a high score reflected a high DSP
adherence. The next two subscales contained items pertaining to general environmental concern (seven items) and the perceived need for
general change (seven items). These were derived from Cotgrove (1982)
and La Trobe and Acott (2000). A high score on these subscales indicated
a higher level of general concern and a greater perceived need for change.
Two further subscales measured local environmental concern (seven
items) and the perceived need for local change (seven items). These
referred to a range of local environmental issues that, it was reasoned,
would engender an increased awareness of personal impacts. As before,
higher scores reflected higher environmental concern and perceived need
for change locally. A final subscale measured attitudes toward the greenfield development proposal (eleven items), including concerns about the
consequences for local wildlife as well as the economic benefits the development might bring. A high score signified a more positive attitude to the
development. The scale items are displayed in appendix A.

Analysis
Our analysis comprised three distinct stages using multiple regression
techniques. For each of the regressions, predictor variables were entered
simultaneously in a specified order. Also, any outlying cases were removed
where necessary and the regression analysis was rerun. The first stage
examined the link between adherence to the DSP, general environmental
concern, and the perceived need for change. In accordance with prior
research, we expected an inverse relationship between DSP adherence on

one side and general environmental concern and the perceived need for change on the other. In regression one, general environmental concern formed the dependent variable. The predictor variables incorporated the technological, economic, and political DSP dimensions. This was followed by a second regression, which substituted general concern with the perceived need for general change. Given the scoring system, it was expected that the resulting relationships for both multiple regressions would be inverse. The second stage of the analysis was to test whether the DSP could predict local environmental concern and the perceived need for local change. The next three multiple regressions incorporated local environmental concern, the perceived need for local change, and opposition to the greenfield development as the dependent variables in turn. The opposition variable was considered to comprise a more acute test of the DSP given the perceived personal impact of the issue. As in stage one, the three DSP variables formed the predictor model each time. Two final regressions were included to ascertain the extent to which general and local environmental attitude variables predicted the perceived need for change at the general and local levels. Consequently, general and local change formed the dependent variables in turn, and the predictor model comprised the remaining general and local attitude variables, including the strength of opposition to the greenfield development.

Results

The following section provides a statistical interpretation of the findings of our study. For those who are unfamiliar with behavioral statistics, a more discursive assessment of our results may be found in the discussion section below.

   Following the collection of the completed surveys, the raw scores were compiled and aggregated for each scale using Excel for Windows (version 7.0). The data were then pasted to SPSS for Windows (version 10.0) for statistical analysis. With regard to multicollinearity, there were no predictor variables that correlated above .8 in any of the multiple regression analyses. Furthermore, all variance inflation factors were below 10, in line with the conventional threshold set by Myers (1990). Additionally, variance inflation tolerance levels were above .02, in accordance with Menard (1995).

The first stage of the analysis tested whether the DSP variables were good predictors of general environmental concern and the general perceived need for change. We predicted that the DSP would be inversely related to both variables, so that as DSP adherence increased, general concern and the need for change would decrease. The two general environmental attitude measures therefore constituted the two dependent variables. The three measures of DSP adherence encompassing attitudes toward technological, economic, and political institutions formed the regression predictor model. The results of the analysis are displayed in table 6.1. The DSP variables were found to explain 23.1 percent of the variance within general environmental concern (r square adj = .231, $F(3,246) = 25.904$, $p < .001$) and 13 percent within the general perceived need for change (r square adj = .130, $F(3,248) = 13.487$, $p < .001$). In terms of the relationship between the DSP and general environmental concern, in studying the table, one can see that all three coefficients are inversely related to DSP adherence to a statistically significant degree.

The beta correlation coefficient for the economic dimension is particularly strong. Exactly the same pattern emerges for the relationship between DSP adherence and the general perceived need for ameliorative environmental change. With the exception of the political dimension, the beta values are lower than in the previous dimension. The accompanying adjusted r square statistic indicates that the DSP is a better predictor of concern than of the perceived need for change.

Table 6.1
Relationships between the technological, economic, and political dimensions of the DSP and general environmental concern and perceived need for change

	General environmental concern		Perceived general need for change	
	Standardized beta	P value	Standardized beta	P value
Technological	−.227	.001	−.179	.005
Economic	−.311	.001	−.186	.003
Political	−.117	.044	−.160	.011
Adjusted R square	.231		.130	

The next three multiple regression analyses examined DSP adherence and its relationship to environmental concern and the perceived need for change at the local environmental level. The results of these tests appear in table 6.2. First, the DSP predictor model was found to predict just 11.9 percent of the variation within the dependent variable of local environmental concern (r square adj = .119, F(3,247) = 12.247, p < .001). Only the correlation between local concern and the DSP economic dimension yielded a statistically significant standardized beta coefficient (−.352) paralleling the general level. Similarly, the DSP model, although statistically significant, predicted just 7.9 percent of the variation within the dependent variable of the perceived local need for change (r square adj = .079, F(3,246) = 8.083, p < .001). As before, only the standardized beta coefficient for the relationship with the DSP economic dimension realized a statistically significant inverse relationship from the table (−.211). As predicted, this highlights a very different set of relationships than those at the general level of environmental attitudes. Clearly, the DSP is a much weaker predictor of concern and the perceived need for ameliorative change in relation to local issues, with the exception of the DSP economic dimension.

To summarize so far, the DSP is confirmed as a good predictor of environmental concern and the perceived need for change at the general level. Moreover, a pattern of relationships in the predicted direction has emerged where as DSP adherence increases, concern and the need for change decrease. The DSP has also explained little of the variance at the local level. Nevertheless, a statistically significant inverse relationship did emerge between the DSP economic dimension and the variables of local concern and the local perceived need for change. This suggests that the DSP economic dimension is a significantly valid predictor of local environmental concern and the need for change in terms of both general and local issues.

The measure of opposition to the greenfield development proposal was also considered as a local environmental attitude variable. Subsequently, a fifth multiple regression was computed with opposition as the dependent variable and the three DSP dimensions as the predictor model. The betas and the r square coefficients are also reproduced in table 6.2. The resulting r square value further confirmed the predictive limitations of the DSP at the local level of environmental attitudes as

Table 6.2
Relationships between the technological, economic, and political dimensions of the DSP, local environmental concern and perceived need for change, including opposition to the greenfield development proposal

	Local environmental concern		Perceived need for local change		Opposition to development proposal	
	Standardized beta	P value	Standardized beta	P value	Standardized beta	P value
Technological	.027	.677	-.112	.086	-.106	.103
Economic	-.352	.001	-.211	.001	-.261	.001
Political	-.048	.436	-.075	.241	.075	.238
Adjusted R square	.119		.079		.079	

only 7.9 percent of the variation was accounted for by the predictor model (r square = .079, F(3,248) = 8.178, p < .001). Again, only the economic dimension was inversely related to opposition to a statistically significant degree, resulting in a standardized beta coefficient of −.261.

The two final multiple regression calculations further examined the relationship between general and local environmental attitude variables in predicting the perceived need for change at both levels. Accordingly, the perceived general need for change formed the first dependent variable followed by the perceived local need for change. The predictor model for each multiple regression was composed of the remaining environmental attitude variables: local change, local concern, general concern, and opposition to the development. This was followed by a model comprising general change, local concern, general concern, and opposition to the development. This was followed by a model comprising general change, local concern, general concern and opposition to the development. The resulting values are presented in table 6.3.

The first batch of aggregated attitude subscales accounted for a moderate 21.4 percent of the variation within the need for general change variable (r square adj = .214, F(4,247) = 18.053, p < .001). The standardized betas in table 6.3 illustrate that the relationship between general environmental concern and the general need for change is quite strong (.427), as would be expected. None of the three local environmental measures yielded statistically significant relationships, supporting the idea that attitudes at each psycho-spatial level are determined differently. The agglomeration of general and local environmental attitude variables predicted over half of the variation within the perceived need for local change (r square adj = .582, F(4,245) = 87.56, p>.001). Furthermore, the local environmental attitude variables were positively associated with the need for local change to a statistically significant degree. While general environmental concern was not related to the need for local change, however, the need for general change was related.

Discussion

Our study aimed to achieve three main goals: to empirically replicate an established model of the DSP of Western industrial societies and its

Table 6.3
Relationships between perceived need for general and local change, and remaining general and local environmental attitude variables

	Need for general change		Need for local change	
	Standardized beta	P value	Standardized beta	P value
General environmental concern	.427	.001	.049	.335
Need for general change			.106	.023
Local environmental concern	−.009	.907	.478	.001
Need for local change	.142	.092		
Opposition to local development	−.061	.382	.340	.001
Adjusted R square	.214		.582	

influence on general environmental concern and the perceived need for change (Kilbourne et al. 2001, 2002); to proceed by using a less restricted public sample; and to extend our range of inquiry to local environmental attitudes. The findings of our study clarify the relationship between the DSP and general environmental concern. The relationship implies that as adherence to technological, economic, and political beliefs paralleling those of the DSP increase, so concern about the existence of general environmental problems decreases. The DSP model accounted for a significant amount of the variation in respondents' attitudes toward concern. Negative relationships were statistically confirmed for all three socioeconomic dimensions in line with our first hypothesis. This supports criticisms of the usefulness of information deficit models, thereby suggesting that measures aimed at raising citizen awareness will be automatically translated into concern and thus action (Kollmuss and Agyeman 2002). Taking cultural factors into account, it becomes apparent that the processes of translating awareness are undoubtedly more complex. One factor is the fundamental contradiction between ecological and economic values, as expressed by citizens of Western industrial societies (Shetzer et al. 1991; Gigliotti 1992, 1994). The cultural influence of the DSP offers one possible explanation for this dichotomy. Essentially, adherence to the DSP requires citizens to place faith in institutions to resolve environmental problems—which does occur to varying degrees. Therefore, the faith placed in the aforementioned institutions leads to citizens becoming markedly less concerned about the threat of environmental issues.

The study also confirms a similar relationship between the three DSP dimensions and the perceived need for change to ameliorate general environmental issues. That is, as adherence increases, so the need for change follows the same pattern as concern. This is interpreted as a means of ideological control, whereby industrial institutions make assurances and promote particular lifestyles in order to sustain their own narrow interests. We propose it is this that contributes to the measured contradiction in ecological and economic values. With reference to ecological citizenship, the message of the DSP obfuscates the need for an ecological shift in values as it would threaten industrial interests. Dobson (2003) points out that notwithstanding their differences, liberal and civic republican forms of citizenship involve the same contractual relationship to the state. This raises the issue that traditional forms of citizenship will also be commensurate with dominant state interests. The state is hardly likely to promote any ecological initiatives that might threaten economic growth in favor of ecology. Thus, an ecological citizenship bound to the state is likely to be unsuccessful in delivering social and environmental justice as it is more preoccupied with satisfying industrial elites. We may exercise our green sensibilities by purchasing organic foodstuffs, using recycled products, or driving more environmentally friendly vehicles. And yet the DSP maintains economic primacy, driving consumption and materialism. Moreover, neither liberal nor civic republican forms of citizenship extend beyond the public sphere and into the private realm, where many ecologically damaging consumption decisions are made (Dobson 2003). The value neutrality of liberal political philosophy is fundamental to sustaining the DSP in that citizens are persuaded to occupy themselves only with satisfying their own preferences. Dominant Western ideology, however, shapes those preferences so that people are driven to consume more and accrue more wealth. If our notion of citizenship neglects the private realm, citizens are less likely to question the ecological impacts of their own lifestyles, and so citizenship is less likely to succeed.

Furthermore, the decision-making mechanisms of the liberal democracy are also called into question. As noted, decision-making mechanisms currently extend mainly to independently chaired public inquiries that are then passed to government, which makes the final decision. Yet the privileged position of dominant groups—with greater lobbying power, resources, and expertise—makes for unbalanced judgments (Opotow and Weiss 2000). Meanwhile, ecological and other interests are marginalized, creating an impression of consultation as fait accompli (Davies 2001). Such criticisms of the democratic process have led some to reject it outright in favor of authoritarian forms of governance, as proposed by Heilbroner and Ophuls among others (Eckersley 1992). Goodin (1992) argues that the end justifies the means, highlighting the seriousness of our predicament, and commenting that no democracy could ever ensure that every outcome is ecologically prudent. We do not share this belief wholeheartedly, as additional problems may be envisaged due to the fact that many citizens of Western liberal democratic societies, including environmentalists, would consider an authoritarian government as completely unacceptable.

Further results of our study suggest possible ways of integrating ecological citizenship with democratic principles. At the local level of environmental concern and the perceived need for change, the clear pattern of the negative relationship with the DSP observed at the general level did not emerge. These mixed findings underscore a psycho-spatial division between the creation of general and local environmental attitudes in relation to the DSP. That is, while the DSP was found to be a good predictor of general environmental attitudes, it was in contrast a poor predictor of local attitudes. The distinction between general and local environmental attitudes is documented by Uzzell (2000). He remarks that individuals express a greater sense of responsibility when addressing local issues. This can be linked to the size of general issues and their potential manageability (Dunlap et al. 2000). In terms of efficacy, citizens view global issues such as climate change as too large and complex in scope, leading to the reasoning that individual action will achieve little. The DSP could also enhance the lack of self-efficacy at the general level by persuading citizens to leave problems for institutions to resolve. Conversely, the influence of the DSP at the local level is much weaker. Therefore, the signal of the DSP seems to be disrupted and drowned out by the "noise" created by the more direct nature of sensory experience and personal impacts, and the greater potential manageability of local issues. Additionally, no clear relationship emerged when testing the DSP model as a predictor of concern about the greenfield development proposal, in accordance with our third hypothesis. Our results indicate that adherence to the DSP did not significantly affect concern about the proposal.

How is one to assess the relationship between the DSP and local environmental attitudes with reference to ecological citizenship? Crucially, the weak influence of the DSP on local environmental attitudes offers a means by which its grip may be loosened. We have identified that the top-down dimensions of citizenship, which have traditionally underpinned the concept, create obstacles to reaching a sustainable society. Importantly, it is at the grass roots of bottom-up citizenship processes where initiatives will need to be focused (Soysal 2000). This is needed to build the impetus for a challenge to the status quo. As well as lying beyond the influence of the DSP, local initiatives are important in seizing on the enhanced sense of responsibility and self-efficacy felt at this level. Axelrod and Lehman (1993) have shown that self-efficacy is an important determinant in whether an individual will act proenvironmentally. Yet it may also be that this distinction is enhanced more for reasons of narrow self-interest than the desire to act for the community. We reply by saying that it would be wrong to assume that individuals reason solely within these parameters. The role of the ecological conscience (Leopold 1970) or the sense of a deeper commitment to ecological principles is essential if citizenship is to work. Haste (2004) also adds that environmental knowledge must be of salience to the individual. People must recognize themselves as being a member of the category of citizen. Arguably, the atomistic nature of liberal democracy as it exists will not engender a sense of membership as long as it stresses acting on private interests rather than the broader considerations one would expect from an "ecological citizen" (Carter 2001). Therefore, by exploiting the sense of responsibility at the local level and specializing knowledge and awareness to this context, it will appeal to individuals. A primary message to be put across to citizens is to urge them to question their own lifestyles and make the connection with ecological impacts. At the same time, it must be emphasized that individual interests and the collective interest are not mutually exclusive but are in fact complementary. Local knowledge and awareness may be seen as an important first step.

Once citizens have taken ownership of local issues, a democratic system conducive to citizen-led action is needed, given the significance of self-efficacy as a motivating force. As mentioned above, we believe that authoritarian forms of governance, or an ecologist king, will only serve to coerce citizens and fail to create a true commitment to ecology. While the initiatives for greater local awareness and knowledge may have some impact on self-efficacy, we advocate the need for a more participatory democratic system. Whereas the current liberal democratic system privileges elite groups and promotes individualism, participatory democracy would necessitate a partial decentralization of governance, to wrest power from the elites and make government more accountable to wider interests. This would empower local citizen action further by giving people a much greater degree of involvement in the decisions that affect their communities and lives. As Carter (2001) states, this is not to call for complete decentralization as some environmental risks will lie beyond the local remit. Nevertheless, if ecological citizenship is to take root, local initiatives must be supported by local, participatory democratic mechanisms.

Having highlighted the weak influence of the DSP at the local level, the DSP economic dimension did prove itself to be an exception to this rule. It was found to be negatively related to all three local environmental attitude variables. Therefore, as faith in economic institutions increased, concern about local environmental issues (including the development proposal) and the need for local change was reduced. We might speculate that the strength of influence across the three DSP dimensions is not equally distributed. The economic dimension does appear to differentiate between high DSP adherents, on the one hand, and low DSP adherents, on the other. It is possible that values associated with the economic dimension exert a greater pull on the individual at the local level than technological and political considerations, which are markedly more abstract and less central to citizens' everyday concerns. Consider that environmental conflict is commonly typified as competition between ecological and economic interests, where one is traded for the other. Perhaps economic values straddle both psycho-spatial levels of environmental opinion. Moreover, we would expect economic judgments to be important determining factors in the formation of local environmental attitudes. This would also seem to indicate that environmentalism is still thought of as something of a lifestyle luxury to many. In moving toward ecological citizenship, it will be prudent to destabilize the myth that proenvironmental behavior should not be understood as implying a cost to the individual. This again raises the importance of stressing the mutuality of individual and collective interests.

Another point to note from our findings is that at both psychospatial levels, the DSP model was found to be a better predictor of environmental concern than the perceived need for change. The Kilbourne et al. (2002) model provides some explanation for this. Their model posits that the DSP is more causally distant from the need for change than it is from concern. In other words, adherence to the DSP directly influences environmental concern by causing it to decrease. But the causal link between DSP adherence and the perceived need for change is only indirect. Rather, the measured decrease in the perceived need for change is more attributable to an antecedent lowering of concern. Thus, lowered concern is a necessary precondition of a lowered need for change, as we would logically expect. This would suggest that interventions should be aimed at increasing concern while also arming citizens with the knowledge and awareness needed to guide action. In regard to the issue of the psycho-spatial distinction between general and local environmental attitudes, another pattern was noted when we examined the relationship between concern and the need for change. When all remaining general and local attitude variables were combined to form the predictor model, they were much better predictors of the perceived need for local change than the need for change at the general level. We attribute this observation to the fact that there were more local variables than general in the predictor model each time. This also reinforces the idea that attitudes to general and local environmental issues are distinct from one another.

In summary, the DSP is a dominant ideological set of values influencing the environmental attitudes of citizens and adopted to varying degrees through socialization processes. Despite sustained support for environmental protection, the ideological message of the DSP assures citizens that industrial institutions will address environmental problems for them. In actuality, they are the very values that perpetuate ecologically damaging lifestyles for the sake of the narrow environmental interests of elite groups. This influence prevents many citizens from "making the connection," which might encourage more of us to question our own values. The root of the problem is that Western industrial societies seduce citizens with the allure of economic growth and consumption, while shielding them from the true consequences of their actions. It appears that materialist love is as blind as its romantic counterpart, and as in all classic tales of romance, the lovers' tryst is destined to end in tragedy. Our message is that these narrow institutional values must be challenged. We have prescribed a number of basic first steps that we think will be of some use to encourage a deeper form of commitment to ecological principles. An obvious starting place for ecological citizenship initiatives would be at the level of local issues, where citizens feel a greater sense of responsibility, and where the DSP is weaker. This would involve improving knowledge and awareness, particularly the need to question private interests and consider what is best for the collective good. Additionally, individuals must subscribe to the category of citizen and take ownership of local issues. Citizenship must capitalize on bottom-up citizenship strategies, extend to the private realm, and forgo its traditional contractual format to challenge narrow state interests. At the institutional level, the existing liberal democratic system should be decentralized and transformed into a more participatory form of local governance, to transfer power from the industrial elites to a wider range of interests. Despite our suggestion, the task of reorienting ourselves to a more sustainable course rests ultimately on the commitment of present and future citizens. And we feel that if given the opportunity, more citizens would appreciate the longer-term vision, which bestows a clarity on and an appreciation of our interconnectedness with the world, and opens up the route to better choices.

Appendix A: Attitude Scale Statements Used In The Survey

Section A

Attitude statements measuring agreement with basic technological, economic and political characteristics of the DSP.

1. Humans are allowing technology to run out of control.
2. Scientific progress will eventually result in catastrophe for humankind.
3. Technological progress means a higher standard of living for most people on the planet.
4. Future technology will solve society's problems for many years to come.
5. When environmental problems pose a serious threat, technology will solve them.
6. Science will be unable to solve the problem of future resource shortages.
7. Technology has failed to create a truly better world.
8. Economic growth should be the primary concern of society.
9. Unlimited economic growth is an impossible idea.
10. The preservation of nature is more important to me than a stable economy.
11. Natural resources should be used to satisfy basic needs rather than material wealth.
12. Material wealth is the best measure of human progress.
13. The sole responsibility of a business is to increase its profits.
14. Quality of life is more important than material wealth.

15. Government should decide what is produced rather than the customers who buy the products.
16. Financial markets should be based on the needs of society rather than individuals.
17. The capitalist system is the best way of allocating resources.
18. Government should decide what is best for its citizens.
19. There is no such thing as society, only individuals.
20. Radical political change is needed to save the environment.
21. Politicians should focus more on the individual than society.

Section B

Attitude statements measuring agreement with issues of general environmental concern.

22. Experts will always find a way to solve environmental problems.
23. Humans should live in harmony with the earth.
24. Conserving natural resources is unnecessary as alternatives will always be found.
25. Industry is doing everything it can to prevent environmental damage.
26. Human interference in nature always results in catastrophe.
27. Environmental problems are always portrayed as being greater than they are in reality.
28. Environmental problems in remote parts of the world are of little interest to me.
29. My current lifestyle can be seen as being environmentally sustainable.
30. Families have the right to have as many children as they wish.
31. Eventually every society's standard of living will be raised to that of our own.
32. Humankind needs to radically change its basic values in order to address environmental problems.
33. The rights of other species should be at least equal to humans.
34. Current rates of resource use can be maintained indefinitely.
35. A sustainable future is only possible through lower levels of material wealth.

Section C

Attitude statements measuring agreement with issues of local environmental concern.

36. The disappearance of local green areas is affecting residents' quality of life.
37. I am unconcerned with the development of local green areas.
38. We should be free to develop local green areas if we wish to do so.
39. The local economy is more important than the local natural environment.
40. Local species of plants and animals are disappearing rapidly because of human impacts.
41. The most important concern of the local community should be economic growth.

42. As residents we have a moral obligation to protect our local areas of green space.
43. Local natural habitats are adequately protected against human impacts.
44. Local residents need to be more environmentally aware in the future.
45. Natural resources in the local area should be used if they benefit the community.
46. The urban expansion of Swindon must be stopped to protect remaining green areas.
47. More needs to be done in future to protect local green areas.
48. Local road building plans must continue.
49. Local residents should be doing more to protect the local countryside.

Section D

Attitude statements measuring agreement with plans to develop the Front Garden.

50. The new housing development is a suitable solution to local workforce shortages.
51. The "front garden" development will spill over, leading to further loss of local green areas.
52. The "front garden" blueprint will create a genuinely environmentally friendly development.
53. The new development will damage important natural habitats in the area.
54. The new development will make the local area a more attractive place to live.
55. Residents in the "front garden" development will be affected by motorway traffic noise.
56. An existing brown site (built-up area) should be redeveloped instead of the local greenbelt.
57. The new development will benefit local residents by enhancing the existing natural environment.
58. The need for affordable housing justifies developing this area of greenbelt.
59. Improved public transport, footpaths, and cycle ways will benefit the whole of Swindon.
60. The new development is acceptable if adjoining greenbelt areas are guaranteed to be preserved.

References

Anderson, T., and D. Leal. 1991. *Free Market Environmentalism*. Boulder, CO: Westview Press.

Axelrod, L. J., and D. R. Lehman. 1993. Responding to Environmental Concerns: What Factors Guide Individual Action? *Journal of Environmental Psychology* 13:149–159.

Barnes, R., T. Auburn, and S. Lea. 2004. Citizenship in Practice. *British Journal of Social Psychology* 43:187–206.

Blake, J. (1999) Overcoming the Value-action Gap in Environmental Policy: Tension Between National Policy and Local Experience/Local Environment, 14, 3, 257–278.

Carter, N. 2001. *The Politics of the Environment: Ideas, Activism, Policy.* Cambridge: Cambridge University Press.

Coates, P. 1998. *Nature: Western Attitudes since Ancient Times.* Cambridge: Polity Press.

Clark, M. E. 1989. *Ariadne's Thread: The Search for New Modes of Thinking.* New York: St. Martin's Press.

Clark, M. E. 1995. Changes in Euro-American Values Needed for Sustainability." *Journal of Social Issues* 51, no. 4:63–82.

Cotgrove, S. 1982. *Catastrophe or Cornucopia: The Environment, Politics, and the Future.* Chichester, UK: John Wiley and Sons.

Daly, H. E., and J. B. Cobb Jr. 1990. *For the Common Good: Redirecting the Economy towards Community, the Environment, and a Sustainable Future.* London: Green Print.

Davies, A. 2001. What Silence Knows: Planning, Public Participation, and Environmental Values. *Environmental Values,* 10:77–102.

Department of Environment, Food and Rural Affairs. 2002. *Survey of Public Attitudes to Quality of Life and to the Environment—2001.* London: DEFRA Publications.

De Haven Smith, L. 1988. Environmental Belief Systems: Public Opinion on Land Use in Florida. *Environment and Behavior* 20, no. 3:276–299.

Dobson, A. 2003. *Citizenship and the Environment.* Oxford: Oxford University Press.

Du Nann Winter, D. 2000. Some Big Ideas for Some Big Problems. *American Psychologist* 55:516–522.

Dunlap, R. E., and R. Scarce. 1991. The Polls-Poll Trends: Environmental Problems and Protection. *Public Opinion Quarterly* 55:651–672.

Dunlap, R. E., K. D. Van Liere, A. G. Mertig, and R. Emmet Jones. 2000. Measuring Endorsement of the New Ecological Paradigm: A Revised NEP Scale. *Journal of Social Issues* 56, no. 3:424–442.

Eagly, A. H., and P. Kulesa. 1997. Attitudes, Attitude Structure, and Resistance to Change: Implications for Persuasion on Environmental Issues. In *Environment, Ethics, and Behavior: The Psychology of Environmental Valuation and Degradation,* ed. M. H. Bazerman, D. M. Messick, A. E. Tenbrunsel, and K. A. Wade-Benzoni, 123–153. San Francisco: New Lexington Press.

Eckersley, R. 1992. *Environmentalism and Political Theory.* London: UCL Press.

Evernden, N. 1992. *The Social Creation of Nature.* Baltimore, MD: Johns Hopkins University Press.

Finger, M. 1994. From Knowledge to Action? Exploring the Relationship between Environmental Experiences, Learning, and Behavior. *Journal of Social Issues* 50:179–197.

Foxall, G. 1994. Environment-Impacting Consumer Behavior: A Framework of Social Marketing and Demarketing. *Perspectives on Marketing Management* 4:27–53.

Gigliotti, L. M. 1992. Environmental Attitudes: Twenty Years of Change? *Journal of Environmental Education* 24, no. 1:15–26.

Gigliotti, L. M. 1994. Environmental Issues: Cornell Students' Willingness to Take Action, 1990. *Journal of Environmental Education* 26, no. 1:34–42.

Goodin, R. 1992. *Green Political Theory.* Cambridge: Polity Press.

Haste, H. 2004. Constructing the Citizen. *Political Psychology* 25:413–439.

Jacobs, M. 1994. The Limits to Neoclassicism: Towards an Institutional Environmental Economics. In *Social Theory and the Global Environment,* ed. M. Redclift and T. Benton, 67–91. London: Routledge.

Johnston, R. J. 1996. *Nature, State, and Economy: A Political Economy of the Environment.* 2nd ed. Chichester, UK: John Wiley and Sons.

Kilbourne, W. E., S. C. Beckmann, A. Lewis, and Y. Van Dam. 2001. A Multi-National Examination of the Role of the Dominant Social Paradigm in Environmental Attitudes of University Students. *Environment and Behavior* 33, no. 2:209–228.

Kilbourne, W. E., S. C. Beckmann, and E. Thelen. 2002. The Role of the Dominant Social Paradigm in Environmental Attitudes: A Multi-National Examination. *Journal of Business Research* 55, no. 3:193–204.

Kuhn, T. S. 1970. *The Structure of Scientific Revolutions.* Chicago: University of Chicago Press.

Kollmuss, A., and J. Agyeman. 2002. Mind the Gap: Why Do People Act Environmentally and What Are the Barriers to Pro-Environmental Behavior? *Environmental Education Research* 8:239–260.

La Trobe, H. L., and T. G. Acott. 2000. A Modified NEP/DSP Environmental Attitudes Scale. *Journal of Environmental Education* 32, no. 1:12–20.

Leopold, A. 1970. *A Sand County Almanac: With Essays on Conservation from Round River.* New York: Ballantine.

Mainieri, T., E. G. Barnett, T. R. Valdero, and S. Oskamp. 1997. Green Buying: The Influence of Environmental Concern on Consumer Behavior. *Journal of Social Psychology* 137, no. 2:189–204.

Menard, S. 1995. Applied Logistic Regression Analysis. In *Sage University Paper Series on Quantitative Applications in the Social Sciences,* 07–106. Thousand Oaks, CA: Sage.

Milbrath, L. W. 1995. Psychological, Cultural, and Informational Barriers to Sustainability. *Journal of Social Issues* 51, no. 4:101–120.

Myers, R. 1990. *Classical and Modern Regression with Applications.* 2nd ed. Boston: Duxbury.

Opotow, S., and L. Weiss. 2000. Denial and the Process of Moral Exclusion in Environmental Conflict. *Journal of Social Issues* 56:475–490.

Oskamp, S. 1995. Applying Social Psychology to Avoid Ecological Disaster. *Journal of Social Issues* 51, no. 4:217–239.

Oskamp, S., M. J. Harrington, T. C. Edwards, D. L. Sherwood, S. M. Okuda, and D. C. Swanson. 1991. Factors Influencing Household Recycling Behavior. *Environment and Behavior* 23, no. 4:494–519.

Pirages, D. C., and P. R. Ehrlich. 1974. *Ark II: Social Response to Environmental Imperatives.* San Francisco: Freeman.

Seligman, C., M. Kriss, J. M. Darley, R. H. Fazio, L. J. Becker, and J. B. Pryor. 1979. Predicting Summer Energy Consumption from Homeowners' Attitudes. *Journal of Applied Social Psychology* 9, no. 1:70–90.

Shetzer, L., R. W. Stackman, and L. F. Moore. 1991. Business-Environment Attitudes and the New Environmental Paradigm. *Journal of Environmental Education* 22, no. 4:14–21.

Selman, P., and Parker, J. (1999) Tales of Local Sustainability, Local Environment 4, 1, 47–60.

Soysal, Y. N. 2000. Citizenship and Identity: Living in Diasporas in Postwar Europe? *Ethnic and Racial Studies* 23:1–15.

Stern, P. C., T. Dietz, and L. Kalof. 1993. Value Orientations, Gender, and Environmental Concern. *Environment and Behavior* 25, no. 3:322–348.

Stern, P. C., T. Dietz, L. Kalof, and G. A. Guagnano. 1995. Values, Beliefs, and Proenvironmental Action: Attitude Formation toward Emergent Attitude Objects. *Journal of Applied Social Psychology* 25, no. 18:1611–1636.

Tiles, M., and H. Oberdiek. 1995. *Living in a Technological Culture: Human Tools and Human Values.* London: Routledge.

Twine, F. 1994. *Citizenship and Social Rights: The Interdependence of Self and Society.* London: Sage.

Uzzell, D. L. 2000. The Psycho-Spatial Dimension of Global Environmental Problems. *Journal of Environmental Psychology* 20:307–318.

Waldron, J. 2000. Liberalism. In *The Concise Routledge Encyclopedia of Philosophy,* 486. London: Routledge.

7

Justice, Governance, and Sustainability: Perspectives on Environmental Citizenship from North America and Europe

Julian Agyeman and Bob Evans

Recent years have seen the emergence of environmental justice as a vocabulary for political opportunity, mobilization, and action, initially in the United States (Taylor 2000), and more recently in the United Kingdom (Boardman, Bullock, and McLaren 1999; Agyeman 2000, 2002; Agyeman and Evans 2004) and other parts of the world (Adeola 2000; Agyeman, Bullard, and Evans 2003). Within a somewhat similar timescale, environmental citizenship has become an increasingly central concept within environmental discourses (Selman and Parker 1997). In this chapter, we wish to question the utility of the concept of environmental citizenship. We do not want to dismiss the notion but to argue instead that if citizenship is to be a core theme of environmental discourses, politics, and policy, then it must be more broadly linked to environmental justice, and set within the wider context of first the sustainability discourse and second the current debates on governance.

We recognize that the contemporary debate around environmental citizenship is both vigorous and erudite (see, for example, Barry 1999). For instance, Dobson (2003a) offers a conception of *ecological* citizenship that is more theoretically robust than the rather naive conceptions of *environmental* citizenship typified by the Environment Canada (2001) approach discussed later. Dobson's position is that ecological citizenship is but one part of a wider sustainability project: "One by one, then, the signposts to sustainability are being erected, and I regard ecological citizenship as a key addition to the collection" (8).

We are in broad agreement with this position, and are supportive of his arguments in favor of a postcosmopolitan ecological citizenship. Nevertheless, our contribution to this debate is to suggest that the broader political and policy dimensions of the environmental justice discourse, linked to current debates on governance and sustainability, provide a context for these more theoretical discussions on both environmental and ecological citizenships. We are interested in the political and policy implications and opportunities of the concept of environmental citizenship, and while we recognize the importance of Dobson's distinction between environmental and ecological citizenships, for the purposes of our argument, we will conflate the two.

In pursuit of this, we therefore want to address three themes:

· Environmental citizenship is not, in our view, a particularly useful term on which to base political action. It is important to recognize the need to encourage changes in human behavior in relation to the environment, and that individuals should have both rights and responsibilities with respect to this. It may also be useful to regard environmental citizenship as part of the educational agenda around citizenship. Yet to focus on *the environment* and to a lesser extent the *ecological* is to underplay the broader social as well as political dimensions implicit in the concept of sustainability or sustainable development. In particular, the key questions of equity and to a lesser degree futurity tend to be marginalized.

· Following from this, any conception of citizenship must be more broadly and centrally linked to both justice and equity. In the case of environmental citizenship, we wish to assert that the emergence of environmental justice as both a *vocabulary for political opportunity, mobilization, and action* and a *policy principle* (Agyeman and Evans 2004) gives cause to see this as a more powerful tool for securing change than the concept of environmental citizenship.

· Finally, citizenship is integrally connected to questions of governance and in turn to sustainability. Citizenship for sustainability can only be understood as part of a reconstituted commitment to the processes of governance and justice.

This chapter takes these issues forward by first examining the experience of North America, focusing on the linkages between "civic environmentalism," environmental justice, and sustainability. This is followed by a review of how these issues are being played out in Europe, where the lower profile of environmental justice and environmental citizenship/civic environmentalism is replaced by a stronger commitment to sustainability and the processes of governance, particularly through the European Union. Drawing on these experiences, we offer conclusions around the three themes outlined above.

The U.S. Experience

While the Canadian government has a primer on environmental citizenship on its Environment Canada Web site (<http://www.ns.ec.gc.ca/msc/as/primer.html>), a search on the U.S. Environmental Protection Agency's (EPA) Web site brings up Community-Based Environmental Protection (CBEP) (<http://www.epa.gov/ecocommunity/news/cno6–4f.htm>), a manifestation of the U.S.-based equivalent of environmental citizenship: civic environmentalism. Indeed, in the latest evaluation of the EPA's (2003) CBEP program, nowhere is the word *citizenship* mentioned. This is not to say that the concept is not used in the United States. The Washington, D.C.–based not-for-profit Center for Environmental Citizenship has as its slogan "networking young leaders to protect the environment," an indication that the dominant orientation of citizenship is about getting young people involved in environmental action (Tufts University has a University College of Citizenship and Public Service, and Duke University has the DuPont Professorship in Environmental Citizenship), whereas civic environmentalism is seen as the more adult version.

This seemingly simple, age-related environmental citizenship/civic environmentalism continuum, however, is complicated in the United States by two concepts, which have evolved over the past two decades, that provide new directions for public policy—namely, *environmental justice* and *sustainability*. Both are highly contested concepts (Foreman 1998; Jacobs 1999), yet both have tremendous potential to effect long-lasting change in policy as well as peoples' behavior. The environmental justice movement is typically a grassroots or "bottom-up" political response to external threats, whereas the sustainability agenda emerged largely from international processes and committees, governmental structures, think tanks, and international nongovernmental organizations networks. Despite their historically different origins, there is an area of theoretical compatibility between them, which increasingly is evidenced in practice (Schlosberg 1999; Cole and Foster 2001; Agyeman and Evans 2003). This conceptual and increasingly practical overlap (see the city of San Francisco example below) represents a critical nexus for a broad social movement to create livable, sustainable communities for all people in the future (Agyeman, Bullard, and Evans 2003). Straddling this nexus is the concept of civic environmentalism.

Civic environmentalism (CE) has emerged over the past ten years as the dominant U.S. discourse on environmental policymaking at the subnational level. The first person to articulate and name civic environmentalism as an emergent policy framework that recognized the limits of top-down command-and-control environmental regulation was a former employee of the U.S. National Academy of Public Administration, DeWitt John. The CE approach—and that of its practical, EPA-inspired cousin, CBEP—stems from an increasing awareness that centrally imposed, media-specific environmental policy found in legislation like the Clean Air Act or Clean Water Act is not sufficient for dealing with contemporary environmental problems, and that more flexible and collaborative solutions should be found.

John sees civic environmentalism in a *narrow* sense: it "is *fundamentally* a bottom up approach to *environmental* protection" (1994, 7; emphasis added). Since John's work, there have been a variety of interpretations of the concept of civic environmentalism by a range of authors such as EPA (1997, 2002, 2003), Friedland and Sirianni (1995), Roseland (1998), Hempel (1999), Landy, Susman, and Knopman (1999), Mazmanian and Kraft (1999), Sabel, Fung, and Karkkainen (1999), and Shutkin (2000).

Yet Shutkin, like Roseland, Hempel, and Mazmanian and Kraft, see civic environmentalism as a much more *broadly* based concept than John and their contemporaries. For them, it is the idea that members of a particular geographic and political community "should engage in planning and organizing activities to ensure a future that is *environmentally healthy and economically and socially vibrant* at the local and regional levels. It is based on the notion that environmental quality and economic and social health are mutually constitutive" (Shutkin 2000, 14; emphasis added). While John did not problematize the concept of civic environmentalism, a survey of the range of scholarship on the concept has indicated that there are (at least) two major orientations. Table 7.1 makes the distinction between these different *orientations,* which Agyeman and Angus (2003) call "narrow focus" and "broad focus" civic environmentalism. Some may argue that there are two types of narrowness: one based on *environment*

Table 7.1
"Narrow focus" and "Broad focus" civic environmentalism (Agyeman and Angus 2003)

	"Narrow focus" civic environmentalism	"Broad focus" civic environmentalism
Main contributors	John (1994), EPA (1997), Sabel et al. (1999), Friedland & Sirianni (1995), Landy et al. (1999)	Shutkin (2000), Roseland (1998), Hempel (1999), Mazmanian and Kraft (1999)
Central premise	Stresses limits of top-down command and control environmental regulation. Civic environmentalist policies are best suited to dealing with the local nature of contemporary environmental problems.	Stresses interdependent nature of environmental, social, political, and economic problems. Civic environmentalism is fundamentally about ensuring the quality and sustainability of communities.
Central focus	The focus is on the interconnected nature of *environmental* problems. Using an ecosystem focus, the argument is that environmental problems do not correspond to political boundaries.	The focus is on the connections between *environmental, economic, and social* issues such as urban disinvestment, racial segregation, unemployment, and civic disengagement.
Contribution to sustainable communities	Can only help achieve the *environmental* goals of a sustainable community, namely, to *protect and enhance the environment* e.g., pollution control, protection of biodiversity, etc.	Can help to *protect and enhance the environment,* while *meeting social needs* and *promoting economic success*—i.e., meets all the goals of a sustainable community.

Table 7.1
(continued)

	"Narrow focus" civic environmentalism	"Broad focus" civic environmentalism
Nature of change	*Technical, reformist.* Policy change to incorporate community perspectives.	*Political, transformative.* Change requires paradigm shift.
On the role of the citizen	*Passive citizenship,* focus on *rights* of citizen access to legislative and judicial procedures, community right-to-know laws	*Active citizenship,* focus on *responsibilities* of the citizen to the environmental, social, and economic health of the community.
Role of social capital	Builds social capital as citizens gain access to the regulatory and public interest arena. But "narrow focus" precludes broader conception of and growth of social capital because of unrepresentative nature of local environmental action.	Environmental, economic, and social decline mirrors decline of social capital. Increasing social capital and networks of social capital is essential for developing sustainable communities.
Stance on environmental justice	Environmental injustice is mostly related to lack of access to, and protection from, public policy. The primary focus is on *procedural justice.*	Environmental injustice is a result and cause of social, economic, and racial inequity. The focus is on both *procedural and substantive justice.*

to the exclusion of justice, and the other on *justice* to the exclusion of environment. The former is our interpretation of narrow focus civic environmentalism. In this orientation, justice or equity are not mentioned in the survey literature. The latter position does not appear to exist in the literature surveyed. Broad focus civic environmentalism is explicit and clear: environment, economy, and social justice issues are "mutually constitutive" (Shutkin 2000, 14).

An example of narrow focus civic environmentalism is the Chesapeake Bay Program (CBP), a collaborative approach to restore a severely damaged watershed. The EPA, the states of Maryland, Virginia, and Pennsylvania, and Washington, DC, together with the Chesapeake Bay Commission, use voluntary measures such as education and technical assistance to achieve their goals. Since the CBP's inception in 1983, the highest priority has been the restoration of the bay's living resources—finfish, shellfish, bay grasses, and other aquatic life and wildlife. Improvements include the restoration of fisheries and habitat, the recovery of bay grasses, and decreases in nutrient and toxic loads.

An example of broad focus civic environmentalism is one of the classic U.S. cases of community revitalization: Boston's Dudley Street, by the Dudley Street Neighborhood Initiative (DSNI) (Medoff and Sklar 1994). The DSNI was formed in 1984 when residents became increasingly frustrated with the arson, disinvestment, neglect, and redlining practices in their area, and wanted to revive their neighborhood and protect it from outside speculators. The initiative is the only community-based nonprofit in the United States that has been granted eminent domain authority over the abandoned land within its boundaries. The DSNI works to implement resident-driven plans through partnerships with Community Development Corporations, various nonprofit and religious organizations that serve the neighborhood, and other institutions such as banks, government agencies, businesses, and foundations. Unlike the narrow focus of the CBP, the DSNI's approach is broadly focused and comprehensive.

Agyeman and Angus's (2003) distinction between narrow and broad focus civic environmentalism does not imply that narrow focus environmental action is *devoid* of meaningful participation. What they suggest is that it will be far more difficult to achieve what Hempel describes as the "economic vitality, ecological integrity, civic democracy, and social well-being" (1999, 48) that are necessary for the development of sustainable communities without a more broadly based social, economic, and political analysis. This can *only* be provided by broad focus civic environmentalism. This point becomes obvious when one sees—for instance, in table 7.1—that narrow focus civic environmentalism looks at the interconnected nature of environmental problems themselves, whereas the broad focus is on the connections between environmental problems and economic and social issues such as urban disinvestment, racial segregation, unemployment, and civic disengagement.

Within the discourse of broad focus civic environmentalism just described above, together with a vision of political transformation and paradigm shift, lies the hope for a deeper U.S. discourse on sustainability than the dominant discourse of environmental sustainability or environmental stewardship that equates to narrow focus civic environmentalism. It is crucially through this broader, deeper discourse of "just sustainability" (Agyeman, Bullard, and Evans 2003; Agyeman and Evans 2004; Agyeman 2005), not the dominant environmental sustainability discourse, that a space has opened for the exploration of much-needed coalition building between the environmental justice and sustainability movements.[1]

Schlosberg, in his investigation of the prospects for a critical pluralism, contends that there are a growing number of "examples of cooperative endeavors between environmental justice groups and the major organizations" (1999, 194). He adds that cooperative endeavors "offer the environmental movement as a whole a way out of its limited and conventional pluralist approach, into a realm of more diverse, participatory, effective and just environmentalism" (194). Just environmentalism, just sustainability, and broad focus civic environmentalism are, we argue, one and the same.

Schlosberg's "cooperative endeavors" are the small building blocks that are needed to build up to what Cole and Foster call "movement fusion": "the coming together of two (or more) social movements in a way that expands the base of support for both movements by developing a common agenda" (2001, 164). This cooperation, coactivism, and costrategizing on sustainability and environmental justice issues can be found in local fights for, and conferences on, just transportation (see, for instance, Bullard and Johnson 1997; Conservation Law Foundation 1998), community food security (Perfecto 1995; Gottlieb and Fisher 1996), smart growth and sustainable communities and cities (Rees 1995; Roseland 1998; Haughton 1999; Bullard, Johnson, and Torres 2000), among others.

The European Experience

During the last decade, the European Union (EU) has approved a range of initiatives that are collectively creating a policy framework it wishes to see adopted by all of its member states, although there are clearly considerable variations across the EU in terms of levels of compliance. The EU has adopted a *Strategy for Sustainable Development* (European Commission 2002) that seeks to embed the principle of sustainability into all areas of policy development and implementation: "All policies must have sustainable development as their core concern. In particular, forthcoming reviews of Common Policies must look at how they can contribute more positively to sustainable development" (European Commission 2001a, 6).

Sustainable development is clearly defined by the EU as being more than environmental sustainability, important though that is. The "Presidency Conclusions of the Gothenburg Summit" stated that "the Union's Sustainable Development Strategy is based on the principle that the economic, social and environmental effects of all policies should be examined in a coordinated way and taken into account in decision making" (European Commission 2002, par. 22).

This commitment to a broadly based sustainable development is closely linked to an emerging European policy on governance, as presented in *European Governance—A White Paper* (European Commission 2001b). In this white paper, a modernization of European governance is seen as a necessary precondition for European integration through a process of decentralization, combating the impact of globalization, and a restoration of the faith in democracy via wider citizen involvement in decision making. The white paper identifies five principles that underpin good governance—openness, participation, accountability, effectiveness, and coherence—which should apply to all levels of government from the local to the global. The white paper recognizes that the creation of the EU and the challenges of policy in a globalized world necessitate new ways of working that are not possible within a traditional framework of top-down government: "Policies can no longer be effective unless they are prepared, implemented and enforced in a more inclusive way" (European Commission 2001b, 18).

It remains to be seen how the proposals contained in the white paper will develop and be implemented. By implication, the proposals demand a degree of power transference both between levels of government (through the principles of proportionality and subsidiarity) and from government to civil society interest organizations. Such transfers of power, responsibility, and influence have historically met with opposition from the current power brokers.

The sustainable development discourse places heavy emphasis on the need to develop more democratic mechanisms for decision making and taking—for instance, in policy guidance at the international level, "good governance" is seen to be evidenced in a strong and dynamic organization of local government as well as a culture of "institutional learning." According to this perspective, there needs to be creative intervention by political actors to change structures, but in turn citizens should be well informed and seek better "performance" from public agencies.

The emphasis on improving democratic mechanisms for decision making leads to calls for human equity and environmental justice, more effective environmental governance, and greater environmental democracy. Although there is often a blurring of these concepts, the underpinning rationale is clear and may be briefly summarized as follows:

· *Equity*   Moves toward greater sustainability imply a series of difficult decisions that will need to be faced, and the consequences of not taking these decisions (for example, about resource use, consumption, and pollution) will seriously compromise the quality of life for both current and future generations. Those societies that exhibit a more equal income distribution, greater civil liberties and political rights, and higher literacy levels tend to have higher environmental quality (Torras and Boyce 1998). The sharing of common futures and fates (and the difficult decisions involved in this) is more likely when there is a higher level of social, economic, and political equality. This principle applies both within and between nations.

· *Justice*   Environmental problems bear down disproportionately on the poor, although it is the rich nations and the prosperous within those nations that are the greatest consumers and consequently polluters (Agyeman, Bullard, and Evans 2003). The principles of environmental justice demand that environmental decision making does not disproportionately disadvantage any particular social group, society, or nation.

· *Governance*   The changes implied in a move toward more sustainable societies are so immense that they cannot be imposed by governments alone. This central fact was a major impetus behind the agreement at the 1992 Earth Summit to Local Agenda 21, which recognized that change of the magnitude envisaged by Agenda 21 can only be achieved by mobilizing the energy, creativity, knowledge, and support of local communities, stakeholders, interest organizations, and citizens worldwide. More open, deliberative processes that facilitate the participation of civil society in taking decisions will be required to secure this involvement.

• *Democracy*   The right to information, to freedom of speech, association, and dissent, to meaningful participation in decision making—these and other rights underpin most conceptions of modern liberal democracy. Democracy is vital for sustainability in that it facilitates involvement, but through this it also nurtures understanding and education. Moreover, to encourage the involvement of citizens is to develop ownership as well as to combat the alienation and civic disengagement that must undermine the drive to more sustainable societies.

Christie and Warburton argue that good governance is central to sustainability: "The fundamental driver of sustainable development must be democratic debate—decisions reached through open discussion, consensus based on shared goals and trust. Sustainable development needs representative democracy that is trusted and vibrant, and new forms of participatory democracy to complement it that can inspire greater engagement by citizens in creating a better world" (2001, 154). They maintain that a renewal of local democracy and trust in public institutions will be required if the sustainability agenda is to be delivered.

Much of this has resonance with the assertion put forward by Putnam (2000). He charts the erosion of social capital in the United States, and the gradual loss of civic engagement. The consequences of this are, he argues, extremely serious for the prosperity, security, and quality of life—and one might add, sustainability—of U.S. citizens. There seems to be agreement among academic commentators and the sustainability community at least that there is a need to revitalize civic engagement, to support and nurture social capital, and to construct more responsive governmental institutions that can permit a healthy polity and a process of democratic governance.

The fundamental point here is that the societal changes implicit in any move to a more sustainable world will involve substantial changes in lifestyles and patterns of consumption, which will be extremely difficult, if not impossible, to secure without extremely high levels of public debate and civic engagement. Even with this, such changes are likely to be resisted, but if the challenges of common futures and fates implied within the sustainability discourse are to be met, the building of civic engagement and social capital is likely to be crucial.

The final component of this emerging European policy "architecture" is related to rights and citizen participation. The UN Economic Commission for Europe's (1999) *Convention on Access to Information, Public Participation in Decision Making, and Access to Justice in Environmental Matters,* also known simply as the Aarhus Convention, was adopted on June 25, 1998, in the Danish city of Aarhus at the Fourth Ministerial Conference in the Environment for Europe process.

The Aarhus Convention lays down the basic rules to promote citizens' involvement in environmental matters and the enforcement of environmental law. The convention consists of three "pillars," each of which grants different rights:

· The first pillar gives the public the right of access to environmental information.

· The second pillar gives the public the right to participate in decision-making processes.

· The third pillar ensures access to justice for the public.

These three elements of European policy relating to sustainable development, governance, and environmental rights collectively provide a European-wide policy framework that it is anticipated, will eventually determine and condition the policies and practices of European national governments. As might be expected, the actual implementation of these policies across Europe is patchy, and until the European Commission constructs and applies directives with which national governments have to comply, progress is likely to be slow. Moreover, it might be objected that these approaches are "procedural" rather than "substantive," in that they do not necessarily imply any real changes in levels of social inclusion or social justice. But an optimistic position would be that such top-down initiatives, however limited, are steps in the right direction.

The UK government's Sustainable Development Unit, located in the Department for Environment, Food, and Rural Affairs, has established an Environmental Democracy Unit whose remit is to facilitate the ratification of the Aarhus Convention. Although this might be interpreted as a governmental commitment to the principles of environmental justice and citizen participation in decision making, perhaps a more accurate assessment would be to see the unit's remit as predominantly concerned with civil and political procedures rather than outcomes—adherence to the letter rather than the intention and spirit of the convention.

The UK government's Sustainable Development Strategy "Securing the Future" (H.M. Government 2005) is based on the guiding principle of "putting people at the centre". Although the strategy has an environmental focus, it also has the declared objective of combating poverty and social exclusion. This objective specifically refers to the processes of public participation as well as access to justice and human rights, this latter reflecting the requirements of the UK Human Rights Act of 1998. The Sustainable Development Commission (2002)—a national body set up by the UK government to review the strategy, identify policy gaps, and make recommendations to the government, has been more proactive in its promotion of questions of social inclusion and environmental justice.

Nevertheless, the general picture in the United Kingdom with respect to questions of sustainable development, environmental justice, and governance is one of strong policy guidance from Europe, declared support at the national level, but comparatively little activity at the regional and local levels. In the case of environmental justice, there is little evidence to suggest that there is the bottom-up community outrage so typical in the United States. The principal exception to this is the case of Scotland, where Friends of the Earth Scotland has been extremely effective in catalyzing and promoting a coherent environmental justice agenda. Indeed, it is now called Friends of the Earth Scotland: The Campaign for Environmental Justice, and has adopted the slogan "No less than a decent environment for all; no more than a fair share of the earth's resources" (adapted from Carley and Spapens 1997) as its campaign headline.

Although Scottish First Minister Jack McConnell has publicly supported the principle of environmental justice, in general UK politicians have not given much priority to matters relating to sustainable development, environmental justice, governance, or even the environment. As Christie and Jarvis point out, there is a huge reluctance among politicians to take a lead on environmental issues and even less to utilize concepts such as sustainable development: "The 'joined-up' thinking and action required to integrate environmental policy with economic and social strategies are in short supply and hard to do within the fragmented machinery of UK governance. Politicians are also deeply resistant to the environmental movement's critique of economic growth" (2001, 132).

It is this reluctance to engage with the sustainable development agenda that in turn conditions public attitudes to the environment and influences the levels of "environmentally friendly" behavior among individuals. Christie and Jarvis conclude that public attitudes toward the environment in the United Kingdom at the turn of this century have not been dramatically transformed since the early 1990s. They quote the conclusions of an earlier (1994) *British Social Attitudes* report, stating that the survey carried out in 2000 confirms this general picture: "We have shown that many environmental beliefs are rather superficial. Environmental concern is far more widespread than either support for environmental policies or environmental activism. The more specific and costly any proposal to improve the environment seems to be, the more rapidly support dissipates" (Witherspoon 1994).

A somewhat similar picture emerges from a recent National Consumer Council survey into consumer attitudes to sustainable consumption. Consumers are generally happy to "do their bit" toward sustainable consumption, but convenience in pressured daily lives takes precedence. In particular, low-income consumers suffer most from environmental degradation and feel powerless to improve their circumstances, in addition to often being shut out from making sustainable consumption choices (Holdsworth 2003).

Given these circumstances, it is not surprising to find that environmental citizenship does not have a high profile in the United Kingdom, apart from as a potential component of the emerging citizenship element of the national curriculum. As in the United States, where environmental citizenship is rebranded as civic environmentalism, the nearest worked-through equivalent appears to be the concept of "stewardship" as promoted by World-Wide Fund for Nature, Scotland: "Most of us would accept that a sense of responsibility to care for the interests of others, now and in the future, here and in the rest of the world, is deeply embedded in our personal and national psyche. It applies, among other things, to our care for nature and natural resources" (2000, 4).

This report specifically states that stewardship should be seen as a term that equates with sustainable development, but that is likely to be more accessible to a wider public. There is a blending of concepts here that makes environmental citizenship virtually indistinguishable from sustainable development. We will return to this in the conclusion.

Environmental Citizenship?

Environment Canada claims to have first developed the idea of environmental citizenship, defining it as "an idea that each of us is an integral part of a larger eco-system and that our future depends on each one of us embracing the challenge and acting responsibly and positively toward our environment. It's about making changes in our daily lives to be environmental citizens all day, every day" (2001). Laudable though this definition might be, however, it is both aspirational and superficial. The belief that all right-thinking people will eventually respond to rational debate and change individual patterns of behavior for the good of the environment seems a little misplaced coming from the environment agency of a country with one of the highest consumption and pollution records in the world. As we have seen above in the UK context, changing behavior is not so simple.

The key point here is that in most societies, a significant number of inhabitants are effectively removed from citizenship of any sort by virtue of race, ethnicity, class, gender, or age. In the United Kingdom Hutton (1996) has argued that a forty-thirty-thirty society exists. Forty percent of Britons are economically and socially stable, and are participating fully in society. Thirty percent are effectively excluded—they may live in poverty, be disabled, or experience long-term unemployment, and thus are marginalized from the day-to-day benefits secured by the 40 percent. The final 30 percent, contends Hutton, are in between, dipping in and out of exclusion throughout their lives.

It is possible to take issue with the detail of Hutton's assertion, but the general point remains. A substantial proportion of Britain's population are unlikely to qualify as prospective environmental citizens, and of those who are in the privileged 40 percent, a substantial majority are unlikely to want to lose the benefits associated with a high-consumption, resource-intensive lifestyle. Under these circumstances, there must be serious doubts as to the validity of the concept of environmental citizenship, at least in the terms outlined by Environment Canada.

What then of civic environmentalism as discussed above? Agyeman and Angus's (2003) distinction between broad focus and narrow focus civic environmentalism represents differing local-level interpretations both of the agenda at hand (*environmental quality*—narrow focus; versus *just sustainability*—broad focus) and the role of the citizen (*passive*—narrow focus; versus *active*—broad focus). Broad focus approaches represent just sustainability—a more politically radical vision of ways forward, with a strong resonance with environmental justice principles and approaches. Neither of these two variants of civic environmentalism has much in common with the Environment Canada approach.

Does stewardship offer a way forward? The WWF Scotland approach certainly places considerable store on the capacity of individuals and organizations to voluntarily change behavior in order to conserve and protect the environment, as such stewardship may be considered synonymous with environmental citizenship as defined by Environment Canada. As we have seen, however, stewardship is in effect the same beast as the dominant discourse of environmental sustainability—the need to protect and conserve the natural environment for future generations and in the interests of unseen others. How this might be achieved is left open, although reference is made to education and information programs, codes of good practice, and prizes and awards. There is no mention here of questions of equity, exclusion, and justice (WWF Scotland 1999).

Conclusions

We wish to make four points in conclusion. First, in our view, the concept of environmental citizenship as popularly defined (for example, by Environment Canada) has limited utility as an analytic tool or a vehicle for securing change. It may have potential as a mechanism for inculcating responsibilities through the educational process, but we have severe reservations over its use in other contexts. The narrow emphasis on environment rather than a broader emphasis on sustainability is important, but probably not crucial. In contrast, the unproblematic assumption that rational argument, more information, and examples of good practice will somehow change individual behavior is unnecessarily naive (Kollmuss and Agyeman 2002). Sustainable development (and for that matter, environmental sustainability) is a contested approach that will be resisted by powerful lobby interests and the bulk of the privileged consuming classes. Environmental citizenship as currently defined is insufficiently robust a concept to deal with the complex schisms of contemporary society.

Second, in contrast, we are more optimistic about the potential within environmental justice. Environmental justice offers (at least) two different, but complementary paths toward transformation. First, it is a *vocabulary for political opportunity, mobilization, and action,* predominantly at the local level. As Taylor notes, "Discourses about injustice . . . [become] . . . an effective mobilizing tool" (2000, 508). Environmental justice facilitates political organization, and when that "frame" is aligned with other powerful frames, such as that of the U.S. civil rights movement or the South African unions, it offers a wider perspective, a just sustainability that confronts the potential for more powerful interests to displace their problems onto localities and people with less power. It is also a *policy principle:* that no public action should disproportionately disadvantage any particular social group. This principle has been adopted by several U.S. cities and states (Eady 2003), and through former President Bill Clinton's Executive Order on Environmental Justice 12898, environmental justice policy has been institutionalized in EPA programs and those of other government agencies.

It is difficult to construct ethical arguments against this principle, although clearly one would think that there would be substantial political objections if any local government sought to adopt the principle. Combined with other principles, such as the proximity and precautionary principles, environmental justice could become a powerful tool for both the sustainability movement and the quality of life of some excluded groups. Indeed, the city of San Francisco has taken a step toward this combination. The city's Board of Supervisors voted eight to two to adopt the precautionary principle as official policy in June 2003. This is a heady victory for environmental justice and sustainability, as it shifts the burden of proof from citizens to industry. In other words, instead of citizens or communities trying to prove that harm is being done to them, industry has to prove that its operation is harmless. Following this landmark decision, in July 2003 the California Environmental Protection Agency's (Cal/EPA) Environmental Justice Advisory Committee (EJAC) recommended that Cal/EPA adopt the precautionary principle as a way of fixing, or preventing, environmental justice problems in California. The EJAC's decision is all the more important in that the committee included representatives from different government agencies and the corporate sector as well as community activists.

Third, we do not see how a discussion of environmental citizenship can be divorced from wider questions of equity and governance. The linkage between sustainability and equity is well rehearsed, and similarly, the move to more deliberative and open processes of governance, with greater levels of civic engagement and participation, is equally wedded to sustainability, not least through the worldwide Local Agenda 21 initiative (Evans and Theobald 2003). The EU commitment to more open and inclusive approaches to governance is not replicated in the United States, and will inevitably progress slowly in Europe. Nevertheless, the recognition that sustainability, questions of equity, and the processes of governance are integrally connected has now been well established (see, for instance, Boardman, Bullock, and McLaren 1999), and it is difficult to see how a discourse for progress toward sustainability can be adequately based on a concept such as environmental citizenship.

Finally, the ideas of sustainability and justice are also being linked, and used to influence policy at the global level. The Earth Charter (www.earthcharter.org) represents an initiative to form a global partnership that hopes to recognize the common destiny of all cultures and life-forms on earth, and to foster a sense of universal responsibility for the present and future well-being of the living world. The Earth Charter initiative was launched in 1994 by the Earth Council and Green Cross International, and is now overseen by the Earth Charter Commission in Costa Rica. The charter stresses the need for a shared vision of basic values to provide an ethical foundation for the emerging world community. The city of Oslo, a winner of the 2003 European Sustainable Cities award, has like many other localities adopted the charter and is actively pursuing ways of implementing it in the Oslo metropolitan area. It is these linkages between the challenges of sustainability, justice, equity, the awareness of global responsibilities, and the processes of governance that might help to deliver the individual behavior implied in the concept of environmental citizenship. Until these elements are blended together, though, the concept will remain fragile and elusive.

Notes

1. Agyeman (2005) fully explores the concept of just sustainability and the Just Sustainability Paradigm.

References

Adeola, F. 2000. Cross National Environmental Injustice and Human Rights Issues: A Review of Evidence from the Developing World. *American Behavioural Scientist* 43, no. 4:686–705.

Agyeman, J. 2000. Environmental Justice: From the Margins to the Mainstream? *Town and Country Planning Association "Tomorrow" Series*. London: Town and Country Planning Association.

Agyeman, J. 2002. Constructing Environmental (In)justice: Transatlantic Tales. *Environmental Politics* 11, no. 3:31–53.

Agyeman, J. 2005. *Sustainable Communities and the Challenge of Environmental Justice*. New York: New York University Press.

Agyeman, J., and B. Angus. 2003. The Role of Civic Environmentalism in the Pursuit of Sustainable Communities. *Journal of Environmental Planning and Management* 46, no. 3:345–363.

Agyeman, J., R. D. Bullard, and B. Evans. 2003. *Just Sustainabilities: Development in an Unequal World*. London: Earthscan/MIT Press.

Agyeman, J., and T. Evans. 2003. Towards Just Sustainability in Urban Communities: Building Equity Rights with Sustainable Solutions. *Annals of American Academy of Political and Social Science* 590:35–53.

Agyeman, J., and B. Evans. 2004. Just Sustainability: The Emerging Discourse of Environmental Justice in Britain? *Geographical Journal* 170, no. 2:155–164.

Barry, J. 1999. *Rethinking Green Politics*. London: Sage.

Boardman, B., S. Bullock, and D. McLaren. 1999. *Equity and the Environment: Guidelines for Socially Just Government*. London: Catalyst/Friends of the Earth.

Bullard, R., and S. Johnson, eds. 1997. *Just Transportation*. Gabriola Island, BC: Island Press.

Bullard, R., G. Johnson, and A. Torres. 2000. *Sprawl City: Race, Politics, and Planning in Atlanta*. Washington, DC: Island Press.

Carley, M., and P. Spapens. 1997. *Sharing Our World*. London: Earthscan.

Christie, I., and L. Jarvis. 2001. How Green Are Our Values? In *British Social Attitudes: The Eighteenth Report—Public Policy, Social Ties,* ed. A. Park, J. Curtice, K. Thomson, L. Jarvis, and C. Bromley. London: Sage.

Christie, I., and D. Warburton. 2001. *From Here to Sustainability.* London: Earthscan.

Clean Production, Part 1. 1998. *Rachel's Environment and Health News* (May 13): 650.

Cole, L., and S. Foster. 2001. *From the Ground Up: Environmental Racism and the Rise of the Environmental Justice Movement.* New York: New York University Press.

Conservation Law Foundation. 1998. *City Routes, City Rights: Building Livable Neighborhoods and Environmental Justice by Fixing Transportation.* Boston: Conservation Law Foundation.

Dobson, A. 1998. *Justice and the Environment: Conceptions of Environmental Sustainability and Dimensions of Social Justice.* Oxford: Oxford University Press.

Dobson, A. 2003a. *Citizenship and the Environment.* Oxford: Oxford University Press.

Eady, V. 2003. Environmental Justice in State Policy Decisions. In *Just Sustainabilities: Development in an Unequal World,* ed. J. Agyeman, R. D. Bullard, and B. Evans. London: Earthscan/MIT Press.

Environment Canada. 2001. Available at <http://www.ns.ec.gc.ca/msc/as/primer.html>.

Environmental Protection Agency. 1997. *Community-Based Environmental Protection: A Resource Book for Protecting Ecosystems and Communities.* Washington, DC: Environmental Protection Agency.

Environmental Protection Agency. 2002. *Community Culture and the Environment.* Washington, DC: Environmental Protection Agency.

Environmental Protection Agency. 2003. *Evaluation of Community-Based Environmental Protection Projects: Accomplishments and Lessons Learned.* Washington, DC: Environmental Protection Agency.

European Commission. 2001a. *A Sustainable Europe for a Better World: A European Union Strategy for Sustainable Development.* Brussels: European Commission.

European Commission. 2001b. *European Governance—A White Paper.* Brussels: European Commission.

European Commission. 2002. *A European Union Strategy for Sustainable Development.* Luxembourg: European Commission.

Evans, B., and K. Theobald. 2003. LASALA: Evaluating Local Agenda 21 in Europe. *Journal of Environmental Planning and Management* 46, no. 5: 781–794.

Foreman, C. 1998. *The Promise and Peril of Environmental Justice.* Washington, DC: Brookings Institution Press.

Friedland, L., and C. Sirianni. 1995. *Civic Environmentalism.* Civic Practices Network. Available at <http://www.cpn.org/topics/environment/civicenviron/ html>.

Gottlieb, R., and A. Fisher. 1996. First Feed the Face: Environmental Justice and Community Food Security. *Antipode* 28, no. 2:193–203.

Haughton, G. 1999. Environmental Justice and the Sustainable City. *Journal of Planning Education and Research* 18, no. 3:233–243.

Hempel, L. C. 1999. Conceptual and Analytical Challenges in Building Sustainable Communities. In *Towards Sustainable Communities: Transition and Transformations in Environmental Policy,* ed. D. A. Mazmanian and M. E. Kraft, 43–74. Cambridge: MIT Press.

Holdsworth, M. 2003. *Green Choice: What Choice?* London: National Consumer Council.

H. M. Government 2005. Securing the future: delivering the UK Sustainable Development Strategy, London: TSO.

Hutton, W. 1996. *The State We're In.* London: Vintage Books.

Jacobs, M. 1999. Sustainable Development as a Contested Concept. In *Fairness and Futurity: Essays on Environmental Sustainability and Social Justice,* ed. A. Dobson. Oxford: Oxford University Press.

John, D. 1994. *Civic Environmentalism.* Washington, DC: Congressional Quarterly Press.

Kollmuss, A., and J. Agyeman. 2002. Mind the Gap: Why Do People Act Environmentally and What Are the Barriers to Pro-environmental Behavior? *Environmental Education Research* 8:239–260.

Landy, M. K., M. M. Susman, and D. S. Knopman. 1999. *Civic Environmentalism in Action: A Field Guide to Regional and Local Initiatives.* Washington, DC: Progressive Policy Institute. Available at <http://www.dlcppi.org>.

Mazmanian, D. A., and M. E. Kraft, eds. 1999. *Towards Sustainable Communities: Transition and Transformations in Environmental Policy.* Cambridge: MIT Press.

Medoff, P., and H. Sklar. 1994. *Streets of Hope: The Fall and Rise of an Urban Neighborhood.* Boston: South End Press.

Perfecto, I. 1995. Sustainable Agriculture Embedded in a Global Sustainable Future: Agriculture in the United States and Cuba. In *Environmental Justice: Issues, Policies, and Solutions,* ed. B. Bryant. Washington, DC: Island Press.

The Precautionary Principle. 1998. *Rachel's Environment and Health News* (February 19): 586.

Putnam, R. 2000. *Bowling Alone: The Collapse and Revival of American Community.* New York: Simon and Schuster.

Rees, W. E. 1995. Achieving Sustainability: Reform or Transformation? *Journal of Planning Literature* 9, no. 4:343–361.

Roseland, M. 1998. *Toward Sustainable Communities: Resources for Citizens and Their Governments.* Gabriola Island, BC: New Society Publishers.

Sabel, C., A. Fung, and B. Karkkainen. 1999. Beyond Backyard Environmentalism: How Communities are Quietly Refashioning Environmental Regulation. *Boston Review* 1, no. 12. Available at <http://www.bostonreview.mit.edu/BR24.5/sabel.html>.

Schlosberg, D. 1999. *Environmental Justice and the New Pluralism: The Challenge of Difference for Environmentalism.* Oxford: Oxford University Press.

Selman, P., and J. Parker. 1997. Citizenship, Civicness, and Social Capital in Local Agenda 21. *Local Environment* 2, no. 2:171–184.

Shutkin, W. A. 2000. *The Land That Could Be: Environmentalism and Democracy in the Twenty-First Century.* Cambridge: MIT Press.

Sustainable Development Commission. 2002. *Vision for Sustainable Regeneration: Environment and Poverty—the Missing Link.* Available at <http://www.sdcommission.gov.uk/pubs/regeneration02/pdf/regeneration02.pdf>.

Taylor, D. 2000. The Rise of the Environmental Justice Paradigm. *American Behavioural Scientist* 43, no. 4:508–580.

Torras, M., and J. K. Boyce. 1998. Income, Inequality, and Pollution: A Reassessment of the Environmental Kuznets Curve. *Ecological Economics* 25:147–160.

UK Government. 1999. *A Better Quality of Life: A Strategy for Sustainable Development.* London: Stationery Office.

UN Economic Commission for Europe. 1999. *Convention on Access to Information, Public Participation in Decision Making, and Access to Justice in Environmental Matters.* Geneva: UN Economic Commission for Europe.

Witherspoon, S. 1994. The Greening of Britain: Romance and Rationality. In *British Social Attitudes: The Eleventh Report,* ed. R. Jowell, J. Curtice, L. Brook, and D. Ahrendt. Aldershot, UK: Ashgate.

World Wide Fund for Nature, Scotland. 2000. Stewardship of natural resources: A WWF Scotland Report. Aberfeldy, Scotland: WWF.

8

Virtual Environmental Citizenship: Web-Based Public Participation in Rulemaking in the United States

David Schlosberg, Stuart W. Shulman, and Stephen Zavestoski

Rarely, though every so often, a latent progressive tendency emerges through U.S. legislation and brings lasting benefits.[1] In the environmental realm, we think fondly of the early 1970s, when the United States was a leader in the creation of progressive environmental legislation. In an earlier epoch, the Administrative Procedures Act (APA) of 1946 created the "notice and comment" process. Thereafter, agencies were required to take public comments while considering new rules for the implementation of legislation. Agencies originally were not required to take heed of what they had learned from the public. In some respects, the requirement simply enhanced the learning of agencies (Kerwin 1999). Later, however, agencies were required to be directly responsive to this public input in the development of rules (Beierle 2003, 4).

The APA process set the stage for the institutionalization of the broad participatory aspects embodied in the environmental law of the 1970s. This pathbreaking generation of environmental law, still standing though weakened considerably in some instances, helped establish a practice of environmental citizenship in the United States—the participation of diverse stakeholders (frequently ordinary citizens) in the development, enforcement, and defense of many environmental policies. While environmental citizenship is a highly contested concept (as chapters in this book demonstrate), our focus here is on the intersection of the particular progressive tendencies inherent in the APA process and the effects the move to online public comment will have on them. We underscore those aspects of environmental citizenship in the United States that may be characteristic of the next generation of citizen participation in rulemaking.

Over the last decade, numerous U.S. federal agencies adopted electronic, Web-based participation to meet the notice and comment requirements of the APA (OMB Watch 2002). The trend is a result of legislation such as the Government Paperwork Elimination Act, congressional oversight (GAO 2001, 2000; OMB 2002b), and administrative directives (OMB 2002a) that all seek to make the regulatory process open, transparent, deliberative, efficient, and effective. These efforts culminated in the approval by Congress of the E-Government Act, which specifically directs agencies "to enhance public participation in Government by electronic means" (sec. 206[a][2]), and a "citizen-centric" President's Management Agenda under the George W. Bush administration that emphasizes the standardization of access via portals.

On January 23, 2003, the federal government unveiled a new portal for public comment on all proposed rules: Regulations.Gov. As a result, the original opening for public participation created by the APA now has a virtual cousin—an electronic space devoted to citizen and interest group participation. The central question in this chapter is whether or not this information technology–enhanced process makes possible a new type of virtual environmental citizenship. While it is clearly too early to tell, we continue efforts in earlier work to lay out key issues and questions critical to understanding the potential of virtual environmental citizenship (Zavestoski and Shulman 2002; Shulman, Schlosberg, Zavestoski, and Courard-Hauri 2003).

In this chapter, we examine the move to online participation in environmental rulemaking with a particular emphasis on discursive democracy and citizenship. The primary task here is to discuss what we see as some of the main features of a discursive environmental citizenship, and consider how they may or may not be facilitated by existing or proposed systems of virtual participation in environmental rulemaking. So we will explore some possible discursive benefits of the online rulemaking process itself: deliberation on issues rather than preference aggregation, inclusion of diverse voices and points of expertise, a respect for that diverse input and the positions of others, and the possible transformation of preexisting preferences due to discursive engagement. Additional benefits may include issues raised by other authors in this collection: the expansion of discourse on particular environmental rules into the public realm, the potential to move beyond self-interest into expressions of the public good, and the development of more authentic and legitimate institutions influenced by critical and reflexive citizens.

At the same time, we are well aware of the potential dangers of virtual participation and seek to address these key issues: communication may be one-way rather than discursive, mirroring the weakness of the current system of public comment; agencies may simply exclude the voices or values they do not want to consider; power imbalances in the process may mirror the off-line world, with industry continuing to dominate the process; and virtual environmental citizenship may be an isolating rather than community-building citizenship, depleting social and political capital and potential. These promises and concerns are not new to the debate on e-citizenship, as we note below, but our research is focused on examining these issues both theoretically and empirically in the developing practice of Web-based public participation in rulemaking.

Regulatory rulemaking in the United States is a time- and information-intensive process (Shulman 2005). Recent history has propelled rulemaking into the focus of public attention by inviting greater levels of citizen participation. As Kerwin notes, rulemaking offers "opportunities for dimensions of public participation that are rarely present in the deliberations of Congress or other legislatures," and the "involvement of the public in rulemaking may be the most complex and important form of political action in the contemporary American political system" (1999, 32, 116). The process forces agency personnel to sort through facts and opinions derived from numerous sources. With the advent of the Internet and information technology (IT) more broadly, rulemaking is now undergoing a potentially radical transformation (Shulman, Thrane, and Shelley 2005).

Many agencies seem to agree with the General Accounting Office, which optimistically finds that the "use of IT in regulatory management can reduce regulatory burden; improve the transparency of regulatory processes; and, ultimately, facilitate the accomplishment of regulatory objectives" (2001, 1; Thrane 2003). Anecdotal evidence from agencies involved in e–rulemaking supports such claims; it also points to the efficiency of the process in terms of both time and resources. Yet there are few social science data evaluating this major transition in the procedures for mandated public participation.

Before any thorough baseline and/or longitudinal data have been collected, a number of scholars and commentators have nonetheless begun to argue for and against the potential of the Internet to transform democracy and citizenship. Optimism surrounding the Internet's potential originates from a number of political theorists—the so-called digital democrats. As early as 1993, reports appeared in the technology press about using the Internet to conduct global-scale town meetings. By 1995, the Internet was declared the "de facto standard" for citizen access to government information (Noack 1995, 29), and students of democratic theory were turning their attention to digital government because of its potential to increase democratic participation (Grossman 1995; Hill and Hughes 1998). Scholars in the United Kingdom (Coleman and Gotze 2001) argue that Web-based participation could be the answer to the decline in social capital and thus interest in citizenship (as in Putnam 2001).

But the concerns of the skeptics are persistent (Hern and Chauk 1997). Davis (1999) has suggested it is absurd to assume that technological innovation itself can lead to a greater or more meaningful public role in government. Some point out the risk that digital government might serve to widen gaps already separating the information and resource rich from the poor (Malina 1999); others claim the Internet is just as prone to elite domination as were earlier media. Many are critical of the one-way nature of much existing Web communication, saying it deprives the public of the interactive potential of the Internet as well as the possibility of introducing more two-way, discursive deliberation into decision making. And instead of an empowered citizenry capitalizing on more easily available information, some thinkers warn that the Internet could lead to a fragmented and nondeliberative populace (Alexander and Pal 1998; Schlosberg and Dryzek 2002; Sunstein 2001).

Such are the theoretical positions. There is some initial empirical evidence, however, that given the opportunity citizens will use the Internet to participate in decision-making processes. The majority of government uses of the Internet provide information to citizens without offering the opportunity for interaction and the accountability that follows from such interaction. This is confirmed by recent studies of government Web sites and citizen use of these portals (West 2001; Larsen and Rainie 2002). Yet a Pew Internet and American Life study found that

34 percent of those who have used the Internet to access government sites have sent comments or suggestions to their elected officials (Larsen and Rainie 2002). Whereas the tendency in the past has been for the Internet to increase the flow of information from government to citizens, its real promise is the creation of opportunities for citizen-to-government information flows and two-way deliberative communication between the two. Through such substantive citizen deliberation, public values stand to play a role in decision making, and democratic participation may hold agencies more accountable. Still, little empirical research has been done on the claims of either supporters or critics of e-democracy, or the specific practices with which democracy is being brought into the virtual sphere. The basic point of this chapter is to lay out a large research agenda to examine some of these potential benefits and dangers.

One key caution is called for when reviewing the positions of supporters and critics of e-democracy. Many of the arguments for and against the benefits to citizenship of Web-based participation are based in observation or experience with a wide range of Internet practices—Web sites, Usenets, bulletin boards, chats, blogs, and so on. As Froomkin remarks, "The Internet can be seen as a giant electronic talkfest, a medium that is discourse-mad" (2003, 777). But the focus here is on a particular element in that talkfest. Public participation in rulemaking, we want to contend, is unique for three main reasons. First, rulemaking technology often embodies a democratic direction, with the development of open dockets that allow citizens to see and comment on an agency's decision-making process as well as on the comments of other citizens. The first major experiment in Web-based public comment was on the U.S. Department of Agriculture's (USDA) proposed rules for organic foods beginning in 1997. Personnel at the USDA's National Organic Program understood that the public response—over 280,000 comments, some 50,000 of them via the Web—to the proposed rules was a watershed event for the agency. It was also a watershed event for Web-based public participation and the initial experience of virtual environmental citizenship in rulemaking (Shulman 2003). Systems later developed by the Environmental Protection Agency (EPA) and the Department of Transportation kept this crucial open-docket system.[2]

Second, participation in rulemaking is highly structured, and that structure will be revised constantly in new iterations of the technology.[3] Therefore, it is quite different from other Web-based discussion that is merely one-way, or isolated and homogeneous individual or group reflection, or just talk that is often dominated by the loudest/rudest—talk that alienates many and certainly does not lead to any increase in the qualities of citizenship (Davis 1999; Sunstein 2001). Sunstein argues that the Net enables people to pay attention to other, like-minded individuals, and ignore those who are unlike them or who would disagree with their positions on issues. The Web, then, diminishes exposure to heterogeneity and we lose the potential of a real public forum. But the assertion here is that the structure of e-rulemaking, in particular the open-docket system in which citizens can view the comments of others, leads us to engage the positions of others, including those who disagree. The architecture of e-rulemaking helps us avoid some of the dangers Sunstein sees lurking elsewhere on the Web.

The third reason we see e-rulemaking as a unique type of online discourse is that it leads to the actual revision of real rules and laws. One of the reasons we focus on rulemaking is because, of the many forms of virtual citizen participation, it has the real potential to be a forum where citizens learn, experience each others' positions, engage that difference, and develop the rules that will govern a society—or at least small aspects of that society. Such processes are where many critical democratic theorists look for the legitimacy and authenticity of democratic institutions. Here, e-rulemaking differs from other experiments in discursive democracy. A common problem in, for example, collaborative problem solving or citizen juries is disappointment that all of the discursive work goes nowhere.[4] People spend time and energy hammering out a consensus policy, only to see it ignored or rejected by an agency—this is a problem of implementation deficit. By definition, rulemaking requires agencies to respond to and incorporate public comment.

We focus on virtual *environmental* citizenship for a variety of reasons. For one, it is an area of public policy where public interest and participation have always been quite high. Andrews, in his history of U.S. environmental policy, argues that "one of the most distinctive features of modern U.S. environmental protection policy . . . is the unprecedentedly broad right of access to the regulatory process, which extends not only to affected businesses but to citizens advocating environmental protection" (1999, 240). Rosenbaum notes that more than 75 percent of all public participation programs in the United States originated in federal statutes since 1970, and the vast majority of those are in environmental legislation (1989, 215). Paehlke (1989) maintains that in the last three decades, the environmental area has led all others in the scope and extent of democratic innovation, not just in legislative politics, but also in environmental administration and law. Such innovations include public inquiries, right-to-know legislation, alternative dispute resolution, advisory committees, and policy dialogues. The history of environmental policy, then, illustrates that the leading edge of citizenship and public participation in the United States is in the environmental field; there has developed a culture of participation in environmental issues. It is thus fitting that we look at environmental initiatives in our examination of this new online avenue for environmental citizens.

Second, and not surprisingly, environmental issues have been central in the development of Web-based public comment. The USDA Organic Rule was first. More recently, the U.S. Forest Service took comments for a new Roadless Area Conservation Ruling. The Forest Service posted the proposed rule, the considered alternatives, background information, and a schedule of public meetings on its Roadless Area Conservation Web site (<http://www.roadless.fs.fed.us>). In addition to 430 public meetings, the Forest Service also received more than a million postcards or other form letters, and approximately 60,000 original letters, 90,000 e-mails, and several thousand faxes. As we will discuss below, however, the Forest Service reverted to a one-way system that denied the possibility of interactive discourse. Finally, the EPA Dockets or "EDOCKETS" system was developed to allow citizens to read others' comments in an open docket; as such, it embraces public discourse where the Forest Service system did not.

Third, environmental issues historically have been characterized by intense conflict and controversy. The ethic of involvement nurtured by the environmental movement, as discussed above, has had the result of pitting environmentalists against economic interests in zero-sum, no-win battles. If a central feature of citizenship is the willingness to compromise for the good of the community (Kemmis 1990), the seemingly inherent conflict over environmental policies seems a ripe place to begin exploring the possibility of virtual citizenship. All of this demonstrates that environmental issues are central in this current transition to electronic rulemaking, and that virtual environmental citizenship will be the vanguard of virtual citizenship for the near future.

The Project and the Methods

Our ongoing research project on democracy, e-rulemaking, and virtual environmental citizenship brings recent theoretical writings on democratic values and processes to bear on what will be a central transformation of the administrative state in the twenty-first century: the crafting of policy using the input of the public via the Internet. This radical change in the way agencies will relate to the public is upon us, yet there is little social science evaluating this transformation from traditional forms of public comment to Web-based processes.

To date, the move to e-rulemaking has been justified using the value of efficiency. Electronic commentary costs less to manage, takes less space to store, and makes the inevitable legal requirements for docket review easier to meet. Technological developments are also currently being driven by a desire for efficiency, such as filters that will distribute comments to appropriate agency personnel. While efficiency is not inherently undemocratic, such a focus can have a detrimental impact on democratic process and values; the potential of Internet technology to expand democratic discourse and participation may be lost. The APA championed democratic values such as the transparency of information, expanded public participation, and the accountability of agencies; our research explores precisely these values in the context of the development and practice of e-rulemaking.

Our data are coming from a variety of rulemaking cases on environmental issues, chosen for both diversity and public interest in the issues. These include the original e-rulemaking experience of the USDA's National Organic Program, highly controversial proposals about CAFÉ standards (mileage requirements for cars and trucks in the United States) at the Department of Transportation, and EPA proposals regarding clean water and mercury regulations. We are interviewing both agency officials and the staff of major environmental organizations based in Washington, DC. We are conducting a qualitative textual data analysis of both traditional and electronic citizen comments, revised rules, and our interviews. Toward this end, we have trained undergraduates to code for our issues of interest using NVIVO content-analysis software. We are also conducting a quantitative analysis of a telephone survey of citizens who commented using either traditional or electronic formats; questions in that survey have been informed by both our interviews and the content analysis of comments.

The first step in evaluating the move to virtual citizen participation is to see if there really is a difference between traditional and electronic, Web-based participation—on the part of both citizens and the agency responses to them. This is the present stage of the research. The point here is not just to look at e-participation from some Habermasian (or other) ideal of discursive democracy or citizenship but to compare the new process to the existing, traditional, and highly problematic practice of public participation (or the lack thereof) in rulemaking in the United States. There is certainly room for improvement.

The project findings will provide evidence as to whether current uses of the Internet as a public participation mechanism are expanding democratic practice, and agency legitimacy, by implementing the values and practices of current deliberative democratic theory. As for broader impacts, given the complete absence of data with respect to Internet-based public participation in regulatory rulemaking, our findings will serve as guideposts for the ongoing development of e-rulemaking practices. Such findings will provide key information for agencies now required to bring e-rulemaking systems online as well as empirical data for deliberative democratic theorists on issues central to current debates. In this sense, we hope to offer some reflexivity to a process that has to date been driven by technology and efficiency.

What We Are Looking for: Potential Discursive and Citizenship Benefits and Dangers

While public participation and the practice of civic engagement continue to be a hallmark of democratic theory (e.g., Boyte 1990; Sirianni and Friedland 2001), numerous political theorists over the past decade have refocused on deliberation as a crucial aspect of citizenship and participation in democratic practice. There is a renewed interest in the place of discussion, reasoning, and engagement across lines of difference in this citizen engagement in democratic politics. In the deliberative model, democracy is the practice of public reasoning. Participants make proposals, attempt to persuade others, listen to the responses of those others, and determine the best outcomes and policies based on the arguments and reasons fleshed out in public discourse.

Some deliberative democrats (e.g., Bessette 1980, 1994; Rawls 1996) make the argument that deliberation and public reasoning already occur in current liberal democratic governments, legislatures, and/or courts; often these theorists are content to stop there. Yet most deliberative democrats (including Barber 1984; Bohman 1996; Dryzek 1990, 2000; Habermas 1996; Young 2000) insist on expanding the practice of discourse to the public engagement in and deliberation of policy issues. Importantly, this renewed interest—along with specific deliberative prescriptions—is addressed to the governmental sphere, the public sphere, and the intersection of the two. As Dryzek says in his recent reflection on the past ten years of deliberative democratic theory, the essence of democracy itself is now widely taken to be deliberation, as opposed to voting, interest aggregation, constitutional rights, or even self-government. The deliberative turn represents a renewed concern with the authenticity of democracy: the degree to which democratic control is substantive rather than symbolic, and engaged by competent citizens (Dryzek 2000, 1).

Our key aims in examining Web-based public participation are based in these concerns of discursive democracy. We wish to understand the development of virtual environmental citizenship in terms of the type of citizen participation and communication engendered by the new technology, and with attention to the authenticity and legitimacy of the rule-making process. Participatory democrats (e.g., Pateman 1990) have long advocated the benefits of public involvement in the rules that govern society. Participation supposedly fosters important personal and social virtues; it is the way that citizens learn how to be citizens. More specifically, deliberative democratic theory helps us bring numerous broad and particular concerns to bear on the examination of the potential of virtual citizen participation.

Deliberation, Not Preference Aggregation

In light of the deliberative turn in democratic thinking, it is important to democratic citizenship that reflective as opposed to unreflective preferences get expressed and addressed. This is contrasted with unreflective comments that are simply aggregated, as in polling or voting. We plan to examine comments and survey commenters to see if people are referring to one another or agency-provided information in the text of their own comments.

Unfortunately, there are many barriers to deliberation in e-rulemaking. One-way electronic participation, in which a citizen simply sends a message presenting a preference and agencies balance such preferences, leaves us in an "aggregative" mode of democracy (and leaves the mechanics of that aggregation to the experts in agencies). No engagement with the position of others is required, and no reflection on one's own position is induced. Both governmental agencies and citizen groups are guilty of such behavior.

The processes developed over the past few years of electronic participation in rulemaking are varied. Numerous agencies independently designed their own systems in-house, and the result has been quite a diversity of interfaces. This was one of the primary reasons for the development of the Regulations.Gov Web site—a move from the existing fragmented system to one with a single portal with a single process for public comment on any proposed rule in any agency.[5] One of the crucial differences in the architecture of e-rulemaking has been whether comment from the public has been one-way or on an open docket. In a one-way design, citizens simply post an e-mail or Web-based comment to the agency; in an open-docket design, those comments are posted online, and anyone can read—and respond to—the comments of others. The standard form of one-way communication of positions used by some agencies leads to the simple aggregation of preferences, rather than any sort of public deliberation on the issue. With deliberation, there is the possibility of citizens rethinking and transforming their preferences given the input of others.

The USDA organic rulemaking allowed public comment on the Web site, and maintained an open docket. The architecture was not purposely designed to be so democratic, yet the process was certainly the most open, discursive, and transparent rulemaking in the history of the agency. One of the striking things about the process was the way that citizens commented on not only the agency's proposed rule but also the previous comments of other citizens. There was, in a sense, discourse in that citizens demonstrated that they had paid attention to one another, learned from one another, and engaged one another in differences of fact, science, and values.

Some agencies improved past practices with the move to e-rulemaking. The EPA, for example, has long had a "de facto guideline" for two-way communication (Covello and Allen 1988), but rarely implemented the suggestions contained therein (see Schlosberg 1999; see the EPA's recent rethinking in EPA 2001). Yet the EPA developed an open, two-way rulemaking system, EDOCKETS, which allows citizens to read and respond to the comments of others.

In contrast, another highly controversial rulemaking process, this time defining the protection of existing roadless (yet not officially wilderness) lands in the United States, was designed as a one-way system. This obviously precluded any Web-based public discourse. Citizens were only allowed to submit comments, not to see the comments of others or engage in a dialogue, as they were in the National Organic Program process. While it is clear that there was much more of a difference of opinion among the public on the issue of roadless areas, and on the science and values attached to those positions, the process did not tap into the potential of the Internet to provide a discursive framework to resolve these differences. With deliberation, as mentioned above, there is the possibility of citizens rethinking and transforming their preferences given the input of others; we see this in both the big changes and some of the fine-tuning of the specifics in the organics case. But the form of public participation in the roadless ruling preempted the possibility of preference transformation, and in fact, required citizens to present (and the government to interpret) hard-and-fast positions. The inability for a deliberative interaction certainly did not help citizens engage one another's symbolic or value-laden perspectives, or develop a notion of the public good. Worse, agencies such as the Forest Service claim to be looking only for unique comments, and so ignore bulk e-mails or petitions—making even the aggregative approach problematic. Such agencies may argue that they are looking for unique comments to add to the *internal* discussion regarding rules, but their approach exemplifies neither authentic aggregation nor deliberative democracy.[6]

Finally, there is the potential of strategic one-way communication employed exactly to avoid discourse. Regular players in the rule-making process (both industry and environmental groups) often wait until the last day of the comment period to submit their remarks. This effectively prevents the opposition from seeing and countering one's argument, and avoids the illuminating light of discourse. We are exploring whether this process continues in the move to Web-based rulemaking.

Many environmental groups do no better in the deliberative realm. For example, most simply ask visitors to their Web sites to "click here" to send a message to a congressional representative or an agency. In this, they are also guilty of promoting one-way—and genuinely unreflective—discourse. The motivation here is clearly aggregative; these organizations are more interested in getting the sheer numbers of those who agree with a group's position across to agencies. In focus groups, representatives of environmental organizations contend that the rulemaking process allows them to make their substantive contribution in the form of their own detailed comment to the agency—and agencies are bound by law to listen. But they often do not trust that the public has any additional expertise to add to the conversation and fear that a move to a more deliberative process would cost them the aggregative strength of public opinion on many environmental issues. In light of contemporary democratic thinking's stress on deliberation and authenticity, this focus on an exclusively aggregative approach constitutes a giant step back.

Still, in interviews with officials across many agencies, we have found praise for the new system for bringing more and new information into the rulemaking process. These officials offer two reasons for this. First, officials honestly believe they are getting information and expertise they otherwise would not receive. This was one of the points of the APA in the first place. Second, agency employees claim that they need more informed comment from the public in order to counter the comments (and political pressure) they receive from the industries being regulated (and the political appointees at the top of the agencies). Here it is important to note that we are talking with career personnel, not the political appointees who may be more averse to public input—and who control the development of any system for citizen participation.

It may be that while the technology offers the potential of deliberative citizen participation on environmental decision making, neither agencies nor environmental organizations support such a move. In fact, preliminary data in this study show exactly that: a large increase in electronic click-and-send form letters, and comparatively few original comments. Both parties may design their interactive systems to avoid deliberation, for their own political reasons. We do not mean to imply that existing traditional procedures are any paragon of deliberative authenticity, merely that if the new technology is not diverted away from mechanical aggregation, it will deplete any potentially beneficial deliberative aspects that may exist for virtual citizenship (Schlosberg and Dryzek 2002).

The Transformation of Preferences

Discursive democracy differs from standard liberal democracy in one key way: preferences and interests are not brought into the conversation as in a battle—with one person or group winning and others losing. The ideal of deliberation is that of communication that actually changes the preferences of participants in the face of the arguments and positions of others. In other words, citizens *learning* from agency information and from one another is absolutely critical to the process, as is agencies learning from citizens (one of the original APA aims). Such a transformation in individual preferences demands an exposure to and integration of a variety of perspectives, including legal, scientific, and value-based ones. In this way, a process of democratic rulemaking cannot just be one-way, with either an agency positing a position for citizens to accept or that agency simply taking note of objections to proposed rules without revisions. There must be room in the design of the online procedure for individuals to not only deliberate with others but also note changes in their own position.

The research we are currently conducting is examining whether commenters refer to agency materials and/or other commenters in the development and articulation of their own comments. It is hard, however, to measure the transformation of preferences without a control group. People do not often say that they've changed their minds in comments, and we do not have the benefit of pre- and post-tests of opinion. We are going to have to rely on participants surveys and interviews with the rule writers to see if the engagement influenced people to change their positions.

Inclusion of Difference

Other than deliberation and preference change, we are interested in particular qualities of the public discourse within rulemaking. Deliberative democratic theory has paid particular attention to the issue of the plurality of participation (Bohman 1995; Dryzek 1990; Hanson 1985; Young 1996). A more authentic discourse—and a more authentic democracy—includes the diversity of voices present in a society (and in particular, those who are affected by the outcome of the deliberation). This inclusion takes a variety of forms. First, obviously, it means the equal participation of more individuals and groups in the development of policy. Such a focus on inclusive participation is the essence of environmental justice demands for participation for traditionally excluded groups (Schlosberg 2003; see also Ageyman and Evans, this volume). The "digital divide" will always be an issue, but the question here is whether digital participation can be *more* inclusive than the traditional comment process, where the vast majority of the "public" is actually made up of business lobbyists and unelected agency officials (Coglianese 2003).

This brings us to another key benefit of a broad virtual discourse: while traditional comment during the rulemaking process is overwhelmingly corporate in origin, the move to electronic participation has the potential to make more diverse participation easier, especially if the user interface is friendly and simple to use. This will potentially help allow for a broader discussion of the implications of environmental policies under consideration—economic, cultural, and political, beyond the corporate, legal, and/or scientific considerations that now drive the process.

An inclusion of difference also means opening the discussion to modes of expression beyond those traditionally accepted. Young (1996, 2000) wants to move beyond simply rational argumentation—which she sees as exclusive—to include storytelling, greeting, and rhetoric in discourse. At present, agencies really only pay attention to either scientific or legal discourse—comments that directly address technical issues or existing legal standards. Often, comments that are more value based or symbolic in nature are not addressed. One of the current authors witnessed a public hearing session where a woman, dressed as an endangered Fender's blue butterfly, gave her testimony from the point of view of the butterfly after wetlands were filled for a proposed construction project. The agency official in charge of the hearing was visibly uncomfortable in his seat; he had previously admonished the crowd to keep their comments limited to the legality of the proposed action with regard to the Clean Water Act. When contacted later, the agency admitted they could not incorporate such testimony into their ruling, which was strictly legal in nature. In practical terms, the inclusion of difference would mean giving value to citizen participation that is outside the realm of either scientific or legal argumentation. Personal narrative or moral urging, for example, would weigh into both the public deliberations on rules in virtual discussions and the revisions of those rules themselves.

There is the potential to include such diverse citizen discourse in rulemaking, but again, only if the technology is designed to allow it. Web-based systems may help introduce more and more value-based public participation, while simultaneously making the exclusion of such comments easier for agencies. As the process is being developed, programmers are designing software filters to "read" the content of electronically submitted comments, so that the mention of a particular word or issue in a comment will have that comment directed to the relevant agency employee—for example, the mention of a soil additive in the discussion of organic farming rules would be sent to an expert in the field at the USDA. But what if a comment does not include reference to a particular legal point or scientific issue? Will they be filtered into an electronic wastebasket? Already, the potential of exclusion is clear. The Forest Service recently declared that it would not consider electronic comments that were not "unique."[7] The point here is to filter out mass-mailed messages from the members of interest groups (in this case, environmental groups). Oddly enough, this means that widely held opinions will be ignored.[8]

Interestingly, these techno-exclusionary tactics would leave the appearance of allowing more diverse comments, as they would appear on an open docket; yet those comments outside the acceptable lines of argument would be left out of the revision of rules. A more authentic and diverse system would find a place for alternative modes of communication as well as the expression of symbols, values, and beliefs in rule revisions, in addition to broadening the discourse in the visible docket.

Respect for a Variety of Positions

Linked to the above is the issue of *respectful* engagement in a discourse across differences. Deliberation is aimed not just at a singular outcome in terms of policy at the end but also at the understanding and mutual respect of participants—deliberative citizens—in the process itself. This means respect in terms of both the tone and character of a discourse, and the willingness to listen and engage with others. As Benhabib argues, the emphasis is "on sustaining those normative practices and moral relationships within which reasoned agreement *as a way of life* can flourish and continue" (1992, 38). Young (2000, 24–25) notes that participants in democratic discussion listen to others, treat them with respect, make an effort to understand them by asking questions, and do not judge them too quickly. This calls on people to be able to understand the positions of the others with whom they engage, and engage respectfully with differences.

Anyone familiar with Web-based discourse knows that it is often filled with intemperate speech, flames, insults, and attempts at intimidation.[9] But Web civility can often be improved with rules, guidelines, and/or moderation. Certainly, the different tone of Usenet groups versus moderated discussion lists demonstrates the potential of a few guidelines to bring about more respect—or at least lessen the strategic use of insults and the like (Davis 1999). In the highly structured realm of online public participation in agency rulemaking, discourse should be closer to a more moderated version of online communication. Within this context, participants should develop arguments that are agreeable to those with different interests and ends (Gutman and Thompson 1996; Bohman 1995), which will require, at the least, that participants feign virtual respect for each other.[10] Yet such expressions may be authentic; there is some evidence that Internet users are actually more supportive of diverse and tolerant points of view than nonusers (Robinson, Neustadtl, and Kestnbaum 2002, 300). Virtual citizen engagement might help improve toleration toward others both online and off-line. Again, we are coding the public comment record for respect, and comparing traditional forms of comment with electronic comment.

From Self-Interest to the Public Good

Here, the key question is not only how the public sphere participates in discourse but how the public *good* is represented in such deliberations. In environmental politics, the question was put best by Sagoff (1990): How can we include the preferences of citizens as citizens, rather than just as consumers? One of Habermas's (1993, 448–449) hopes for public discourse is that it might help us bridge the gap between enlightened self-interest and an orientation to the public good. In other words, it may help us move from the role of client to that of citizen. The opportunity here is in a public discourse that will bring people out of their selfish individual interests and into a diverse discussion of the common good.

Current modes of public participation in rulemaking do not require such a transformation. Traditional comment and one-way communication do nothing to appeal to the shared public good; they actually encourage self-interested comment in order for participants to attempt to bring revised rules closer to their own preconceived individual interests. People may offer comments from completely self-interested positions (as do the industries that attempt to revise a rule more to their favor) or they may address the larger public interest (as do many citizen groups). An open rulemaking platform, where people can address the comments of others and engage their arguments as well as motives, may move discussions on the rules that govern society away from self-interest. The potential here is to move beyond such individual interests (aggregated by the agencies) toward agreement on a public good. If an open rulemaking process is designed properly, a notion of the public good might be where we start to find common ground among citizens. Participants will have to convince others that their suggestions are not just good for one party or another. Deception will always be an issue; often, participants will couch their self-interest in terms of the public good (as in "tax cuts for the rich will increase employment and wages for everyone"). But engagement is a way to cut through such transparent framings.

Expanding Discourse in the Public Sphere

Digital democracy is a way of extending participation into civil society, beyond elected representatives and agency employees. Yet civil society contains not just individuals but groups as well. Environmental citizenship—virtual or not—must address both individual- and group-level analysis. It is widely recognized that flourishing associational life in civil society is crucial to the well-being of democracy. Theorists of "social capital" such as Putnam (2001) stress the supportive role of nonpolitical groups in inculcating trust that in turn makes people good citizens. More radical theorists emphasize social movements that often oppose the state (Dryzek, Downes, Hunold, and Schlosberg 2003). Barry (this volume) concurs regarding the vital nature of resistance in a critical environmental citizenship. More, and more open, public discourse on crucial issues through participation in rulemaking may be a way to strengthen groups in civil society and expand discourse among them.

The organic rule, as described earlier, is a good example here. When the USDA first introduced the rule, it allowed for crops fertilized with "biosolids" (previously known as sewage sludge), foods treated with irradiation, and organisms that were genetically modified to all count as organic. The public outcry was tremendous, and the discussion ranged from the pages of the nation's newspapers to talk radio.[11] Key in building public interest were the responses of numerous environmental, public interest, and organic farming groups. Obviously, not every proposed rule will engender such widespread discussion in the public realm. There are two central questions here: Does electronic participation expand the role for the public sphere in governmental decision making? And what role is there for public discussion specifically and the public sphere generally in a digital democracy? While there is potential here for an expanded public sphere, there are also dangers of isolation, which we will address below.

In addition to discourse, a critical environmental citizenship embodies action as well. We have found it quite interesting that while so much focus is on discursive participation in online rulemaking, many environmental groups see the process as a possible site of resistance and source of media attention. E-activists we have interviewed note the attention the media has given when groups have organized members to overwhelm the Web servers of various agencies. There, a statement is made not just on the merits of a particular argument but on the strength of the "public" feeling too. So while there is potential for more and more broad civil society involvement in state policymaking, there is also the possibility of e-activism, and the potential of that activism to generate discussion and coverage in the public sphere.

Impact and Authenticity

Of course, democratic processes are authentic only if those processes have an actual impact on the development and implementation of policy that affects people's lives. Habermas (1996) defines democratic legitimacy as one that enables meaningful participation in the development of norms and rules. Many theorists make clear the importance of authenticity and legitimacy as measures of democratic process (Dryzek 2000; Young 2000). In addition, numerous social theorists have discussed the importance of a "reflexive modernization" (Beck 1995, 1997, 1998; Beck, Giddens, and Lash 1994; Giddens 1990). Here, democratic processes are used to reflect on the impact of modernity (especially on environmental issues), and to actively redirect policy in less risky and more sustainable directions. Beck argues that "reflexive modernization is the attempt to regain a voice and thus the ability to act, the attempt to regain reality in view of developments that are the consequences of the successes of modernization. These developments call the concepts and formulas of classical industrial society fundamentally into question from the inside, not from crisis, disintegration, revolution or conspiracy, but from the repercussions of the very ordinary 'progress' on its own foundations" (1997, 15).

Such a critical, reflexive engagement is rare, though possible in e–rulemaking. It certainly was observable in discussions regarding the national organic rule. It may even be the case that a discursively designed process would allow not only diverse human interests, but nature itself to be "represented" or considered more thoroughly. This could lead to a practice not only of reflexive modernization, but of "ecological reflexivity" as well (Schlosberg 2005).

As a matter of practicality, there are numerous examples of these sorts of authentic democratic processes leading to both public acceptance of environmental risks and more positive opinions of agencies (Fischer 2000; Williams and Matheny 1995). But there are also many examples of inauthentic and co-opting mechanisms that only offer the veneer of democratic participation without the reality of a substantive impact on policy. Citizens need to be vigilant about such efforts, no matter the process. Yet the basic question here is whether virtual processes *may* enable a reflexive citizenry to have authentic impact. Again, we will compare the inclusion of traditional versus electronic public comments on revised and final rules.

Additional Dangers of Virtual Citizenship Mechanisms

The list above is not meant to be exhaustive, and as we noted at the start, it focuses on aspects of discursive democratic citizenship rather than on citizenship more generally. Also, the list is not meant to imply that virtual participation is now meeting, or can or will meet, such lofty ideals. But the criteria are key in any ongoing social science evaluation of such procedures, in particular in our comparison of traditional forms of comment with electronic comment. Finally, we wish to lay out two main concerns regarding e–rulemaking noted in both the literature and our initial round of interviews with agency and nongovernmental organization representatives.

Power

Much has been written about the potential of Web-based discourse to free us of shyness, stereotypes, socioeconomic status, and various other social cues that come into play in face-to-face communication. The supposed blindness of cyberspace is said to allow people to act as equals. Dahlberg notes that "arguments are said to be assessed by the value of the claims themselves and not the social position of the poster" (2001, 14). Some insist that the Web helps us shed the clear power differentials we have in the "offline" world—based, for example, on race, economic status, appearance, and gender.[12] As with most questions about behavior on the Internet, there are mixed reports on this question, with anecdotes on either side. It does seem to be the case, for example, that students who do not participate in the classroom are often the most talkative in online discussions. The anonymity of Web-based discussion may help citizens overlook their usual initial assumptions regarding the "place" or talents of others. It may also be the case that while equality is not actually achieved, participants may *feel* more equal in online forums than in person.

Still, there are issues beyond the discursive exchanges on the Web. Many environmental groups have said in our interviews that they still see the rulemaking process as being run by a close alliance between industry and agencies. The concern is that the agency is in the pocket of the corporations and will do what they want; this leads the environmental organizations to take a defensive stance in both their comments and approach to the process, reproducing the power relationship existent in the traditional rulemaking process. Given this assumption, environmental groups have told us that they are not interested in online dialogue with their "enemies." The existing culture and power relations of policymaking and public participation is such that all the parties have clearly defined roles. Simply moving to online discourse does nothing to reverse these relations of power, control, domination of the process by industry, and the defensive posture of environmental groups. Nevertheless, we see some potential given the response of agency personnel; many government employees have told us (off the record) that they see increased public participation—from both individual citizens and environmental groups—as a way to counter the traditional power of industry as well as political appointees at the top of agencies in the rule-making process. Substantive comments that critique industry positions, they assert, will help them write better, more balanced rules.

As rule making is now dominated by the power of industry, and those most articulate in legal and scientific discourse, it will certainly be key to actually examine the way agencies respond to public comments. How the inputs from different individuals and constituencies are brought into the revisions of proposed rules will be telling, and will help us understand how a move to virtual participation affects the current power imbalance in the rulemaking process.

Isolation versus Community

One of the supposed virtues of electronic access to, for example, agency Web sites is that access can be achieved by individuals without reference to groups. This possibility might constitute one less reason to join and support a group, however. Sunstein's (2001) thesis in *Republic.com* is that without some major guidance, the Internet's use with regard to government and the public realm will be isolating, and will not build any sort of public sphere or community life. The virtual citizen, then, would seem an oxymoron.

Agency officials are quite interested in this process; they see breaking down the barrier between themselves and citizen groups as a positive development, and look forward to citizens commenting directly, rather than through the Web sites and influence of interest groups. Environmental groups worry about this phenomenon, as they see the potential loss of members. Many groups are staying keenly on top of the developments in agency e-comment Web sites in order to continue to enable comments to come from their own Web sites. But the practice of many environmental groups themselves is more isolating than community building. In the "Action" sections of many major environmental organization Web sites, action simply entails pushing a button to add one's name to an electronic petition or send an e-mail to a member of Congress. While e-tactics of this sort demonstrate resistance to the process and may help generate media coverage to expand the public debate, this type of electronic action may also simply be isolated, one-way, and largely unthinking. While Putnam's (2001) thesis regarding bowling alone focuses on the depletion of *social* capital, a move to commenting alone—driven by either agencies or interest groups—may deplete the *political* capital of a populace becoming ever-more isolated. Critics argue that the Internet may fragment communities and diminish discourse.[13] No interchange or opportunity for questioning means little reflection and little attachment to groups. The hazard, then, is a further loss of democratic authenticity.

Such critiques may not hold for electronic participation in rulemaking, however. This argument may work for some parts of the Internet experience, but as we noted earlier, the structure of e-rulemaking—especially in an open-docket format—enables engagement with others who disagree. In fact, that is the very point of the public comment process. So a key question to explore here is whether the architecture of e-rulemaking brings real engagement across difference. We believe that given a proper structure, digital democracy need not be inherently isolating. Still, isolation is obviously a danger worth studying, and we will be comparing traditional versus electronic comments for mentions of group membership or information. We are also examining whether comments are unique or simply mirror the language of particular groups; initial findings show that while the pure numbers of unique comments are up, the majority of growth in the numbers of public comments are electronic form letters.

Conclusion

The point of all this is to examine the citizenship and environmental potential of Web-based public participation in rulemaking in the United States. Again, the process is upon us, and yet there are many predictions without much real research on these crucial questions. The central issue is the potential of this transformation—the potential good that may come, and the potential dangers that are present. We think, for the variety of potential reasons above, that this particular Web-based process holds promise. Froomkin has probably put the issue best: "It is too early to predict, but not too early to hope, that the Internet supplies at least a partial answer to the powerful challenge raised against the possibility of ever applying discourse theory to broad ranges of public life" (2003, 856). We would add that it is also too early to predict, but not too early to hope, that participation in Web-based decision making may make for more involved citizens—and more space for environmental citizenship.

On the particular point of environmental citizenship, Smith has recently offered a word of caution regarding increased discourse in environmental decision making: "If we are looking for decisive evidence that the institutionalization of deliberation will lead to . . . the greening of liberal democracies and, in particular, the emergence of an environmentally enlightened citizenry, we will be disappointed. The evidence is no more than suggestive" (2004, 150). We think there is something to the argument that in the United States at least, environmental issues and policy have historically been the leading edge of democratization.[14] We do not think it is coincidental that the most popular rules in the short history of e-rulemaking in terms of general public attention and numbers of comments on rules concern environmental issues: organic food, forests, fuel mileage standards, water, mercury, and so forth. It may be that Smith has looked at the issue from the wrong direction; it may be the case that an environmentally enlightened citizenry will lead to the increased use of deliberation in democracies, and so bring both more citizenship and more democracy to bear on environmental issues in the United States. This project simply offers to keep looking at these issues in this new, possibly promising direction.

Notes

1. This research agenda has been partially supported by a grant (SES–0322662) from the National Science Foundation, Social Dimensions of Engineering, Science, and Technology, Ethics and Values Studies program. A previous version of some of these ideas has appeared in Stuart Shulman, David Schlosberg, Stephen Zavestoski, and David Courard-Hauri, "Electronic Rule-Making: New Frontiers in Public Participation," *Social Science Computer Review* 21, no. 2 (Summer 2003): 162–178. Any opinions, findings, conclusions, or recommendations expressed in this material are those of the authors, and do not necessarily reflect those of the National Science Foundation. The authors wish to thank Andy Dobson, Derek Bell, and reviewers for The MIT Press for their helpful comments on previous versions of this chapter.

2. Unfortunately, the first iteration of Regulations.Gov reverted to a one-way system, where people can offer comments, but not read the docket. The focus of this system has so far been on efficiency over transparency; we hope that the next generation of the site will return to the open-docket system.

3. Importantly, these revisions to the technology may come, in part, from studies like this. The developers and operators of Regulations.Gov, for example, are quite open to input from both computer and social scientists on how the system might be improved.

4. Another popular discursive democratic devise, Fishkin's deliberative polling, is aimed at collecting, improving, and evaluating public opinion—not implementing it.

5. Though it should be noted that the motivation for this portal most likely had more to do with efficiency and financial cost than democracy. A single centralized system will cost much less than independent in-house systems in every agency of the U.S. government. It was the White House's Office of Management and Budget that pushed hard for the establishment of the Regulations.Gov portal.

6. One might assert that the very fact that agencies publish a rule, accept public comment, and offer a revised rule illustrates a deliberative process. Agencies may deliberate internally, or the public may think reflectively about an issue in order to make a persuasive argument to that agency. These assertions may be true, but they illustrate only a weak or internal deliberation—not the public, interactive deliberation that is the ideal of discursive democracy.

7. Interestingly, agencies could use the ideal of discursive democracy to dismiss such comments; there is certainly no attempt at democratic engagement with others in a mass-mailed comment.

8. Though we can be sure that savvy programmers at these organizations are working on ways to make each e-mail message "unique" by changing a word here or there.

9. Though this is not a quality unique to the Web, as any listener to conservative radio and television stations in the United States can attest.

10. Note how this differs from traditional interest group communication, wherein the norm consists of denigrating others and/or their points of view.

11. Personally, one of the authors knew the USDA would have to make changes after he heard the proposed rule lambasted on a weekend National Public Radio show dedicated to the humorous discussion of cars and their owners. *Click and Clack, the Tappet Brothers* often take conversation on their show beyond the bounds of automobiles, but the move to a critique of a government *agricultural* agency demonstrates how far into the public sphere the rule-making discussion went.

12. For a response, see Streck (1998).

13. These critics include one of the current authors; see Schlosberg and Dryzek (2002).

14. See, for example, Andrews (1999); Paehlke (1989).

References

Alexander, Cynthia J., and Leslie A. Pal. 1998. Introduction: New Currents in Politics and Policy. In *Digital Democracy: Policy and Politics in the Wired World,* ed. Cynthia J. Alexander and Leslie A. Pal, 2–22. Don Mills, Ontario: Oxford University Press.

Andrews, Richard N. L. 1999. *Managing the Environment, Managing Ourselves: A History of American Environmental Policy.* New Haven, CT: Yale University Press.

Barber, Benjamin. 1984. *Strong Democracy: Participatory Politics for a New Age.* Berkeley: University of California Press.

Beck, Ulrich. 1995. *Ecological Enlightenment.* Trans. Mark A. Ritter. Atlantic Highlands, NJ: Humanities Press.

Beck, Ulrich. 1997. *The Reinvention of Politics: Rethinking Modernity in the Global Social Order.* Cambridge, UK: Polity.

Beck, Ulrich. 1998. *Democracy without Enemies.* Cambridge, UK: Polity.

Beck, Ulrich, Anthony Giddens, and Scott Lash. 1994. *Reflexive Modernization: Politics, Tradition, and Aesthetics in the Modern Social Order.* Stanford, CA: Stanford University Press.

Beierle, Thomas C. 2003. Discussing the Rules: Electronic Rulemaking and Democratic Deliberation. Resources for the Future Discussion Paper 03–22. Washington, D.C.: RFF.

Benhabib, Seyla. 1992. *Situating the Self: Gender, Community, and Postmodernism in Contemporary Ethics*. New York: Routledge.

Bessette, Joseph M. 1980. Deliberative Democracy: The Majoritarian Principle in Republican Government. In *How Democratic Is the Constitution?* ed. Robert A. Goldwin and William A. Shambra, 102–116. Washington, DC: American Enterprise Institute.

Bessette, Joseph M. 1994. *The Mild Voice of Reason: Deliberative Democracy and American National Government*. Chicago: University of Chicago Press.

Bohman, James. 1995. Public Reason and Cultural Pluralism: Political Liberalism and the Problem of Moral Conflict. *Political Theory* 23:253–279.

Bohman, James. 1996. *Public Deliberation: Pluralism, Complexity, and Democracy*. Cambridge: MIT Press.

Boyte, Harry C. 1990. *Backyard Revolution: Understanding the New Citizen Movement*. Philadelphia: Temple University Press.

Coglianese, Cary. 2003. The Internet and Public Participation in Rulemaking. Paper presented at the Democracy in the Digital Age conference, Yale Law School, April 4–6.

Coleman, Stephen, and John Gotze. 2001. *Bowling Together: Online Public Engagement in Policy Deliberation*. London: Hansard Society. Available at <http://bowlingtogether.net/about.html>.

Covello, Vincent, and Frederick Allen. 1988. *Seven Cardinal Rules of Risk Communication*. Washington, DC: Environmental Protection Agency.

Dahlberg, L. 2001. The Internet and Democratic Discourse. *Information, Communication, and Society* 4, no. 4:615–633.

Davis, Richard. 1999. *The Web of Politics: The Internet's Impact on the American Political System*. New York: Oxford University Press.

Dryzek, John S. 1990. *Discursive Democracy: Politics, Policy, and Political Science*. New York: Cambridge University Press.

Dryzek, John S. 2000. *Deliberative Democracy and Beyond: Liberals, Critics, Contestations*. New York: Oxford University Press.

Dryzek, John S., David Downes, Christian Hunold, and David Schlosberg. 2003. *Green States and Social Movements: Environmentalism in the United States, Britain, Germany, and Norway*. Oxford: Oxford University Press.

Environmental Protection Agency. 2001. Stakeholder Involvement and Public Participation at the U.S. EPA: Lessons Learned, Barriers, and Innovative Approaches. Office of Policy, Economics, and Innovation. EPA–100–R–00–040. Available at <http://www.epa.gov/publicinvolvement/pdf/sipp.pdf>. Washington, DC: EPA.

Fischer, Frank. 2000. *Citizens, Experts, and the Environment: The Politics of Local Knowledge*. Durham, NC: Duke University Press.

Froomkin, A. Michael. 2003. Habermas@Discourse.Net: Toward a Critical Theory of Cyberspace. *Harvard Law Review* 116, no. 3:751–873.

Government Accounting Office. 2000. *Federal Rulemaking: Agencies' Use of Information Technology to Facilitate Public Participation.* GAO–00–135R. Washington, DC: Government Printing Office.

Government Accounting Office. 2001. *Regulatory Management: Communication about Technology-Based Innovations Can Be Improved.* GAO–01–232. Washington, DC: Government Printing Office.

Grossman, Lawrence K. 1995. *The Electronic Republic: Reshaping Democracy in the Information Age.* New York: Viking.

Gutman, Amy, and Dennis Thompson. 1996. *Democracy and Disagreement.* Cambridge: Harvard University Press.

Habermas, Jürgen. 1993. Further Reflections on the Public Sphere. In *Habermas and the Public Sphere,* ed. Craig Calhoun, Cambridge: MIT Press.

Habermas, Jürgen. 1996. *Between Facts and Norms: Contributions to a Discourse Theory of Law and Democracy.* Cambridge: MIT Press.

Hanson, Russell L. 1985. *The Democratic Imagination in America: Conversations with our Past.* Princeton, NJ: Princeton University Press.

Hern, Matt, and Stu Chauk. 1997. The Internet, Democracy, and Community: Another.big.lie. *Journal of Family Life* 3, no. 4:36–39.

Hill, Kevin A., and John E. Hughes. 1998. *Cyberpolitics: Citizen Activism in the Age of the Internet.* Lanham, MD: Rowman and Littlefield.

Kerwin, Cornelius. 1999. *Rulemaking: How Government Agencies Write Law and Make Policy.* Washington, DC: Congressional Quarterly Press.

Larsen, Elena, and Lee Rainie. 2002. The Rise of the E-Citizen: How People Use Government Agencies' Web Sites. Pew Internet and American Life Project. Available at <http://www.pewinternet.org/ PPF/r/57/report_display.asp>.

Malina, Anna. 1999. Perspectives on Citizen Democratisation and Alienation in the Virtual Public Sphere. In *Digital Democracy: Discourse and Decision Making in the Information Age,* ed. Barry N. Hague and Brian B. Loader, 23–38. New York: Routledge.

Noack, David R. 1995. Of, by, and for the People. *Internet World* 6, no. 8:28–31.

Office of Management and Budget. 2002a. E-Government Strategy. Available at <http://www.whitehouse. gov/omb/inforeg/egovstrategy.pdf>.

Office of Management and Budget. 2002b. OMB Accelerates Effort to Open Federal Regulatory Process to Citizens and Small Businesses. OMB 2002–27. Washington, DC: OMB.

Office of Management and Budget Watch. 2002. Administration Pushes E-Rulemaking. Available at <http://www.ombwatch.org/article/ articleview/846/1/39/>.

Paehlke, Robert. 1989. *Environmentalism and the Future of Progressive Politics.* New Haven, CT: Yale University Press.

Pateman, Carol. 1990. *Participation and Democratic Theory.* Cambridge: Cambridge University Press.

Putnam, Robert. 2001. *Bowling Alone: The Collapse and Renewal of American Community*. New York: Simon and Schuster.

Rawls, John. 1996. *Political Liberalism*. New York: Columbia University Press.

Robinson, John P., Alan Neustadtl, and Meyer Kestnbaum. 2002. The Online 'Diversity Divide': Public Opinion Differences among Internet Users and Non-users. *IT and Society* 1, no. 1:284–302.

Sagoff, Mark. 1990. *The Economy of the Earth: Philosophy, Law, and the Environment*. Cambridge: Cambridge University Press.

Schlosberg, David. 1999. *Environmental Justice and the New Pluralism*. Oxford: Oxford University Press.

Schlosberg, David. 2003. The Justice of Environmental Justice: Reconciling Equity, Recognition, and Participation in a Political Movement. In *Moral and Political Reasoning in Environmental Practice*, ed. Andrew Light and Avner de-Shalit. Cambridge: MIT Press.

Schlosberg, David. 2005. Environmental and Ecological Justice: Theory and Practice in the U.S. In *The State and the Global Ecological Crisis*, ed. Robyn Eckersley and John Barry. Cambridge: MIT Press.

Schlosberg, David, and John Dryzek. 2002. Digital Democracy: Authentic or Virtual. *Organization and Environment* 15, no. 3 (September): 327–330.

Shulman, Stuart W. 2003. An Experiment in Digital Government at the United States National Organic Program. *Agriculture and Human Values* 20, no. 3 (Fall): 253–265.

Shulman, Stuart W. 2005. E-Rulemaking: Issues in Current Research and Practice. *International Journal of Public Administration*.

Shulman, Stuart W., David Schlosberg, Stephen Zavestoski, and David Courard-Hauri. 2003. Electronic Rulemaking: New Frontiers in Public Participation. *Social Science Computer Review* 21, no. 2:162–178.

Shulman, Stuart W., Lisa Thrane, and Mack C. Shelley. 2005. E-Rulemaking. In *Handbook of Public Information Systems*, ed. G. David Garson. 2nd ed. New York: Marcel Dekker.

Sirianni, Carmen, and Lewis Friedland. 2001. *Civic Innovation in America: Community Empowerment, Public Policy, and the Movement for Civic Renewal*. Berkeley: University of California Press.

Smith, Graham. 2004. Liberal Democracy and the 'Shaping' of Environmental Citizenship. In *Liberal Democracy and Environmentalism: The End of Environmentalism?* ed. Marcel Wissenburg and Yoram Levy, 139–151. London: Routledge.

Streck, J. M. 1998. Pulling the Plug on Electronic Town Meetings: Participatory Democracy and the Reality of the Usenet. In *The Politics of Cyberspace: A New Political Science Reader*, ed. Chris Toulouse and Timothy W. Luke, 18–47. New York: Routledge.

Sunstein, Cass R. 2001. *Republic.com*. Princeton, NJ: Princeton University Press.

Thrane, Lisa. 2003. Agency Representatives: Focus Group Report. Available at <http://erulemaking.ucsur.pitt. edu/doc/reports/Final_Agency_Summary.pdf>.

West, Darrell M. 2001. State and Federal E-Government in the United States, 2001. A. Alfred Taubman Center for Public Policy and American Institutions, Brown University. Available at <http://www.brown.edu/Departments/ Taubman_ Center/polreports/egovt01us.html>.

Williams, Bruce A., and Albert R. Matheny. 1995. *Democracy, Dialogue, and Environmental Disputes: The Contested Languages of Social Regulation*. New Haven, CT: Yale University Press.

Young, Iris Marion. 1996. Communication and the Other: Beyond Deliberative Democracy. In *Democracy and Difference: Contesting the Boundaries of the Political*, ed. Seyla Benhabib, 120–136. Princeton, NJ: Princeton University Press.

Young, Iris Marion. 2000. *Inclusion and Democracy*. Oxford: Oxford University Press.

Zavestoski, Stephen, and Stuart W. Shulman. 2002. The Internet and Environmental Decision-Making. *Organization and Environment* 15, no. 3:323–327.

9

Encouraging Environmental Citizenship: The Roles and Challenges for Schools

Monica Carlsson and Bjarne Bruun Jensen

The starting point for this chapter is that today's environmental problems are structurally anchored in our societies and our ways of life. Solving these problems requires fundamental changes at the societal as well as personal level, which is why education in school must strive to help pupils become better at making decisions about their own lives and influencing their surrounding environment.

But how realistic or authentic should environmental education be? Should it be theoretical and hypothetical, or should it be practical, with students involved *now* in decisions and actions that affect their environment? Is it possible to build students' capacity for environmental action without enabling them to engage directly in environmental action? And what kinds of barriers and problems will appear if students—as part of their education—take action in society? These are some of the questions that will be explored here, first from a theoretical perspective and then drawing on experiences from schools in Denmark.

We view environmental citizenship as a contested concept and as closely related to the notion of action competence, and we find the educational research and evaluation carried out in this field of importance for developing and further operationalizing environmental citizenship.

Action Orientation and Action Competence

In the following, a definition of the concept of action is introduced. A particular point is made of demarcating action from behavioral change and activity, respectively. Then the difference between direct and indirect actions is made, and finally, the concept of action competence is introduced.

Action versus Behavior Change and Activities

It is often admitted that knowledge does not necessarily lead to action (read: changed behavior) (for a review, see, for instance, Kollmuss and Agyeman 2002) and that other means must therefore be used. Many attempts at action orientation are characterized by the fact that efforts are made to influence pupils directly—outside the "knowledge component," as it were—and thus, students are not necessarily allowed to make up their own minds and decide on the intended behavioral change.

Yet this is exactly where there is an important difference between behavioral change and action, and also between the two fundamentally—or paradigmatically—different goals for environmental education: behavior modification and action competence. Before an action, there will always be a conscious making up of one's mind, while this is not necessarily the case with a behavioral change. The first element in the definition of action is that students themselves are involved in making the decision to do something, whether it is a question of a change in their behavior or an attempt to influence the broader living conditions in the school or the community.

Another strong tendency in environmental education in schools is to integrate different practical activities. For example, these activities might include excursions to more or less untouched natural areas, or physical, chemical, and biological investigations of a polluted lake or stream. These various activities are obviously valuable and productive to the extent that they increase motivation and further the acquisition of knowledge, but in order to be characterized as actions, they must be aimed at solving the problems that are being addressed. This is the second element in the definition of action.

If, for instance, work is done with problems connected with fertilizer consumption in agriculture, investigating the amount of oxygen in a nearby lake would therefore not be characterized as an action but rather as an activity (which as mentioned, can easily be valuable in the educational context). An example of involving the action perspective in this sphere would be to work with how, by boycotting products from conventional agriculture, the opportunities for products from ecological agriculture could be promoted and in that way help to solve the problems of nitrate pollution. In other words, an action must be targeted toward solutions of the problem that is being worked with. This is the second element in the definition of action.

The above distinctions can be formulated as two criteria for actions (Jensen and Schnack 1997). The first criterion concerns the boundary between behavior and action, and hence the question of whether the pupils themselves decide to "do something." The second criterion concerns the difference between activity and action, and thus focuses on whether what "is done" is aimed at reaching a solution of the actual problem or not.

Different Kinds of Environmental Actions

Environmental actions can be grouped into two main categories: namely, actions that directly contribute to improving the environment, and actions whose purpose is to influence others to do something to contribute to solving the environmental problem in question—indirect environmental actions (Jensen 2002). In other words, indirect actions may be characterized as dealing with "people-to-people" relations, while direct actions refer to relations between people and their environment.

One example of a direct action could be a motorist who decides to take public transportation to work, whereas the laws and taxes imposed by the politicians to encourage car owners to do this can be described as indirect actions. The politicians' actions can also be seen as a result of the indirect actions of public groups, such as letters of protest, demonstrations, lobbying, voting, and so on. The indirect environmental actions of the public may be influenced by other indirect actions, such as debate evenings on traffic and the environment arranged by students working on air pollution problems in the local community. In other words, indirect actions may lead to direct actions, and a direct action is typically caused by a web of indirect environmental actions.

A specific case of indirect actions might be the so-called social investigative actions such as interviews. One could argue that interviews can be viewed as environmental actions. When students decide to test a farmer's knowledge of and attitudes about the environmental problems caused by agriculture with the help of questionnaires and interviews, for example there is a possibility that these activities in themselves influence the farmer's way of thinking about the environment. Therefore, these

	Direct actions	Indirect actions
Individual	1	2
Collective	3	4

Figure 9.1
Four types of action.

social investigative actions can to a certain extent be characterized as indirect environmental actions.

In addition to this, actions may be individual or collective, and collective and individual actions may be direct or indirect. The model in figure 9.1 illustrates the different combinations (Jensen 2002).

If a student decides to turn off the light when leaving the room as the last person, that action can be characterized as an individual direct action. If a group of students decides to build a recycling container as part of an environmental education project, that is a collective direct action. If the same group of students writes a letter to the principal or the school board suggesting that the school develop a political position about garbage and waste, that is a collective indirect action.

If the proposed actions only deal with the individual level, we will run the risk of teaching students only the individualist approach to environmental problems and their causes. Does the action of turning out the light when leaving the room necessarily give more insight into problems concerning energy consumption and change of climate? Or more to the point, how does one ensure that the specific action contributes to developing students' understanding of the environmental problem in question?

If environmental-based action competence, among other things, means that insight into solving environmental problems requires knowledge about social and structural changes, then major demands are put on the teacher's ability to put individual actions and their potential into perspective—both locally and globally. The model above might be used as a framework to structure these kind of discussions.

Action Competence
The ability to take environmental action is dependent on a number of factors (Jensen 2002).

· *Insight and Knowledge*   Students need a broad, positive, coherent, and action-oriented understanding of environmental problems. This component involves students acquiring a coherent knowledge of the problem of concern to them—a knowledge about the nature and scope of the problem, how it arose, who and what it affects, and the range of possibilities that exist for solving it.

· *Commitment*   Students need the motivation to become involved in change in relation to their own lives and so as to create a dynamic society. It is important to build up this component if the knowledge acquired is to be transformed into actions. Commitment is often developed within a social context, so group work is an essential part of the learning environment when developing environmental citizenship among young people.

· *Vision*   Students need the ability "to go behind" the environmental issues and think creatively. This involves developing visions of what their own lives could be like, and how society and the environment could be improved in relation to the particular problem of concern. This component deals with the development of pupils' ideas, dreams, and perceptions about their future lives and the society in which they will be growing up.

· *Experience*   Students need real-life experiences by participating individually or collectively in facilitating changes, and considering how barriers can be overcome. This component stresses the benefit of taking concrete action during the learning process.

· *Social Skills*   A number of basic social skills can be added to the list of components of action competence. These include, among others, self-esteem, the ability to cooperate, self-consciousness, and self-confidence. "Critical thinking" or "critical decision making" has been suggested as an independent component, closely linked to visionary thinking along with the ability to identify and analyze conflicting interests in relation to environmental problems (Breiting et al. 1999).

Based on this discussion of different central concepts, action-oriented environmental education should be defined as *education in which working with students' authentic environmental actions is an essential and integrated element.* Actions will often overcome barriers in the form of, for example, an insufficient response or no response at all. If actions such as these are to result in increased action competence, then demands must be made on teachers to put these barriers into perspective so that the teaching does not lead solely to incompetence and indifference.

Furthermore, it is important that the actions are not viewed as end products of an environmental education project. On the contrary, students' environmental actions should be continuously integrated into the educational processes. It is crucial that students have the opportunity to evaluate, reflect on, and restructure their actions—within a certain environmental education project and together with their teachers—in order to develop their action competence.

Collaboration and Participation

In order to clarify the potential for collaboration between schools and external partners, the notions of power and participation will be introduced. In the following, we distinguish between two different forms of participation—real and symbolic participation—and between two different models of collaboration—"the school as a consumer" and "the school as a political agent."

Schools' collaboration with external partners in society can be seen as a significant contribution to the development of environmental citizenship. Among other things, it supports pupils in

- developing knowledge about authentic environmental issues;
- gaining experience with interaction and action;
- developing engagement and motivation;
- perceiving themselves as people who can influence their surroundings;
- developing a sense of membership and belonging.

The term collaboration comprises normative expectations about mutuality and equality, but collaboration is also a process that involves a sharing of an arena for action. Consequently, it is also an arena of power with different interests, wishes, and needs. This arena makes it possible for students to experience essentially political situations, and thereby to develop the ability to identify and analyze conflicting interests in relation to environmental problems. Among other things, this involves working with questions such as: Who makes the decisions? Who was for and against, and why? How can we as young people gain influence in relation to environmental issues and with whom can we ally ourselves?

Forms of Participation

Schools' collaboration with external agents on environmental issues is closely linked to students' participation opportunities, through the extended space it gives for developing experiences with participation. Hart defines participation as the fundamental right of citizenship and "the process of sharing decisions which affect one's lives" (Hart 1992, 4). He uses the metaphor of a ladder to describe different forms of "non-participation" and several degrees of "real participation" depending on the level of initiative and influence over the decisions that children have. Hart is hereby referring to the notion of "real democracy," where participation is developed through concrete experiences such as being asked to work in students' environmental councils in schools, being consulted and informed, and participating in decision making, sharing decisions, and taking action with other children and adults alike.

At the same time, children's position in society must be viewed as a barrier for real participation since they are not generally included in making decisions that affect their lives. Consequently, one precondition for children's participation in the school and the local community is that those with power—the adults—are willing to delegate power to the children. Evaluations of projects on children's participation point out that children are often held in a position between being included and excluded (Danish Children's Council 1998). They are heard and consulted, but are seldom encouraged to participate genuinely in decision making and action. Furthermore, the evaluations stress that it is important to create nonformal, constructive, and issue-oriented forums for children's participation such as try-it-yourself projects—where children administer a pool of money for their own projects, such as computer clubs, along with the formal framework for participation, such as representation on school councils.

On the basis of Hart's (1992) and Simovska's (2000) work on children and participation, we distinguish between two different forms of participation: real and symbolic participation.

• Real—or genuine—participation is directed toward pupils' critical reflections, through a process in which the students' construction of knowledge and meaning about environmental issues is in focus, based on a belief in students' abilities to identify and find solutions to problems, individually or in collaboration with others. Furthermore, the focus is on an identification of values and interests related to environmental issues, which can be seen as a reaction to the moralistic approaches that often dominate environmental education, where certain values, knowledge, and actions are presented as given or natural, and alternative perspectives are ignored or left out. Real participation targets "individuals in a context," recognizing that the individual's lifestyle has to be related to structural, cultural, and economic conditions in the society.

• Symbolic—or token—participation is related to an environmental behavior modification approach, where students are expected to adopt predetermined environmentally friendly lifestyles and behaviors. Within this form of participation, environmental knowledge is understood as information that is passively transferred from the "teacher" to the "learner." Symbolic participation targets individuals and individual action possibilities, and the aim of the actions is prescribed by external institutions and organizations. The responsibility and blame for environmental problems are placed at the individual level, and conditions of life influencing the individual's lifestyle are ignored.

In an educational sphere connected with concerns for citizenship and the environment, we find the focus on an action-oriented *and* a participatory learning approach essential.

Two Models of Collaboration

In the following, two models of school collaboration are outlined, describing the school as a consumer and a political agent (Carlsson 2001). Each of these models is embedded in different basic understandings of the role of the school in society.

In "the school as a consumer" model, the world outside is brought into the school and the classroom, for example, by inviting guest teachers from environmental institutions and organizations in the local community, or through classes visiting energy and wastewater centers. The outside actors provide information for the school—which gives the school the role of a passive consumer.

The underlying educational philosophy of this model, which is widespread in our current educational systems, is the scientific-rational "conditioned-socialization" one (Hellesnes 1976). This discourse underlines that the school aims to educate pupils to follow the societal development outlined by existing knowledge and expert cultures as the "best."

Within this understanding, the school is seen as a preparation for real life—a democratic laboratory or a rather closed societal subsystem—and the pupils are perceived as the citizens of tomorrow—who have to learn good values and habits. The students gain experience from excursions in society and nature, but do not participate directly in society as they are not yet viewed as citizens. The students' actions do not therefore directly influence the decisions that are made in the surrounding society.

The "school as a political agent" model utilizes a two-way process. Schools and students gain insight into environmental issues by utilizing information that is brought to them by outside experts. In addition to this, students also play an active role in society by informing the public about environmental issues, suggesting new initiatives to the municipal government, and so on. Through these processes, schools and students are involved in establishing social relations with, for example, municipal technical departments and nongovernmental organizations in the surrounding society. This leads to collaboration processes, in which to a higher degree than in the model described above, the partners in school and society are in dialogue with each other. This means that the collaborating partners not only make contact and inform each other but also negotiate issues, make agreements, and initiate joint actions. As this process increases the possibilities for schools to gain political influence on environmental issues both inside and outside the school, this model gives the school the role of a political agent.

The underlying democratic discourse of this model—"political literacy" (Hellesnes 1976)—stresses that the school should educate pupils so that they can participate as critical individuals in the making of the future society. The notion of action competence can be placed within this discourse, with action competence defined as an ability to participate in society or, in other words, to be a citizen (Schnack 2003). In this understanding, the school and the students are seen as catalysts of change (including environmental change) or as mediating actors. Here, the school and the students collaborate with "outside actors" in society. The students act in institutions, organizations, and the local community—for example, as initiators, innovators, and local "experts" in environmental projects. The students' actions can therefore directly influence decisions made in society. From an educational point of view, the basic premise is that students learn to be critical citizens by practicing democracy and they develop their capacity for environmental citizenship by taking action in relation to authentic environmental issues.

The two outlined collaboration models are quite different in nature, as will be illustrated in the two cases from the Danish school context described in the next section.

Cases from the Danish School Context

To illustrate, clarify, and discuss the concepts outlined above, the Danish school cases both focus on action and participation, but from different angles. Furthermore, they illustrate different models of school/community collaboration.

The first case (Jensen et al. 1995)—*Children as Catalysts of Environmental Change*—was part of a European research-based development project (Uzzell et al. 1997) aimed at clarifying potentials for and barriers to students/schools being agents for local environmental change. In this case, the focus was on students' genuine participation and concrete action taking in the area of environmental issues. Regarding the collaboration with the local community, the school and the students were seen as potential agents for environmental change.

The second case (Hoffmann and Carlsson 2003)—*The School as an Authentic Arena for Students' Actions and Participation*—describes experiences from Danish schools' work with the energy theme in the Eco School project—an international nongovernmental organization–initiated project (<http://www.eco-schools.org>) supported by the European

Union. The guiding principle of this project is the need to solve environmental problems originating from the use of fossil energy; CO_2 and the greenhouse effect were viewed as the central problem, and savings in energy consumption as the primary solution. The overall educational aim is constructed as action competence related to the need for concrete changes that can be realized through environmental education.

Case 1: Children as Catalysts of Environmental Change

This project was carried out as part of an environmental education initiative including all students and teachers in three schools in a municipality in Denmark (Jensen 2002; Jensen et al. 1995). The research and evaluation connected to the project included a variety of methods: document analysis, observation studies, interviews with different stakeholders (politicians, technicians, headmasters, teachers, and students), and questionnaires to all teachers and students.

A preparation phase, in which teachers and other key people from the local community participated in various in-service activities, took place during an eight-month period prior to the actual project. During this period, teachers and their collaboration partners developed the main pedagogical approach (which did not include selecting the specific environmental topics that students were expected to work with). The project itself lasted for six full days (of which three were consecutive). The agreed-on criteria for the project included:

· The environmental problems and the actions must be jointly chosen by the participating parties (i.e., students, teachers, and other adults involved).

· All projects must involve students concrete actions as integrated elements of the learning processes.

· The changes in the community should be permanent and continue after the schools' initiatives come to an end.

· The insight, commitment, and visions of the participating teachers and pupils should be strengthened.

· Political and economic support from the school boards and the municipality is required.

The students in the schools went through various brainstorming exercises as well as walking tours in the local area to identify environmental issues. These groups, which contained students from different age groups (seven to fourteen years old), further specified the environmental problems they wanted to address in the project.

The guidelines for the project included ambitions for teachers, students, parents, and other adults from the local community to work and act together. The majority of the groups chose to work with traffic conditions in the neighborhood, and one of the groups decided to organize a demonstration as part of their work (in fact, it came as a big surprise to many teachers that traffic was chosen as the first priority by many pupils as they imagined that students would select garbage as *the* issue because it had been a priority issue in the municipality for a number of years). A demonstration against traffic on the main street in the town involving 150 students was an example of broad cooperation, where teachers, students, parents, the police, and politicians were involved, and where each did their bit concerning actions.

The police carried out speed tests and gave twenty-seven fines to motorists who had been driving too fast the day prior to the demonstration. Students were involved in measuring traffic intensity, speeds, and so forth, and they also discussed various mechanisms by which the traffic and the speed could be diminished. They developed their own visions with regard to collective transport, bicycle paths, and so on, in the local area. During the demonstration, the students put up a transportable homemade zebra crossing in places where they felt that zebra crossings should be established. Furthermore, signposts were made, indicating speed limits and giving reminders to motorists. The demonstration ended with the students arriving at the town hall, where they received moral support from the director of the municipality for their wishes concerning traffic reorganization. Several other groups worked with traffic issues, and as a consequence, a number of concrete effects and changes occurred in the months after the project. They were, among others,

• an intensified local media debate on traffic between local politicians and citizens;

• the earmarking of DKK 1,000,000 (approximately US $150,000) by the town council for the reorganization of traffic in one of the local areas (a rotary, etc.).

- the establishment of a Toronto-flash and zebra crossing by one of the schools.
- a reduction of the speed limit to thirty mph by one of the schools.
- speed reduction measures on Jaegerspris's main street.
- the planting of trees along the bicycle paths between two neighborhoods.

The evaluation addressed the various changes initiated from the project as a whole. The changes can be separated into three different categories. The first category comprises the changes that came about as a result of individual groups' direct environmental actions. These are groups that through their *direct actions* attempted to change the environmental conditions. This includes setting up compost containers and various embellishment-like changes. It is characteristic that each of these changes can be traced back to the actions of one single group.

The second category of changes also originates from a single local group. This includes establishing public places, a children's village board, playgrounds, and so on. These changes stemmed from a number of *indirect actions* where the group approached the relevant authorities (politicians, technicians, city corporation, etc.) with the aim of getting them to act or to widen the action space for citizens.

The third category deals with changes concerning traffic. These changes can hardly be traced back to one single group's actions as many different groups' projects concerning traffic contributed to intensifying the debate and attention drawn at all levels within the municipality. Moreover, there were a number of changes already being discussed when the project was initiated. There is, however, no doubt that the local groups' projects and actions contributed to influencing these changes, especially hurrying up the decisions and influencing their content. This latter category illustrates how a number of *indirect actions* can form a web and may jointly work to promote the same solutions.

The conclusions regarding the pupils' experiences were optimistic and in favor of the approach. During the evaluation afterward, many of the students commented on the authentic and action-oriented part of the approach (quoted in Jensen et al. 1995, 81–89):

Because we're the next generation, and we're the ones that'll have to pay the price for somebody else not really caring . . . who has just used nature's resources and polluted . . . we have a right to say something about it, haven't we? . . . so we can try to do things in a better way.

Obviously pupils have to do that, it's their future. Everybody should get involved in them . . . everybody that can form an opinion on them should get involved.

When you're living in your own area, and you begin to realize there are problems, then you are more likely to go to the authorities, go to people's houses, and get signatures. And you don't give up just because they say "But I'm sorry, it just can't be done." You just keep on.

Now I just don't worry, now I'll phone and complain . . . if there's any traffic problem again. I've learned a lot from this. Like giving them a kick in the backside.

For one thing it's our democratic right. And for another it's important for society and for us that we become visible, and that we have an opinion.

Although teachers felt the educational approach was demanding, the questionnaires and the interviews with teachers indicate that this way of working increases the students' commitment toward taking action, understanding of power relations in the area of local environmental policy, and insight in developing action strategies for change.

The cooperation with the technical department of the municipality was an essential prerequisite for the authenticity of the project and for the initiated actions to possibly lead to actual environmental changes. This collaboration therefore had two aims. First, it was to ensure the necessary course of action for the local groups. Further, the collaboration was to take place in authentic surroundings with the possibility of creating professional, long-term, and sustainable solutions. One might of course argue that the openness of the municipality that had been generated through the preparatory work in some respects provided a less authentic experience. This means that school projects where the inclusion of a preparatory phase is not a viable strategy, cannot expect the same degree of willingness to listen, cooperate, and act from their municipality.

The technical department has reacted positively toward the project, partly because it has led to increased dialogue between citizens and the municipality. Furthermore, the department now has a more precise impression of attitudes and interests in the area—which previously had been influenced by the most vocal citizens. As a consequence, it became clear that the project could contribute to developing the democratic processes within local government concerning especially physical and environmental planning. As the chair of the technical and environmental committee of the municipality of Jaegerspris commented, "We see how ideas from the local groups, in which children and adults participate, can be used in a concrete way. They can be voiced at the environmental committee and city council, they can be integrated into theme groups and then become part of the local government planning and local planning. These perspectives are targeted at the future" (quoted in Jensen et al. 1995, 101).

The technical department's view of the school's role is of great importance to the project. As long as the department is influenced by a centralist ideology, where both school and children are regarded as means through which to achieve some of the department's goals, the participating schools will have little room for action. The technical department in Jaegerspris has instead put emphasis on regarding the school and children as dialogue partners, and has thus given the local project groups ample room for action. Politically, the technical department was aware of this. Accordingly, the chair of the technical and environmental committee of Jaegerspris said that "the technical department of the municipality should perceive itself as more like a helper than an authority carrying out directives from above" (quoted in Jensen et al. 1995, 106).

This understanding is fundamental and is one of the major conclusions of the whole project. If the technical department could perceive this role of being "a helper" more than "an authority," one of the major obstacles to children as catalysts of environmental changes would be removed. One of the preconditions for this attitude was the in-service training that was linked to the project. At these courses, which were carried out as study circles with a consultant from the pedagogical field, both teachers and key people from the technical department participated on equal terms. During these activities, the participants had the opportunity to develop a shared understanding of the project along with its goals and basic principles.

Case 2: The School as an Authentic Arena for Student's Actions and Participation

The second case study was part of an evaluation project researching children's roles and possibilities for taking action in the energy area (Hoffmann and Carlsson 2003). The data were generated through interviews with a school principal, a municipal educational consultant, the coordinator of the Danish Eco School project, and teachers and students working with the project. Furthermore, data were obtained through document analysis of material from the Danish Eco School project's Web page (<http://www.groentflag.dk>), the school projects' Web pages, and from student- and teacher-produced materials.

In this project, the school setting—together with the local community and the students' families—was viewed as an arena for environmental changes. An overall criterion in the project was that the schools should establish *environmental councils* and involve students in these councils. The students were also encouraged to participate as technicians in an *eco-audit scheme*—where they learned about the procedures that lead to environmental certification. This certification was symbolized by a green flag, which could be obtained by the school if the following four project criteria were met:

1. Pupils had to undertake investigations in order to "get to know" energy.

2. The school had to save at least 10 percent on electricity consumption.

3. Pupils had to produce a visible model—for example, a windmill.

4. Pupils had to communicate their results to the media, to the local community, and at home.

The criterion of informing others about the project and its findings (e.g., advice on how to save energy at school and at home) could be viewed as the main action dimension of the Eco School project. There were a number of these indirect actions in the case while there were no examples of students taking direct environmental action.

At one of the schools, two teachers planned the project and made most of the decisions. Within the overall energy theme, the students chose the subtopics they wanted to work with. The students researched the technical infrastructure in the school and the local community through visits to the local energy center, a wastewater center, and a center for sustainable energy. They also searched for information on the Internet. In the interviews, the students talked about the visit to the wastewater center and that they received some materials from there. The outside actors were obviously perceived as informers by the students and not as social actors with their own interests.

According to the project criteria, the students had to communicate their results. At one of the schools, however, a teacher took the initiative to set up a poster exhibition about the project in the public library. She made the exhibition herself because, as she said in the interview, she was not sure that the students could do it. And she wanted the school to live up to the criteria in order to get the green flag. In the interviews, several pupils said that they didn't know there was an exhibition. One of the students saw it in the library and expressed a skeptical attitude because it was situated in the children's library—she didn't think that the children could read and understand the exhibition, and the adults wouldn't see it there.

Moreover, several pupils emphasized that they discussed energy use with their parents, but that they were not sure if what they said mattered—and whether or not they were listened to and taken seriously. Some students pointed out that they could do something in the future—when they become adults. The overall demand to the schools to establish an environmental council constituted a possibility for real participation by the students. Within these councils, there would in principle be conditions for framing a genuine dialogue between the different council members—students, teachers, the school principal, and outside actors such as parents, technical departments in the municipality, nonprofits, and so on. The coordinator of the Eco School project commented, "It is interesting to see if the environmental councils can motivate the children who also are sitting in the council, since it is a practical tool for planning and coordinating the work" (quoted in Hoffmann and Carlsson 2003, 157).

As the quotation illustrates, there was from the beginning a concern about whether students would take ownership of the councils. At one school, the school principal described the environmental council as having a core function involving the different partners in environmental debate and work: the parent representatives, the after-school activity center, the teachers, the school principal, and the students. Nevertheless, he admitted that the participation of students had demanded a lot of "motivational work" by the teachers in both the council and the classes. Two teachers at this school were coordinating the project, and the task for each class was written down in the minutes from the council meetings. In other words, the environmental council in this school functioned as a planning tool in the project, emphasizing practical details.

A teacher from another school gave an example of an environmental council that to a higher degree offered possibilities for genuine student participation. Here, the school formulated curriculum guidelines for environmental education for all classes in the school with a starting point in the Eco School project. The students in grade 7 were facilitators of the project and choose tasks from the Eco School material. On the basis of the suggestions from grade 7, the council worked out specific plans to be carried out by the whole school.

Although the last example illustrates how students can be genuinely involved in making plans for the whole school, the Eco School project coordinator, the educational consultant from the municipality, and many of the teachers involved underlined the lack of students' engagement and ownership in the councils. Consequently, the project coordinator suggested having two different councils: one for the students and one for the adults.

Finally, the eco-audit schemes also created possibilities for involving students in the project. A teacher from a third school described how the Eco School project was hooked up with the municipality's Eco-audit scheme and the use of economic incentives:

We got self-administration of expenses for water, heating and electricity, and the savings that we could make we were offered to share with the municipality. A part of this was put aside for pupils' self-formulated projects administered by the pupil council. That is pure motivational education. We were not sure if it was the right thing to do: It was motivating in a way that you could explain to the children that we received the 10.000 kr., because they did so and so. But there is a danger there, because then "thinking green" doesn't have to originate from an inner conviction, but from an economic incentive. But we got the results. (quoted in Hoffmann and Carlsson 2003, 164)

Eco-audit schemes can be seen as a potential initiative for providing authentic arenas for learning about environmental issues in schools, but as the teacher pointed out, the criterion that the school had to save at least 10 percent on electricity consumption was not in immediate accordance with the students' own interests: "The children are doing it because it is something that other people expect, because it is described in the concept and because we can get the flag, but it is a quantitative success criterion. It is not qualitative in the way that it describes what we actually did" (quoted in Hoffmann and Carlsson 2003, 158).

Regarding the environmental council, the main conclusion was that it—under certain circumstances—provided a setting for genuine student participation in planning and decision making related to environmental problems at their school. Whether or not this potential was utilized depended on how the adults looked at their own roles and the role of the council in the project. There was, for instance, a big difference between the council being used as a planning tool only or as a medium for creating ownership among all the stakeholders.

Regarding the community eco-audit scheme, it was of importance that this tool was at the time one of the primary societal strategies for dealing with environmental problems. Students participating in the eco-audit schemes had the opportunity to develop their insight into this strategy and also to make a real contribution to the solution of environmental problems at their school. But it was a problem that students often were given predefined tasks as technicians with little room for genuine participation and few opportunities for fundamental reflections such as, What are the links between the local and global levels? What are the root causes behind the problems? What are the different interests involved?

The Eco School approach, with its concrete top-down-formulated project criteria, does indeed challenge participatory educational approaches directed at real participation. The main challenge with such a project is therefore to balance this top-down steering strategy with a bottom-up educational strategy directed at strengthening the students' opportunity to participate in the identification of environmental problems and solutions in their school projects. This means involving the students in a way that promotes their development of action competence—not only promoting predefined solutions to environmental problems.

One could argue that the Eco School project opens up the possibility of the school being a political agent, since schools and students inform the surrounding community about environmental issues, and make deals, that are in their interest with the municipal eco-audit scheme. Schools can gain political influence over environmental issues and strategies in the school, especially if the strategies are related to saving energy. But it is doubtful if the Eco School approach promotes the role of the school as a political agent in the sense that teachers and students can influence principal political issues and decisions made in society.

One of the teachers questioned whether students might be more motivated by self-interest (money) than by so-called green values. Green values inspired by the ideal of sustainable development are based on reflections on what is in the interests of the local *and* global communities as well as in the interests of present *and* future generations. This means that green values are to a higher degree related to public interest than to self-interest. Micheletti (2002) points out, however, that it might not be fruitful to draw a sharp line between self-interest and public interest, since motivation based on the fulfillment of self-interest can lead to the development of motivation and ownership in relation to principal political issues. Building on this, we do not find the use of economic incentives in environmental certification processes to be problematic in itself.

Indeed, we believe it can be useful, since it can illuminate the relation between environmental issues and the economy—between green interests and economic ones—in concrete everyday environmental politics. The crucial question is rather how environmental education can promote students' understanding of the connection between individual and collective actions, and local and global environmental actions—an understanding that can be seen as a prerequisite for the development of environmental citizenship. If schools could use environmental certification projects like the Eco School one as a tool for discussions of concrete environmental politics and its built-in challenges as well as dilemmas, this could be a step toward encouraging students' environmental citizenship.

Challenges for Schools in Encouraging Environmental Citizenship

Based on the issues that emerged from contrasting the theoretical concepts with the two case studies, a few conclusions can be drawn. For each of these conclusions we outline some challenges for schools and future research.

Students' Actions

The overall conclusion is that students' actions—as integrated parts of teaching and learning—further improve their commitment and willingness to take action. In addition, action-oriented projects demonstrate that under certain circumstances, students are able to influence the school agenda on environmental issues and facilitate environmental changes in the local community.

The case studies raise the following issues for discussion and further research:

· When students take action as part of school projects, they will often meet resistance or barriers of different kinds (case 1). It is crucial for the development of students' commitment that these barriers are put into perspective, and therefore it is necessary to further explore what kinds of knowledge and insight teachers need in relation to the local community and its power relations to be able to support students in these processes.

· When students are involved in reducing, for example, the energy consumption of the school, the process is often considered action oriented by the teachers. But if these activities are defined by external partners (case 2, where the Eco School concept demands that a number of specific activities take place), it is strictly speaking not the students who are the actors, as they have not been involved in selecting the issues or the concrete actions that are being carried out. Seen from the perspective of the school, the overall criterion will always be "what students learn from what they are doing" and not simply "what they are doing." How can we support schools, teachers, and students in developing ownership when they are approached by external agencies with "environmentally friendly intentions," but where the goals, criteria, and actions are predefined?

· In environmental projects and campaigns, economic incentives are often used as motivational factors. In principle, such projects provide many opportunities for students and teachers to discuss and explore "economy versus environment" dilemmas in authentic settings. But as seen in case 2, it can also lead to a situation in schools where educational decisions are being directed by economic factors and not integrated with the value-based steering of schools, such as teachers' normative expectations of what the school is about and in which direction it should go. How do we support schools in using projects to illustrate such fundamental conflicts of interests, which are of central importance to environmental citizenship?

Students' Participation

The overall conclusion is that genuine participation in environmental education in schools facilitates the development of pupils' ownership. And that students' ownership is a crucial precondition for the development of the ability to take action and thus for environmental citizenship. The core element in genuine participation in schools is the dialogue between students, teachers, and other partners. The teachers' and collaborating partners' roles as facilitators—asking provocative questions, coming up with suggestions and ideas for action strategies, putting barriers in perspective, pointing out possible collaboration partners, and so forth—is critical for the whole process as well as students' learning in the process.

The case studies raise the following issues for discussion and further research:

• The teachers see participatory approaches as demanding teaching strategies since they feel a lack of control (case 1), and therefore it is necessary to explore and define the competencies and skills needed by teachers to facilitate these processes.

• Externally defined goals and criteria (in materials, campaigns, etc.) will challenge the idea of participation (case 2, where the teacher made the exhibition herself), which makes it important to explore the notion of participation in more detail. This means that we need to go beyond the distinction between real and symbolic participation, clarifying different possible ways and "levels" of participation.

• The difficulty of strengthening genuine student participation increases with the number of stakeholders involved in the school projects. Are there ways to ensure pupils' participation when many teachers or a whole school collaborate and when external actors (partners) are involved? How do we make sure that the students are not forgotten in the name of "more collaboration"?

School-Community Collaboration

The overall conclusion is that collaboration with external stakeholders might contribute to initiating and sustaining students' environmental actions. Furthermore, such collaboration might increase students' understanding of situations, relations, and interests—the dynamics in the local community. Nevertheless, there are many examples of external partners approaching schools because they want to utilize students as a means to reach their predetermined goals. Such an attitude about the role of the school in the community runs counter to the action-oriented and participatory approach advocated here. If development of students' environmental citizenship is the aim, schools and students should be viewed and approached as partners and resources in their own right.

The case studies raise the following issues for discussion and further research:

· Collaboration between schools and external stakeholders can be discussed in light of the different school roles illustrated in the two cases. The challenges for the collaborating partners are quite different in nature depending on whether the collaboration is based on an understanding of schools as political actors (case 1) or consumers (case 2).

· As illustrated in the dialogue collaboration model in case 1, it is crucial that the external stakeholders develop a sense of membership in relation to the school project and its principles, in collaboration with the teachers and students involved. What kind of political support and what forms of professional support are needed to facilitate such processes? Are current models of in-service training, where each professional group attends separate training and support activities, inadequate in relation to an open and collaborating school aiming to develop environmental citizenship among the students?

· Institutions and organizations working with environmental change offer ready-made packages to schools and teachers who view these as time-saving offers. These outside actors are partly neglected by educational researchers, and deserve much more attention in order to strengthen the development of materials and programs so that they leave space for students' genuine participation and action, and hence for the development of environmental citizenship.

We believe that the different forms of participation and collaboration discussed in this chapter are related in a nonsymmetrical way. If the school is seen as a consumer, it does not necessarily imply that students' participation in this school is symbolic. And an example of real student participation doesn't necessarily involve the school as a political agent in society. Yet we hypothesize that a school guided by an understanding that it has a role in society as a political agent provides more opportunities for students' real participation. In the discussion of the case studies, we recognize the need to go beyond the distinction between real and symbolic participation, and consequently the challenge for research is to clarify different possible ways and categories of participation. The case studies also demonstrate the need to further explore the distinction between the school as a consumer and the school as a political agent. Societal changes related to decentralization, liberalization, and public management lead to a development of new roles and challenges for schools and citizens. Research on environmental education needs to reflect these changes, with further research to identify and study these new conditions as well as the possibilities for action, participation, and collaboration, and how they are related to each other.

References

Breiting, Søren, Kristian Hedegaard, Finn Mogensen, Kirsten Nielsen, and Karsten Schnack. 1999. *Handlekompetence, interessekonflikter og miljøundervisning—MUVIN projektet (Action Competence, Conflicting Interests, and Environmental Education)*. Odense, Denmark: Odense Universitetsforlag.

Carlsson, Monica. 2001. Evaluering af sundhedsundervisning i folkeskolen—didaktisk set (Evaluation of Health Education in the Danish Elementary School). PhD diss., Danish University of Education.

Danish Children's Council. 1998. *Børn på banen—inddragelse af børn i lokale beslutningsprocesser (Involvement of Children in Local Decision-Making Processes)*. Statens Information.

Hart, Roger. 1992. Children's Participation: From Tokenism to Citizenship. In *Innocenti Essays,* no. 4, 3–44. UNICEF, United Childrens' Fund.

Hellesnes, Jon. 1976. *Socialisering og teknokrati (Socialization and Technocracy)*. Copenhagen: Gyldendals pædagogiske bibliotek.

Hoffmann, Birgitte, and Monica Carlsson. 2003. *Undervisning om energi. Børns roller og handlemuligheder på energiområdet (Children's Roles and the Possibilities for Taking Action in the Energy Area)*. Copenhagen: Danish University of Education. Available at <http://www.dpb.dk>.

Jensen, Bjarne Bruun. 2002. Knowledge, Action, and Pro-environmental Behaviour. *Environmental Education Research* 8, no. 3:325–334.

Jensen, Bjarne Bruun, Jens Kofoed, Gorm Uhrenholdt, and Christian Vognsen. 1995. *Environmental Education in Denmark: The Jaegerspris Project.* Copenhagen: Royal Danish School of Educational Studies.

Jensen, Bjarne Bruun, and Karsten Schnack. 1997. The Action Competence Approach in Environmental Education. *Environmental Education Research* 3, no. 2:163–178.

Kollmuss, Anja, and Julian Agyeman. 2002. Mind the Gap: Why Do People Act Environmentally and What Are the Barriers to Pro-environmental Behaviour? *Environmental Education Research* 8, no. 3:239–260.

Micheletti, Michele. 2002. Individualized Collective Action. Paper presented at the meeting of the Nordic Political Science Association, Aalborg, Denmark, August 14–17.

Schnack, Karsten. 2003. Action Competence as an Educational Ideal. In *The Internationalization of Curriculum Studies*, ed. D. Trueit, W. E. Doll, H. Wang, and W. F. Pinar, 271–291. New York: Peter Lang Publishing.

Simovska, Venka. 2000. Exploring Pupil Participation within Health Promoting Education and Health Promoting Schools. In *Critical Environmental and Health Education, Research Issues, and Challenges,* ed. Bjarne Bruun Jensen, Karsten Schnack, and Venka Simovska, 29–43. Copenhagen: Danish University of Education.

Uzzel, David, Jean Davallon, Patricia Fontes, Hanna Gottesdiener, Bjarne Bruun Jensen, Jens Kofoed, Gorm Uhrenholdt, and Christian Vognsen. 1997. *Children as Catalysts of Environmental Change.* Lisbon: Instituto de Promoçao Ambiental, Ministerio de Ambiente.

10

Promoting Environmental Citizenship through Learning: Toward a Theory of Change

Stephen Gough and William Scott

This chapter seeks to articulate a credible theory of change linking learning, environmental citizenship, and sustainable development. In doing so, its main purpose is to make a (necessarily partial) contribution to the understanding of the wider potential processes of democratization.

The classic definition of sustainable development (WCED 1987) concerns itself with the meeting of present and future *needs*. For its advocates, sustainable development is an essentially democratic concept. To put this another way, *unsustainable* development is seen as evidence of socially unjust allocations of resources, opportunities, and influence. If this is so, it follows that a form of environmental citizenship conducive to sustainable development is a necessary component of any wider concept of democratic citizenship. What people learn and how they learn it have been important focuses in the literatures of sustainable development, environmental citizenship, and wider democratic theory. Sustainable development, then, is a concept that necessarily has implications for our view of the environment, the notion of democratic citizenship, and the role of learning.

Much has been written about appropriate content, processes, and models of learning in relation to particular views of sustainable development. Different views tend to be informed by, among other things, different theories of change linking the one to the other. Many of these theories cast environmental citizenship (which is sometimes, but not always, also seen as necessarily *global* citizenship) in a key role. Of course, not all such models of learning and sustainable development have an explicit theory of change; but since sustainable development clearly implies some sort of change from the status quo, all must have at least an implicit theory of how change might happen, whether their proponents are aware of this or not.

Some sort of link clearly exists between sustainable development and the environment. While this point will seem obvious to some, it is interesting to note that there are others for whom the environment appears not to be central to their conception of sustainable development. For example, at the time of this writing, the UK government's Department for Education and Skills works with a range of indicators of sustainable development in which social and economic goals are very much emphasized (<http://www.dfes.gov.uk/sd/indicators.shtml>). We have explored this issue from our own particular perspective elsewhere (Scott and Gough 2003).

Here, we are particularly interested in the connection between sustainable development and learning—by which we generally mean all the learning that happens, both in formal and informal settings, whether in one's youth or throughout one's life, and regardless of whether or not it has been planned or sought by anyone.

It is widely believed that there must be a connection between citizenship and learning, or at least between citizenship and *education*. Hence, we can describe the object of inquiry in this chapter as the three-way relationship between environment, citizenship, and learning. Yet it is important to note the following:

• Everyone is not equally interested in all three elements, and may have different ideas about which of the three elements is the change *target* and which are merely the means to that end. For example, environmental educators have sometimes written as if the historic mission of education is to "save" the environment; political activists of one sort or another may assume that both education and the environment should be managed so as to create social and political arrangements of a particular kind; and those of a spiritual turn of mind may advocate both (citizenly) care for others and the environment as routes to inner learning by the self.

• The most common reason for anyone to be interested in this interrelationship is that they want to *change* one or more of its elements, which as noted above, necessarily involves an implicit or explicit theory of change.

In the remainder of the chapter we discuss the elements of this three-way relationship in light of theoretical constructs, examples, and research evidence. Finally, we articulate some of the elements that a theory of change would need to have in order to provide a credible vehicle for the promotion of effective environmental citizenship within the wider democratic project normally associated with sustainable development.

Learning and Citizenship

A range of issues surrounding the relationship between learning (or at least the narrower concept of *education*) and citizenship have been explored by Crick (1999). Crick's work was influential in the development of citizenship education in England. He chaired the advisory group to the secretary of state for education and employment, whose report *Education for Citizenship and the Teaching of Democracy in Schools* was published by the Qualifications and Curriculum Authority (QCA 1998). His remarks are of great interest both in themselves and also in light of subsequent developments in citizenship, which is now specifically linked to sustainable development within the English national curriculum.

Crick notes that active citizenship (which seems likely to include any worthwhile form of environmental citizenship) cannot be made compulsory. Attempts to make it so result either in its trivialization (as in the Australian voting system) or in the absence of any meaningful citizenship at all (as in one-party states). Indifference to active citizenship is a risky stance for any state, however, since it runs the risks of lawlessness and being unable to respond to crises. This has two consequences. First, because citizenship cannot be mandated, a presumption develops that it must be learned (or more accurately, *taught*) through education programs. Second, where one finds arguments for such citizenship education, these tend to be driven by a sense of emerging crisis (including, it should be said, a sense of environmental crisis) rather than "a reflection that knowledge of the political and social institutions of a country should be a normal entitlement of children growing toward an all too adult world" (Crick 1999, 338). In the terms we have developed above, what we see most typically in relation to arguments for citizenship education is a theory of change wherein education is a tool by which social behaviors may be inculcated to serve the greater end of social maintenance. *Political* arguments in England in recent times for compulsory citizenship education in schools appear to have been of this form.

Crick's own prescription sounds quite different: "Any worthwhile education must include some explanation and, if necessary, justification of the naturalness of politics: that men both do and should want different things, indeed have different values, that are only obtainable or realisable by means of or by leave of the public power. So pupils must both study and learn to control, to some degree at least, the means by which they reconcile or manage conflicts of interests and ideals, even in the school" (1999, 339).

It is important to note Crick's emphasis on "manag(ing) conflicts of interests and ideals . . . in the school," where the school serves as a crucible in which citizenship values can be learned ("caught") through the practice of those values *by* the school in the way that it lives day-by-day *as* a community. Further, as Crick himself briefly suggests, this argues for continuity of learning beyond schooling into adult life, since the "reconciling" and "managing" that are central to the process are open-ended skills applicable in developing social (and environmental) contexts. It should be remarked that this need for continuity of learning is also key to a wider literature within the field of lifelong learning. For example:

Central to a learning society is the proposition that the economic, social and cultural challenges confronting individuals and social formations in the late twentieth into the twenty-first century make reliance on initial education as a preparation for the full extent of adult life unsustainable. The capacity to meet those challenges requires continuing learning and recurrent opportunities to learn. As with individuals and organisations, the notion of a learning society signifies a reflexivity to processes of change which is characteristic of contemporary times. (Edwards 1997, 174)

If it seems, on the face of it, that the notion of a "learning society" (on the one hand) and Crick's conception of individual citizenship (on the other) are rather different points of origin from which to arrive at the view that there needs to be continuity between learning in school and learning in later life, then it should be remembered that both are to some extent responses to perceived social challenges that seek to employ learning in an instrumental way, and accepting of the idea that *learning is implicit in the practice of citizenship* and *citizenship is implicit in the practice (not just the content) of learning*—that is, as we learn, we live; as we live, we learn. In simple graphic terms, the relationship we are describing here looks *not* like this:

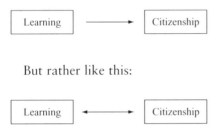

But rather like this:

Of course, this would apply as much to learning in relation to environmental and/or sustainable development–related aspects of citizenship as to any other.

Learning and the Environment

We have developed elsewhere a threefold typology of approaches to learning in the context of sustainable development (Scott and Gough 2003), and further developed this through an ongoing joint Lancaster University/University of Bath project, funded by the UK Economic and Social Research Council and titled Natural Capital: Metaphor, Learning, and Human Behavior.

Type 1 learning interventions are identified as those in which it is assumed that environmental problems have environmental causes. This leads to an attempt to identify solutions through natural scientific inquiry. In the process, new information may be identified that must be communicated. Once this communication has taken place, appropriate behavior change is expected to follow.

Type 1 interventions would include the production of leaflets, advertisements, or other forms of publicity to inform people of scientific arguments supporting, for example, the use of energy-saving lightbulbs, the addition of cavity-wall insulation to houses, the fitting of double glazing, smarter car driving techniques to get better fuel efficiency, recycling domestic waste to create compost, and so on. In these more or less straightforward cases, a real benefit can often be gained by individuals (and some pressure taken from "the environment") by the application of science/technology. A wider example is offered by the development, across a number of Caribbean countries, of an educational response to the degradation of coral reefs that aims to teach children the basic science of such reefs (Hindson et al. 2001). It seems plausible to us that interventions of the type 1 kind are those that enable the taking of the "personal steps" that are seen by some (NEETF 2004) as precursors in one way or another to environmental literacy (Volk and McBeth 1999).

Type 1 approaches commonly depend on a notion of an environmentally responsible citizenry informed by scientifically derived environmental facts. At the very least, this assumes that such facts are available, that countries are run by their citizens, and that the role of "citizen" is of more significance to people than other roles they might have (for example, employee, parent, or businessperson) when they are making environmentally significant choices. The citizen is seen as the vector through which objective knowledge is turned into social action. In short, not only do we have here, in Crick's terms, an impoverished view of the relationship between learning and citizenship but we also have:

• An apparently simplistic view of the relationship between citizens and society. In this, social outcomes are seen as the more or less straightforward expression of the wishes of a majority of independently minded, rational, and empowered individuals.

• An at least arguably inadequate view of environmental sustainability as scientifically determinable and value free (Dobson 2003).

In a recent paper, Kollmuss and Agyeman note:

The oldest and simplest models of pro-environmental behavior were based on a linear progression of environmental knowledge leading to environmental awareness and concern (environmental attitudes), which in turn was thought to lead to pro-environmental behavior. These rationalist models assumed that educating people about environmental issues would automatically result in more pro-environmental behavior. . . . These models from the early 70s were soon proven to be wrong. Research showed that in most cases, increases in knowledge and awareness did not lead to pro-environmental behavior. Yet today, most environmental NGOs still base their communication campaigns and strategies on the simplistic assumption that more knowledge will lead to more enlightened behavior. (2002, 241)

Type 1 approaches, then, cast both learning and citizenship as tools for the achievement of environmental maintenance. They are both widespread and, apparently, resistant to contrary evidence. The model they espouse looks like this:

Type 2 approaches, on the other hand, work from the premise that the problem of environmental sustainability is essentially not environmental at all but social. What citizens need, it is claimed, is not natural-scientific insights and technology but rather social-scientific insights and technology through which they will come properly to understand the social obstacles to sustainability, and thus see the need for appropriate, collective social, political, and environmental action.

Commonplace type 2 examples would include promotion of the use of public transport instead of private cars (or perhaps not making the journey at all), local sourcing of products, and clothing made from renewable (if currently impractical and/or unfashionable) materials. In these everyday cases, although some environment pressure may well be relieved, the benefit to the individual is often nugatory or involves a real cost. Yet learning interventions of this kind often begin from a vision of an alternative society in which things would be different: for example, the social pressure to drive would have vanished, conceptions of the local community would have strengthened, and clothes made from sustainable materials would be all the rage.

In the field of education, type 2 approaches are particularly associated with socially critical theory and the idea of an emancipatory curriculum. An especially lucid exposition of this tradition is Fien (1993). This view, however, is open to critique on the grounds that it oversimplifies the nature and distribution of both environmental and social disadvantage (Gough 1995), pictures practitioners and students as passive victims of wider economic forces (Robinson 1994), overspecifies in advance what people are supposed to decide to do when they are "emancipated" (Scott and Oulton 1999), lacks an appropriate theory of implementation through which practitioners and researchers can make improvements to their practice (Walker 1997), and offers little practical educational purchase in a world in which socialism and (particularly) false consciousness appear widely discredited (Gare 1995; Robinson 1993). A final point is that socially critical approaches have also been criticized by Bowers (1993, 1995) on the grounds that they work with exactly the same underlying industrial metaphor of nature as informs the market capitalism they both deprecate and seek to persuade us all to replace. Nevertheless, this is a view that continues to be influential—for example, in relation to teacher professional development in England (Huckle 2004). The model essentially entails two rounds of learning. In the first, people's eyes are opened to social and environmental truths. In the second, they learn (with others) how to live sustainably, through collective action.

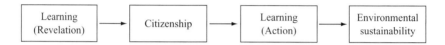

None of the above should be read as an attempt to deny that both type 1 and type 2 approaches can achieve success (see, for example, Hungerford and Volk 1990; Hungerford, Volk, and Ramsey 2000; Greenall Gough and Robottom 1993). A particular example of valuable work developed broadly within the type 2 tradition is the United Nations Educational, Scientific, and Cultural Organization (UNESCO) *Teaching and Learning for a Sustainable Future* multimedia teacher education program. The focus of this program is the professional development of teachers. It is available from UNESCO free of charge, both as a CD-ROM and at <http://www.unesco.org/education/tlsf/>.

This program draws on and develops previous work in this area in many countries around the world, particularly in the Asia Pacific region and South Africa. It takes as axiomatic that education is a potentially effective means through which society can confront its problems. The program is technologically and pedagogically sophisticated, and well set out. It is organized into five main sections: "Getting Started," "Curriculum Rationale," "Across the Curriculum," "Curriculum Themes," and "Teaching and Learning." The belief of the authors in the power of education is quickly in evidence, since the problems that are to be confronted through education could hardly be more all-embracing. There is, we are told in "Getting Started," a global crisis of a fundamentally cultural nature facing humanity as a whole. The most serious aspects of this crisis are subsequently identified as demographic trends; poverty; pressures on the natural environment; a lack of democracy; problems of human rights abuses, conflict, and violence; and difficulties surrounding the very concept of development. The change mechanism that is to link education to the resolution of this suite of issues is that of influencing learners on a global scale to think in terms of, and commit themselves to, the "common good" as they participate as citizens in society and make decisions. Education can cope with issues on this scale because, it is noted, there are over sixty million teachers in the world.

Finally, the program places emphasis on both formal and nonformal learning of an interdisciplinary nature. Eight "interdisciplinary curriculum themes" are identified: culture and religion for a sustainable future; indigenous knowledge and sustainability; women and sustainable development; population and development; understanding world hunger; sustainable agriculture; sustainable tourism; and sustainable communities. In each case, information is provided (with detailed sources), ideas are elaborated, and activities for learning and teaching are proposed. A range of pedagogical approaches are also presented in the "Teaching and Learning Strategies" section. No one could use this product without learning something, or being impressed by its scholarship and presentation. Many teachers will use it, and their teaching will be the better for it. For a further perspective on this resource, see Parry (2003).

And yet in spite of such examples, the existence of a "gap" between rhetoric and reality, and between awareness and behavior, is widely acknowledged. Learning may be happening, but the results in terms of environmental citizenship action remain disappointing. To discover why this may be, we turn now to the third of our pairs of relationships—that between citizenship and environment. Before doing so, however, we should note the existence of *type 3* approaches to learning and the environment, to which we shall return in due course.

Citizenship and the Environment

As we have seen, both Type 1 and Type 2 approaches to learning and the environment entail a conception of environmental citizenship that is, to a greater or lesser degree, driven by the imperative of crisis aversion identified and critiqued by Crick in relation to citizenship more generally.

Citizenship-through-learning is seen as integral, one way or another, to ameliorating the perceived environmental crisis. Still, the expected nature of this process depends on the view taken of the relationship between society (a collective concept of which the citizen is taken to be the unit) and the environment.

One possibility here is to see society as a product of the biogeophysical environment; that is, society is contained within its natural environment and can only survive as long as it responds to that essentially subordinate status. A "hard" version of this position is to be found in the sociobiological view that all social behavior has a biological basis (Wilson 1975). "Softer" versions (from Wordsworth onward) argue that nature provides a model for society. These two versions lead to radically different conclusions, depending on whether the default condition in nature is taken to be extinction (what happens if you don't fight hard enough for survival) or harmony (what happens if you fight no more than is absolutely necessary). The intuitive response to these contradictory foundational assumptions about nature is to observe that both can't be true. But of course, they both are.

Essentially, in all such cases we have the following:

A second possibility is to regard the environment as a social construct. This is to recognize that what is important about *the* environment (i.e., the one that we all live in) is in the end the accrued meanings we (society) have given to it, and how these are developed. To put it somewhat crudely, this is to say that what matters most about an area of tropical jungle is not ultimately the scientific properties of its soils or the catalog of its species but whether it is seen by those who have power over it as a welcoming source of nurture or a (ultimately hostile) source of timber for furniture. Here we have:

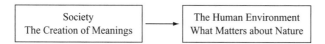

These two ways of thinking about the relationship between society and nature, and therefore about citizenship and the environment, do not necessarily correspond respectively with Type 1 and Type 2 approaches to learning and the environment. For example, deep ecologists see the bio-geophysical environment as foundational, but are likely to advocate learning interventions that seek to model society on its perceived "web-like" characteristics. Nevertheless, we may say that all Type 1 and Type 2 approaches might be expected to be logically consistent with one or other of the possibilities set out above, and so to possess a theory of change that is coherent with these, even if open to empirical questioning.

Of course, things may be so managed in practice that these types and both possibilities become, all together, confused and conflated. This might be expected to result in initiatives with no such coherent theory of change. This would seem to be the case, for example, in some recent educational initiatives focused on food, growing, and cognate areas. The executive summary of a recent review of research in these matters from across the world notes that "in the literature reviewed, a range of major weaknesses was evident including: [1] a lack of recognition of theories of learning or of [2] links to broader conceptual frameworks; [3] a general lack of validity or reliability; [4] a lack of critical reflection and [5] a lack of convincing evidence substantiating claims for better learning or improved attitudes resulting from teaching strategies" (Department for Education and Skills 2003, 5).

Although there is evidence of both type 1 and type 2 approaches to learning in this field (for example, type 1—facts about growing plants supported by practical activities linking soil/plant/crop/cooking/eating; type 2—growing, cooking, and consuming things in appropriate ways is a step to healthy living, whose importance in relation to sustainable development is axiomatic), nowhere is a model apparent that accounts for how any of this can bring about change in either how people *see* food and growing (either in relation to each other or to wider social factors), or how people can *change* how they behave in relation to these issues.

There is, however, a third possibility for thinking about the relationship between society and nature (citizen and the environment). It is uniquely consistent with what we have termed type 3 approaches to learning and the environment. It depends on the notion of the coevolution of society and its environment, and involves quite different perspectives on citizenship and change. It suggests that the great majority of existing educational approaches to bringing about environmental citizenship or indeed promoting the democratic imperatives of sustainable development are doomed to failure by the nature of their design.

The idea of the coevolution of ecological and social systems has been theorized in the context of agricultural development by Norgaard (1984, 1994). For Norgaard, human activities "modify the ecosystem, while the ecosystem's responses provide cause for individual action and social organization" (1984, 528).

Such coevolution is not necessarily beneficial to humans, and does not necessarily result in "development" or "progress." Humans are able to influence ecosystems (i.e., the environment) through their social institutions, including those that promote learning, but in a complex, nonlinear, feedback-modified fashion that is unlikely to result in precisely the outcomes initially planned, and is capable in principle of inducing catastrophe. Similarly, while ecosystem trends may threaten or promote human life, they should be extrapolated with caution since human institutions can be expected to adapt and, in adapting, influence the process of ecosystem change itself. A small-scale, but instructive example of this is found at Velvet Bottom in the Mendip Hills in southwestern England where the natural environment was significantly modified by lead mining in Roman and possibly pre-Roman times. The resulting environmental degradation has over two thousand years led to the development of a unique and biodiversity-rich environment that is now a nature reserve and tourist attraction. Further, social institutions have now come into being to actively prevent further ecosystem change.

Accepting the idea of coevolution has important implications for learning. Learning seems central to the relationship between society and nature, and therefore to any theory of change capable of dealing with reality in its full complexity. People learn (or fail to), organizations learn (or not), but in a sense, the environment always "learns" as nature responds to the results of human learning and activity.

Yet human learning (whether individual or institutional) is essential because we cannot depend exclusively for guidance about how to behave on *either* extrapolations of present trends into the future (regardless of whether these indicate catastrophe or abundance), or our understanding of the past. A consequence of the coevolutionary view is that except in creation myths, there has been no "golden age" of the environment to which we can seek to return. Times past should be seen as points on a continuum of change, not as natural equilibrium positions capable of restoration by one means or another.

Further, *within* a coevolutionary understanding, scope remains for debate, and hence learning, about the degree of *independent* influence over social and natural processes that humans can hope to have. Type 1 or type 2 approaches suppose that what counts as "proenvironmental," "pro–sustainable development," or "good citizenship" behavior can be specified, and that, through learning, appropriate cognitive (thinking), conative (action), or affective (feeling) skills can be induced or developed that will contribute to bringing these about. In this view, the main debate is about *which* set of skills or competencies should be the primary target for learning. From a type 3 perspective, however, the key skill is learning to manage, individually and collectively, a nexus of environmental and citizen behavior in the context of problems that may have multiple, contested definitions and shifting, contingent solutions.

This seems likely to involve constantly striving to improve our scientific understanding while simultaneously examining and reexamining the values we bring to bear. It is certainly not in any sense an anti-scientific approach. On the contrary, it involves the rigor of being clear about:

· when we *really* know something (we might decide to teach it);

· when we *really* don't (we might decide to teach the parameters of the doubt involved);

· the need to sometimes make important choices in the *absence* of incontestable (natural or social) scientific guidance.

It is also clear that complexity, uncertainty, risk, and necessity are ineluctable facets of a coevolutionary understanding that cannot be wished (or educated) away.

These matters derive added significance from one other aspect of a theory of change based on the idea of coevolution: its recognition that change of some kind will happen whether it is planned and managed

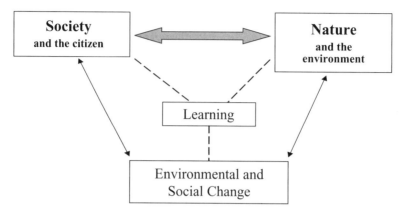

Figure 10.1
Relationships between society, nature, learning, and change.

well, badly, or at all. Diagrammatically, we might represent this view as shown in figure 10.1.

This is a conceptualization that seems to us to be the only one fully consistent with Crick's call for citizenship education that provides learners with "the means by which they reconcile or manage conflicts of interests and ideals" (1999, 339) in the environmental context, and potentially with his further insistence that such education must "begin at the beginning, that is to build a citizenship teaching relevant to all the school population from concepts that children actually hold or that are at least familiar to them" (342). The following example illustrates these points.

Sustainable Development and Education in North Borneo

The work described here took place from 1996 to 1998. It has been selected for inclusion in this chapter because it is both a substantial and completed example. Alongside a number of smaller-scale engagements, work to develop these ideas continues at the time of this writing through a research and development project, funded by the UK National Health Service Purchasing and Supply Agency, that explores innovative approaches to the training of health-sector managers in sustainable procurement.

The research discussed here was for the most part carried out in the small Sultanate of Brunei. Nevertheless, the designation "North Borneo" is also used here as a wider descriptor to include the East Malaysian state of Sarawak, which surrounds Brunei and in fact divides it into two dis-connected parts. This is done because:

· Some official policies that had a bearing on the work were conceived, at least in part, at this scale (e.g., tourism development).

· Some environmental impacts relevant to the work crossed international boundaries (e.g., forest fires and the smoke they produced).

· This wider setting of North Borneo was used in conceptualizing the work (Gough 1995).

From the point of view of sustainable development, North Borneo has a number of interesting characteristics. It is located approximately five de-grees north of the equator, has a hot, humid climate year-round, and was until as recently as the end of World War II entirely covered in tropical rain forest (Harrisson 1959). Three main cultural forms are present: Mus-lim Malay, overseas Chinese, and indigenous Dayak. Citizenship status is not fully extended to all these groups; Malays exercise political power.

These social arrangements are framed by a unique and rich tropical environment. North Borneo provides a fascinating example of tensions between "sustaining" the natural environment, on the one hand, and "development," on the other. Economic growth is rapid; environmental degradation is widespread but uneven.

The work began by considering a form of education that was

· in high demand;

· likely to influence both learner behavior and social as well as environ-mental outcomes in relation to sustainable development;

· a focus of frequent official exhortations to young people to contribute to "nation building."

This was management education, which at the time was being intro-duced for sixteen- to twenty-five-year-old students across the country. Courses were oversubscribed, no doubt in part because of the perceived need and opportunity for managers in a developing economy in which the number of public-sector jobs had been effectively frozen, and offi-cial messages stressed strongly and repeatedly the need for entrepre-neurship and management skills, particularly on the part of citizens (many Chinese entrepreneurs were noncitizens).

In keeping with Crick's point about beginning with the understandings of learners, the most crucial test for this work was simply whether it was perceived by learners to be good *management* education. If not, they would be likely to conclude that they had been misled at some cost to themselves.

The work took place with two cohorts of approximately 150 young people ("the students") aged between seventeen and twenty-four years. The ethnic distribution of this group approximated to that of wider Brunei society, with Dayaks underrepresented. All the students had applied, and been accepted, to study management through an accredited program. The work also focused on the lecturers (at different times, between five and eight in number) teaching the program as well as educational administrators, local businesspeople, and officials in more than one government department. Note that *none* of these individuals indicated *any* initial interest in sustainable development. They were people who saw themselves as students or teachers of business management, administrators of programs that favored the dissemination of business management skills, or potential employers of graduates. Citizenship, however, was a powerful, overarching concern of educational provision in general because of the priority given in official circles to nation building and national development.

In the first phase of work, all students were provided with a nine-page resource booklet by their regular lecturers, who had approved and, at their own discretion, adapted and/or expanded the contents. The booklets directed students to four group-based activities, making clear that the work was time limited and would be integrated in normal assessment procedures. It was also announced that some students would have the opportunity to present their work at a seminar organized by the Ministry of Development.

The activities related to a fictional proposal by a local/foreign joint venture company called Progressive Plastics to establish an industrial plant for the manufacture of plastic bags. This facility was to be located at an industrial estate (which really existed) near the mouth of the Brunei River. Though fictional, such a proposal was entirely credible for that location given that plastic bags are manufactured from ethane gas, which is produced as a waste product by the oil and gas refineries there, and was therefore potentially available as a raw material. Further, industrial chemical industries were officially favored with "pioneer industry" status and so subject to tax advantages. Each activity required students to engage with the proposed development from a different perspective. These perspectives were those of

• a local manager hired by Progressive Plastics to report on the local policy situation with regard to quality and environment;

• a Ministry of Development official charged with the regulation and monitoring of the proposed plant;

• a citizen responding to debate in the local paper, the *Borneo Bulletin*, about plastics and the quality of life (mirroring an actual debate in the *Bulletin* that weighed the visual pollution caused by plastic waste in the Brunei River and elsewhere against the convenience value of plastic containers);

• a scenario writer for the multinational joint-venture partner of Progressive Plastics (a role loosely modeled on that of a real individual, employed by Shell; credibility was added by this, as Shell has an absolute monopoly on oil production in the region);

• a *Ketua Kampong*, or village head, at the site of the proposed development.

In the second phase of work, students were required to prepare a detailed projection of the most appropriate use of the North Borneo coastline over the next five years, and in light of this to write a conventional ("product, price, promotion, place") marketing mix for the nascent Brunei tourism industry. It was announced that in this case, the Ministry of Industry and Primary Resources wished students to present work at an official function. Once again, work took place over an intensive weeklong period as well as at other points in time over a year.

The following outcomes are of note for the present discussion:

• There was evidence of environmental learning by students against two separate (and competing) sets of criteria derived from the literature of environmental education.

• It was felt by lecturers, and confirmed by analysis of students' work submitted for examination, that the interventions had enhanced students' business management learning.

• Senior officials at the Ministry of Development and the Ministry of Industry and Primary Resources expressed themselves satisfied that the interventions had been helpful from their separate perspectives.

Similarly, the Ministry of Education was satisfied with the work as an aspect of the introduction of top-quality business management education.

• Not only students but also local businesspeople, college administrators, and management lecturers were exposed to an environmental perspective on particular issues, perhaps in many cases for the first time. This happened particularly through the functions at which students presented their work.

• In the case of the second phase of work in particular, there was evidence of frequent enthusiasm and involvement on the part of students' family members.

Caution is in order in interpreting these outcomes, but to claim that both some degree of capacity for sustainable development was built and the national educational goal of developing an active citizenry was progressed does not seem unreasonable. The following are suggested as examples of type 1, type 2, and type 3 learning arising from this work.

Type 1
There were limited opportunities within this project for type 1 learning. In the first phase of work, students became familiar with some chemical aspects of plastics manufacture. They developed an awareness of the possible environmental implications of the construction and operation of a facility at the mouth of the Brunei River—for example, for fish stocks and mangroves. In the second phase of work, they were able to compare and contrast these technical implications with those arising from the construction and operation of tourism facilities of various kinds.

Type 2
A minority of students took an extreme view of the major society-wide social issue surrounding development in this context. This minority consisted of

• a group that felt that the past should simply give way to the future (for these students, economic development was central, and environmental and cultural costs only to be expected);

• a group that felt that development on the Western model was for the most part something they could well do without.

At a more everyday scale, however, there was a good deal of type 2 learning relating to, for example,

· the free issuing of plastic bags by businesses, particularly supermarkets, to customers;

· the use and reuse of such bags by members of the public;

· the declining use of traditional rattan bags;

· the decline of traditional river-borne distribution of food and other products;

· tourism as a possible means to revive and reward traditional skills and practices in, for instance, music, dance, woodworking, and metalworking;

· tourism as a threat to these same traditional activities, though a process that tended to turn them into little more than fairground attractions;

· the environmental impacts of increased motor transport and building-site construction, the developmental and market drivers of these changes, and the implications in relation to established religious and ethical positions in society.

Type 3

Most important, this work identified the existing environmental, social, and economic context in which students were endeavoring (in part through their training in management) to make their way, as a developing product of interactions between humans and nature. This was achieved through the focus on the Brunei River and the coastline adjoining its outflow into the South China Sea, which has been the site of a settlement, the Kampong Ayer, for more—and perhaps much more—than five hundred years. It has been modified over that period by human economic activity, including the construction and habitation of the Kampong, which is built entirely over water and accessible only by boat. The area has great cultural significance for Bruneians. The impacts of recent rapid development are apparent and locally controversial. Both Progressive Plastics and tourism developments would clearly be critical for the environment, people's lifestyles, and *each other*. Hence, by encouraging students to consider these developments sequentially, in relation to both modern (e.g., a local manager) and traditional (e.g., a *Ketua Kampong*) roles in their own society, and in a context of the involvement of business and administrative communities that they themselves realistically aspired to join, it was possible to create a sense of shared engagement with (but not resolution of) issues of the ongoing, adaptive, and uncertain development of the local environment. Particular evidence for this claim was the large number of "dilemmas" identified through the research—that is, instances in which individual students reported strongly held but apparently conflicting views. These included, for example, that

• a pleasant environment was characterized by *both* many tall trees and many tall buildings;

• Brunei needed to modernize to attract and provide for tourists, while at the same time tourists would come to Brunei because they were interested in it as it was;

• plastics had both improved and worsened local living conditions;

• only experts can judge environmental impacts, but that judging such impacts must be a matter for the population as a whole;

• coastal tourism would *both* increase employment opportunities and put fishermen out of work;

• modern lifestyles are more convenient *and* traditional lifestyles are more relaxing.

To the extent that students were exposed to the difficulties of decision making in relation to these dilemmas, we would contend that type 3 learning was occurring.

Concluding Thought

This chapter has argued that effective policies relating to sustainable development require an elaborated theory of change built on an understanding of the relationship between the environment, citizenship, and learning. Learning is thus seen as integral to such a theory of change.

In the earlier discussion of types of environmental learning intervention, we noted that both type 1 and type 2 approaches root our thinking about the future firmly in what we know (or think we know) in the present. Type 3 learning interventions, on the other hand, assume that for the present, uncertainty is irreducible; that society and its environment coevolve, each reacting in incompletely predictable ways to changes in the other. We might have added that deliberate actions that produce environmentally desirable outcomes at particular geographic and temporal scales may produce less desirable outcomes at other scales (Holling 1995). Type 3 learning interventions are characterized by open-endedness, negotiation, and the juxtapositioning of competing perspectives. Further, it might be asserted that type 1 and type 2 approaches to environmental learning are often essentially noneducative because they seek to manipulate learners into behaviors designed to support the policy choices of others, even though there may be extensive continuing debate about both the science and the values underpinning those choices. Type 3 learning avoids this difficulty by focusing on developing the abilities of learners to make reasoned choices for themselves.

There is some evidence that policymakers in different fields may be increasingly receptive to this view. In a plenary session at the U.S. National Council for Science and the Environment meeting in January 2003, the UN director general's special envoy for sustainable development, Jan Pronk, argued that education's main contribution should be to familiarize learners with perspectives other than their own. This is a recognizably similar position to that taken by Crick in setting out the characteristics of worthwhile (citizenship) education. If it represents a small step in the right direction, it might prove to be a significant one.

Nevertheless, eventual progress depends on initial clarity of thought. It is to this that we hope we may have contributed.

References

Bowers, C. A. 1993. *Critical Essays on Education, Modernity, and the Recovery of the Ecological Imperative.* New York: Teachers College Press.

Bowers, C. A. 1995. Toward an Ecological Perspective. In *Critical Conversations in Philosophy of Education,* ed. W. Kohli. New York: Routledge.

Crick, B. 1999. The Presuppositions of Citizenship Education. *Journal of the Philosophy of Education* 33, no. 3:337–352.

Department for Education and Skills. 2003. *Improving the Understanding of Food, Farming, and Land Management amongst School-Age Children: A Literature Review.* Research Report 422 (ISBN 1–84185–988–5). London: Department for Education and Skills.

Dobson, A. 2003. *Citizenship and the Environment.* Oxford: Oxford University Press.

Edwards, R. 1997. *Changing Places? Flexibility, Lifelong Learning, and a Learning Society.* London: Routledge.

Fien, J. 1993. *Education for the Environment: Critical Curriculum Theorising and Environmental Education.* Geelong, Australia: Deakin University Press.

Gare, A. E. 1995. *Postmodernism and the Environmental Crisis.* London: Routledge.

Gough, S. 1995. Environmental Education in a Region of Rapid Development: The Case of Sarawak. *Environmental Education Research* 1, no. 3:327–336.

Greenall Gough, A., and I. Robottom. 1993. Towards a Socially Critical Environmental Education: Water Quality Studies in a Coastal School. *Journal of Curriculum Studies* 25, no. 4:310–316.

Harrisson, T. 1959. *World Within: A Borneo Story.* Singapore: Oxford University Press.

Hindson, J., J. Dillon, S. Gough, W. Scott, and K. Teamey. 2001. *Mainstreaming Environmental Education: A Report with Recommendations for DFID.* Shrewsbury, UK: Field Studies Council.

Holling, C. S. 1995. Sustainability: The Cross-Scale Dimension. In *Defining and Measuring Sustainability: The Biogeophysical Foundations,* ed. M. Munasinghe and W. Shearer, 65–75. Washington, DC: United Nations University/World Bank.

Huckle, J. 2004. *Education for Sustainable Development: A Briefing Paper for the Teacher Training Agency.* London: Teacher Training Agency.

Hungerford, H., and T. Volk. 1990. Changing Learner Behaviour through Environmental Education. *Journal of Environmental Education* 21, no. 3:8–21.

Hungerford, H., T. Volk, and J. Ramsey. 2000. Instructional Impacts of Environmental Education on Citizenship Behavior and Student Achievement: Research on Investigating and Evaluating Environmental Issues and Actions, 1979–2000. Paper presented at the twenty-ninth annual conference of the North American Association for Environmental Education, South Padre Island, TX, October 17–21.

Kollmuss, A., and J. Agyeman. 2002. Mind the Gap: Why Do People Act Environmentally and What Are the Barriers to Pro-environmental Behaviour? *Environmental Education Research* 8, no. 3:239–260.

National Environmental Education and Training Foundation. 2004. *Understanding Environmental Literacy in America and Making It a Reality.* Washington, DC: National Environmental Education and Training Foundation. Available at <http://www.neetf.org/roper/ELR.pdf>.

Norgaard, R. B. 1984. Coevolutionary Agricultural Development. *Economic Development and Cultural Change* 32, no. 2:525–546.

Norgaard, R. B. 1994. *Development Betrayed: The End of Progress and a Co-evolutionary Revisioning of the Future.* London: Routledge.

Parry, J. 2003. Book review. *Environmental Education Research* 9, no. 2:276–277.

Qualifications and Curriculum Authority. 1998. *Education for Citizenship and the Teaching of Democracy in Schools.* London: Qualifications and Curriculum Authority.

Robinson, V. M. J. 1993. *Problem-Based Methodology: Research for the Improvement of Practice.* Oxford: Pergamon Press.

Robinson, V. M. J. 1994. The Practical Promise of Critical Research in Educational Administration. *Educational Administrative Quarterly* 30, no. 1:56–76.

Scott, W., and S. Gough. 2003. *Sustainable Development and Learning: Framing the Issues.* London: RoutledgeFalmer.

Scott, W., and C. R. Oulton. 1999. Environmental Education: Arguing the Case for Multiple Approaches. *Educational Studies* 25, no. 1:119–125.

Volk, T., and B. McBeth. 1999. *Environmental Literacy in the United States.* Rock Spring, GA: North American Association for Environmental Education.

Walker, K. E. 1997. Challenging Critical Theory in Environmental Education. *Environmental Education Research* 3, no. 2:155–162.

Wilson, E. O. 1975. *Sociobiology: The New Synthesis.* Cambridge: Harvard University Press.

World Commission on Environment and Development. 1987. *Our Common Future: World Commission on Environment and Development.* Oxford: Oxford University Press.

Contributors

Julian Agyeman is an assistant professor of urban and environmental policy and planning at Tufts University. He is the cofounder and the coeditor of *Local Environment: The International Journal of Justice and Sustainability*. His books include *Local Environmental Policies and Strategies* (1994), which he coedited with Bob Evans; *Just Sustainabilities: Development in an Unequal World* (2003), which he coedited with Robert D. Bullard and Bob Evans; *Sustainable Communities and the Challenge of Environmental Justice* (2005); and *The New Countryside? Ethnicity, Nation, and Exclusion in Contemporary Rural Britain* (forthcoming).

John Barry is director of the Institute of Governance, Public Policy, and Social Research, and a reader in politics at Queen's University, Belfast. He is the author of *Rethinking Green Politics: Nature, Virtue, Progress* (1999), winner of the Political Studies Association's W. J. M. MacKenzie prize for best book published in political science and *Environment and Social Theory* (1999), and the coauthor (with John Proops) of *Citizenship, Sustainability, and Environmental Research* (2000). He is the coeditor of *Sustaining Liberal Democracy: Ecological Challenges and Opportunities* (with Marcel Wissenburg, 2001); *The International Encyclopedia of Environmental Politic* (with E. Gene Frankland, 2001); *Europe, Globalization, and Sustainable Development* (with Brian Baxter and Richard Dunphy, 2004); *The State and the Global Ecological Crisis* (with Robyn Eckerlsey, 2005), and *Intervening in Northern Ireland: Critically Representing the Conflict and Its Legacy* (with Marysia Zalewski), a special edition of *Critical Review of International Social and Political Philosophy* (2005).

Derek Bell is a lecturer in political thought at the University of Newcastle, United Kingdom. His principal research interests are in political liberalism and environmentalism, especially the relationships among justice, democracy, and the environment. He has published widely on these subjects, including articles in *Environmental Ethics, Environmental Politics*, and *Political Studies*. He is currently working on a book on global justice and the environment.

Monica Carlsson is an assistant professor in the Department of Curriculum Research at the Danish University of Education. Her research area is curriculum and evaluation research within environmental and health education. She is the coauthor (with Birgitte Hoffmann) of *Samarbejde om bæredygtig udvikling. Nye perspektiver på samarbejde mellem skole og eksterne aktører* (*Collaboration on Sustainable Development: New Perspectives on Collaboration between Schools and External Actors*) (2004), and the author of "Evaluerer vi det, vi tror, vi evaluerer?" ("Do We Evaluate What We Think We Evaluate?"), *KVAN* 65 (March 2003).

James Connelly   is a professor of political thought at Southampton Institute, United Kingdom. Among his publications are *Politics and the Environment: From Theory to Practice* (with Graham Smith, 1999, second edition 2003), and *Metaphysics, Method, and Politics: The Political Philosophy of R. G. Collingwood*, 2003. He coedited the books *Philosophy, History, and Civilization: Interdisciplinary Perspectives on R. G. Collingwood* (with David Boucher and Tariq Modood, 1995), and *R. G. Collingwood: An Essay on Philosophical Method* (with Giuseppina D'Oro, new edition, 2005).

Andrew Dobson   is a professor of politics at the Open University, United Kingdom. Among his publications are *An Introduction to the Politics and Philosophy of José Ortega y Gasset* (1989), *The Politics of Reason: Jean-Paul Sartre and a Theory of History* (1993), *Green Political Thought* (third edition, 2000), *Justice and the Environment* (1998), and *Citizenship and the Environment* (2003). He has edited or coedited *The Green Reader* (1991), *The Politics of Nature* (with Paul Lucardie, 1993), *Fairness and Futurity* (1998), *Political Theory and the Ecological Challenge* (with Robyn Eckersley, 2005), and *Citizenship, Environment, Economy* (with Angel Valencia, 2005).

Bob Evans   is a professor at and director of the Sustainable Cities Research Institute at Northumbria University, Newcastle, United Kingdom. He is author of many books, book chapters, and articles on land use planning, environmental policy, and local governance. He is the cofounder and the coeditor of the international journal *Local Environment,* and has worked as a town planner in the public, private, and community sectors. He is the UK chair of the European Union's Working Group on Urban Environmental Management. His most recent book is *Governing Sustainable Cities* (2004).

Stephen Gough   is a senior lecturer in education and a member of the Centre for Research in Education and the Environment at the University of Bath, United Kingdom. He is currently researching the role of learning in sustainable procurement management in a project funded by the UK National Health Service Purchasing and Supply Agency. He is a fellow of the Royal Geographical Society. His most recent books are *Sustainable Development and Learning: Framing the Issues* (2003), and *Key Issues in Sustainable Development and Learning: A Critical Review* (2004), both written with William Scott.

Dave Horton   is an Economic and Social Research Council postdoctoral fellow at the Institute for Environment, Philosophy, and Public Policy at Lancaster University, United Kingdom. His ongoing research explores cultures of sustainability, and his main current interest is in the sociology of bicycling. His recent work has appeared in *Critical Mass: Bicycling's Defiant Celebration* (ed. Chris Carlsson, 2002), *Nature Performed: Environment, Culture, and Performance* (ed. Bronislaw Szerszynski, Wallace Heim, and Claire Waterton, 2003), and the journal *Environmental Politics*. He is an environmental activist and cofounder of Shifting Ground, a workers' cooperative dedicated to the creation of new kinds of space between the activist and academic worlds.

Bjarne Bruun Jensen   is a professor in health and environmental education at the Danish University of Education. He is director of the university's Research Programme for Environmental and Health Education. Among his publications are recent articles in *Journal of Curriculum Studies, Journal of Environmental Education Research, Environmental Education Research*, and *Health Education*. He is the coeditor (with Karsten Schnack and Venka Simovska, 2002 of *Critical Environmental and Health Education: Research Issues and Challenges*.

Alan Lewis   is a professor of economic psychology at the University of Bath, United Kingdom. His publications include *The Psychology of Taxation* (1982), *The Comprehensibility of Taxation* (with Simon James and Frances Allison, 1987), *The Economic Mind* (with Adrian Furnham, 1986), *The New Economic Mind* (with Paul Webley and Adrian Furnham, 1995), and *Morals, Markets, and Money* (2002). He has also edited *Mental Mirrors* (with Charles Antaki, 1986), *Ethics and Economic Affairs* (with Karl-Erik Warneryd, 1994), and *Student Debt* (with Adrian Scott and Stephen Lea, 2001).

Sherilyn MacGregor   is a research associate at the Institute for Health Research at Lancaster University, United Kingdom. She is author of *Beyond Mothering Earth: Ecological Citizenship and the Gendered Politics of Care* (2005).

David Schlosberg   is an associate professor at and chair of the Department of Political Science at Northern Arizona University, where he teaches political theory and environmental politics. He is the author of *Environmental Justice and the New Pluralism* (1999), and the coauthor with John Dryzek, David Downes, and Christian Hunold of *Green States and Social Movements* (2003). His current research projects include examining electronic public participation and defining environmental justice.

William Scott   is a professor of education at the University of Bath, United Kingdom, where he directs the Centre for Research in Education and the Environment. He edits the international refereed academic journals *Environmental Education Research* and *Assessment and Evaluation in Higher Education,* is a fellow of the Royal Society of Arts, and works with local and national nongovernmental organizations with interests in environmental, conservation, and sustainability issues. His most recent books are *Sustainable Development and Learning: Framing the Issues* (2003), and *Key Issues in Sustainable Development and Learning: A Critical Review* (2004), both written with Stephen Gough.

Stuart W. Shulman   is an assistant professor in information sciences and public administration at the University of Pittsburgh. He is a senior research associate at the University of Pittsburgh's Center for Social and Urban Research, the Université de Genève, the European Union Institute, and the Oxford Internet Institute–based E-Democracy Centre. His research focuses on electronic rule making, digital citizenship, and service-learning efforts in the United States.

Bronislaw Szerszynski   is a lecturer in environment and culture at the Centre for the Study of Environmental Change as well as the Institute for Environment, Philosophy, and Public Policy at Lancaster University, United Kingdom. He is the author of *Nature, Technology, and the Sacred* (2005), the coeditor (with Wallace Heim and Claire Waterton) of *Nature Performed: Environment, Culture, and Performance* (2003), the coeditor (with Celia Deane Drummond and Robin Grove-White) of *Re-Ordering Nature: Theology, Society, and the New Genetics* (2003), and the coeditor (with Scott Lash and Brian Wynne) of *Risk, Environment, and Modernity: Towards a New Ecology* (1996).

Stephen Zavestoski   is an assistant professor of sociology at the University of San Francisco. His current research examines social movement activism surrounding the environmental causes of illnesses and the use of the Internet as a tool for enhancing public participation in environmental decision making.

Index

PROPERTY OF
SENECA COLLEGE
LIBRARIES
NEWNHAM CAMPUS